The Rules of the Game in the Global Economy:
Policy Regimes for International Business

The Rules of the Game in the Global Economy: Policy Regimes for International Business

Lee E. Preston
University of Maryland

Duane Windsor
Rice University

Kluwer Academic Publishers
Boston / Dordrecht / London

Distributors for North America:
Kluwer Academic Publishers
101 Philip Drive
Assinippi Park
Norwell, Massachusetts 02061 USA

Distributors for all other countries:
Kluwer Academic Publishers Group
Distribution Centre
Post Office Box 322
3300 AH Dordrecht, THE NETHERLANDS

Library of Congress Cataloging-in-Publication Data

Preston, Lee E.
    The rules of the game in the global economy: policy regimes for
international business / by Lee E. Preston and Duane Windsor.
        p.   cm.
    Includes bibliographical references and index.
    ISBN 0-7923-9225-6
    1. International economic relations.   2. International economic
integration.   3. International business enterprises.
    4. International cooperation.   I. Windsor, Duane.   II. Title.
HF1412.P74 1992
338.8′8—dc20   92-2609
                                                                          CIP

Printed on acid-free paper.

Printed in the United States of America

To our wives
Patricia L. Preston
and
Sandra S. Windsor

Summary Table of Contents

Contents

Preface

This study has been long in the making, and the world has changed dramatically while we have been at work. We initially anticipated a substantial section on the Soviet-dominated Council for Mutual Economic Assistance (CMEA or "COMECON"), which offered an interesting contrast to the kind of international business regime typically found among market-oriented countries and industries. As we moved toward publication, the CMEA vanished, and so we mention it only in passing. The USSR subsequently disintegrated into a Commonwealth of Independent States (CIS). On the other hand, we began with the assumption that the historic "rule of capture" no long played a significant role in international economic relations. The seizure of Kuwait's territory and wealth by the government of Iraq suggests that this assumption was heavily influenced by wishful thinking. Even though this seizure has been reversed by military action, the experience remains a challenge to generally held beliefs about the strength of "order" versus "chaos" in contemporary international affairs.

Some readers of this volume have suggested that it gives insufficient attention to the fact that many of the important business and economic regimes of the postwar period are currently under significant pressure, perhaps even in danger of collapse. We acknowledge that there are many evidences of strain in, for example, the free trade and money exchange regimes, and in many areas of environmental protection. However, we defend our belief in the continuing importance of the contemporary set of regimes with two observations:

First, most of the current regime controversies are about the *specific features* of individual regimes, not about whether some system of mutually acceptable understandings and behaviors will be maintained. Efforts of the

USSR and its former East European satellites to become full participants in the entire range of contemporary regimes confirm their vitality.

Second, even as some regimes are weakening, others—for example, the European Community (EC) and the now likely North American Free Trade Area (NAFTA), as well as some environmental regimes—are emerging and growing stronger. Evolutionary change is a typical, not an exceptional, regime characteristic.

Thus, the notion that international business is increasingly governed by a complex system of regimes remains accurate, even though the detailed characteristics of specific regimes are subject to change over time. Our purpose in this analysis is to show what international regimes are like, why they have become numerous and important, and how they adapt to changing circumstances. Our case studies of individual regimes are intended to explain their emergence and evolution over several decades; their status and prospects at any particular point in time must be examined on the basis of then current sources and developments.

During our years of work on this volume, we have received help and support from many sources that must be acknowledged here. For financial support we are indebted to the University of Maryland—both the College of Business and Management, and the Graduate Research Board from which Preston had a one-semester full-salary research grant—and to Rice University's Jesse H. Jones Graduate School of Administration, which has provided financial and other forms of assistance to Windsor. Preston's work was also supported by grants to the University of Maryland from the US Department of Education, Division of International Education. On the research side, we have received valuable help from librarians at both Rice and College Park, and from data collectors and reference sources in many government agencies and international organizations as well. Numerous colleagues have offered references, suggestions, and helpful reviews of portions of the manuscript. Although all of these colleagues must be absolved from any blame for the results, those deserving special mention for their helpfulness are (in alphabetical order): Jean J. Boddewyn, Peter C. Bruce, Martin Dresner, Stephen L. Elkin, George E. Garvey, Virginia Haufler, Martin O. Heisler, Stefanie A. Lenway, Dennis C. Pirages, Robert E. Scott, Julian L. Simon, and Paul Wonnacott.

PROLOGUE

One of the characteristics of global problems is that they affect all inhabitants of the globe—even if not to the same extent—regardless of their social system, nationality, religious convictions, or social situations. Another characteristic is that they can only be handled and solved on a global basis. In an international political system based on the independence of nation states and where the international bodies cannot adopt decisions binding on the nation states, a global basis can only mean broad international understanding and organized cooperation.

—József Bognár
Director of the Institute for World Economy,
Hungarian Academy of Sciences*

* Source: "Global Problems in an Interdependent World," p. 16, in Howard F. Didsbury, ed., *The Global Economy* (Bethesda, MD: World Future Society, 1985), pp. 16–32.

The evolution of an integrated global economy, proceeding with increasing speed over the past two decades, is transforming industries and markets and creating new relationships among governments and enterprises, both domestic and international. Although the process of globalization is far from complete, it is already creating strong pressures for the development of mutually acceptable norms and patterns of behavior among important actors—enterprises, governments, and international organizations—in all areas of international business and economic life. These pressures lead, in turn, to the development of international policy regimes, understandings, and systems of behavior that facilitate and mediate collaboration and competition within the global economy.

The fact that an increasingly interdependent world economy cannot operate without common understandings and norms among the major participants is generally recognized. There is, however, considerable disagreement about the purposes and substantive features of the specific regimes that are evolving. Although the industrial market economies of North America, Western Europe, and the Pacific Rim account for the largest shares of global economic activity, newly industrialized and less developed countries also play important roles. The industries, enterprises, citizens, and governments of these diverse jurisdictions may all stand to gain from the long-term process of worldwide economic development and modernization, but their interests may diverge and conflict in many specific respects. The process of globalization increases the frequency and importance of contacts among these diverse economic actors. As a result, institutions established for the purpose of balancing economic interests and mediating conflicts among them—such as the General Agreement on Tariffs and Trade (GATT) and the UN Conference on Trade and Development (UNCTAD)—have encountered increasing difficulty in performing their functions. Regional economic blocs, such as the European Community (EC) and the now-likely North American Free Trade Area (NAFTA), are emerging as alternatives to (or counterdevelopments within) the trend toward greater worldwide integration and interdependence.

The fundamental issue is the appropriate balance between collaboration and cooperation, on the one hand, and competition and conflict, on the other, within the world economy. Economic relationships among politically separate states, and among industries and enterprises located in different national jurisdictions, are as old as civilization itself. Some of these relationships are based on military conquest or dependency; others arise from mutually advantageous trade and investment; and most involve complex combinations of power, costs, and benefits. All these relationships are governed by some kinds of common understandings among the parties involved, both direct participants and more remote actors and observers. Such understandings may be as simple as the "rule of capture" (whoever grabs the prize can keep it), or may involve formal agreements and sophisticated concepts of "international law." Whatever their precise content, such understandings constitute the "rules of the game" of international economic relations among states, industries, and enterprises.

This study makes a strong statement about the nature and importance of the rules of the international economic game as they are evolving during the closing years of the twentieth century. In brief, we believe that the increasing scale and complexity of the global economy necessarily leads to the development of rules, norms, understandings, and procedures that guide and govern the activities of its major participants. We refer to such systems of standards and accepted behaviors as *policy regimes*, and we believe that such regimes are particularly important in the current international environment, where "hard law" is weak or absent and where dynamic changes frequently occur outside the bounds of pre-existing formal organizational and decision-making structures. We believe that specific regime features may have distinct effects on international business relationships and activities, and that a broader understanding of regimes— their sources, characteristics, and effects—can make a positive contribution to the management of international business enterprises and to the process of worldwide economic development.

International business and economic activities, both among nations and among enterprises, are frequently described as *games*, with corresponding reference to rules and strategies, wins and losses, and ties and stalemates. In addition, concepts from the theory of games—such as the notion of mixed strategies and zero-sum, positive-sum, and negative-sum games —are sometimes encountered in this context. These allusions, both conversational and technical, are generally appropriate. Both cooperation and rivalry are fundamental aspects of international economic contact; and the ultimate choice of playing or not playing, a critical feature of most games, is generally available as well. As in any formal game, the range of acceptable strategic and tactical moves and countermoves is typically circumscribed, although often very wide, and the behavior of participants is governed by an established set of conventions. A special feature of the international economic game is that it involves a large, diverse, and changing group of players over an indefinite time period; hence, there are many possibilities for forming new coalitions and for trading off long-term and short-term benefits and costs.

Every game is governed by a set of rules, which must be accepted by the players if they are to participate. Players may construct rules by chance or for short-term convenience, but in most games—and certainly in the international economic game—players adapt rules over time in response to changing circumstances, which may well include changes in the identities and objectives of the players involved. During the late nineteenth and early twentieth centuries, two very different international economic games were played. One, which had very ancient origins, was the game of *colonialism*, in which more advanced nations gained control of less advanced peoples and territories, exploiting them primarily for home-country advantage; enterprises and governments from the advanced countries usually joined together as "partners" in this game, and they often developed secondary partners in the colonies as well. The other game, *free trade*, a nineteenth-century innovation, was based upon unrestricted market contact among enterprises, regardless of national jurisdiction, with government involvement limited to the maintenance of a suitable framework of monetary exchange. The practice of free trade first developed on a substantial scale in commodities markets, where the identity of parties to any particular transaction is generally unknown or irrelevant. The colonialism game was primarily governed by a *rule of capture* (although if third parties objected to any particular "capture," an "imperialist war" might ensue). The free trade game was governed by the *rule of competition*, meaning that low-price sellers and high-price buyers would complete transactions, and other parties would be left out of the market.

Over the decades since World War II, new and different kinds of games have emerged in the international economy. For the most part, these games involve economic alliances and foreign investment, rather than colonialism, and trade that is to some extent managed, rather than entirely free. The rules of these games are typically established and altered by negotiations and agreements among the participating parties, and are often quite complex. Economic, political, technological, and sociocultural developments are all involved in the emergence of these new games and the evolution of their corresponding rules. National-base enterprises and governments, more numerous and diverse than ever before, continue to be major players. In addition, new dimensions are introduced by the presence of giant global enterprises, many of which operate at least partially beyond the control of individual national governments and which are increasingly linked with each other through ownership and contractual agreements.

P.1. Nature of This Study

The subject of this study is the contemporary system of rules, understandings, and conventions to facilitate and regulate various areas of intimately linked to form a dynamically functioning whole. Our brief and selective summary of this complex collection of material inevitably runs the risk of oversimplification; the purpose, however, is not exhaustive factual coverage but analytical synthesis of major trends and relationships. The role, structure, and impact of multinational enterprises are explored in chapter 3; again, we do not attempt a definitive treatise on the multi-nationals but rather show the way in which the increasing multination-alization of the global economy generates policy developments and regime-enterprise interactions. The final chapter in part I examines some of the theoretical issues and controversies concerning the concept of international policy regimes and explains the way in which this concept is used in our analysis.

The chapters in part II present integrative case studies of five major groups of international policy regimes—global policy developments taking place within the UN system, regional and associative arrangements, and important functional regimes for trade and payments, sea and air transport, and environmental protection. Each of these case studies is based on a survey of the relevant literature, consultation with experts, and integration and synthesis of material from diverse sources. The purpose of the case studies, taken together, is to provide empirical evidence of the nature, operation, and effects of regimes, and of the forces contributing to their creation and evolution over time.

The epilogue draws together some of the main themes of the analysis and focuses them on a potential regime area of great current interest —international services.

P.3. Terminological Note

The language of analysis for international business and policy regimes is not yet standardized, and the terminology suggested by some analysts inevitably strikes others as artificial and unhelpful. It has been our inten-tion here to keep the use of technical terms and academic jargon to a min-imum. Even so, it seems wise to clarify the precise meaning that we attach to certain commonly used terms.

We use the term *enterprise* to refer to any managerial organization through which economic activity is carried out. An enterprise may be owned and controlled by private individuals, by national states or other governments, or in some other or combined fashion; and an enterprise may be organized as a corporation or in some other legal form within its home jurisdiction. These distinctions of ownership and legal form may, or may not, be significant in explaining the behavior and influence of enterprises in the international environment. The appearance of new types of enterprises (e.g., joint ventures, strategic alliances) that do not fit into conventional categories is of special importance.

Business activities are *international* whenever they involve enterprises based in two or more national jurisdictions. Many purely domestic enterprises are regularly involved in *international business* (e.g., sales, purchases, loans to/from enterprises in other countries). Individual national governments regularly make policies with respect to the international aspects of business activities taking place within their own jurisdictions. *Multinational* business relationships arise when participants from more than two—and, as a rule, potentially many—national jurisdictions are simultaneously involved. A *multinational enterprise* is one in which substantial amounts of activity are carried out within and among several different national jurisdictions; again, such enterprises may be organized and owned in many different ways, and such differences may or may not be important for any particular analytical purpose.

International policies involve mutual understandings and agreements among actors—governments, enterprises, or others—representing or based within different national jurisdictions. Although such policies can be *bilateral* (i.e., involving relations between two countries), most of the significant policy arrangements affecting business involve several, possibly very many, different jurisdictions, and hence can be properly termed *multinational*. It is important to remember that *international policies* may relate to enterprises and industries such as those involved in international air transport, that as yet contain no or very few *multinational enterprises*.

When analyzing the role of various nations and regions in international economic and political affairs, it is important to preserve a distinction between geographical and cultural groupings (i.e., *countries*, and various sub- and supranational groupings) and the specific *governments* that may be in power within particular jurisdictions at various times. Throughout most of our analysis, the intended reference should be obvious: "the US share of world trade" refers to data for the nation as a whole; the "US position on . . ." refers to the policies of a particular government at a particular time. When there seems to be any possibility of confusion, we emphasize the reference to "governments" in discussions of policy formation and implementation.

Many acronyms have necessarily been used in this book. Generally the proper name for which the acronym has been used is included. The index includes the acronyms parenthetically, so that the reader can scan for the proper names.

References

Adelman, Carol C., ed. 1988. *International Regulation: New Rules in a Changing World Order*. San Francisco, CA: Institute for Contemporary Studies.

Behrman, Jack N., and Robert E. Grosse. 1990. *International Business and Governments: Issues and Institutions*. Columbia, SC: University of South Carolina Press.

Blake, David, and Robert Walters. 1992. *The Politics of Global Economic Relations*, 4th edition. Englewood Cliffs, NJ: Prentice-Hall.

Strange, Susan. 1988. *States and Markets*. New York: Basil Blackwell.

I THE CONTEXT OF INTERNATIONAL POLICY REGIMES

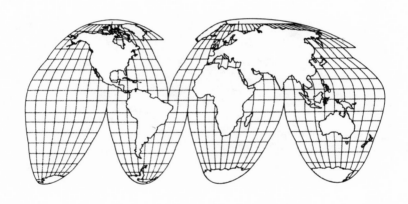

1 COMPLEX LINKAGES IN THE GLOBAL ECONOMY

During the half century since World War II, the international economic system has evolved from a collection of national units, loosely tied together through various economic and political relationships, into a truly "global" economy, an interdependent system of trade, investment, and development that touches nearly all parts of the world. In the course of this evolutionary process, many poor countries have become richer and more active on the international scene, while advanced industrial countries have developed new areas of comparative advantage and disadvantage. Some formal linkages among countries—the colonial empires and the Soviet-dominated Council for Mutual Economic Assistance (CMEA or "COMECON") system—have weakened or disappeared, while new forms of regional and worldwide integration have emerged. In this environment of increasing interdependence and continuing dynamic change, opportunities have multiplied for cooperation and collaboration, and for competition and conflict, among enterprises, industries, nations, and regions.

The new global economy is knit together by three principal types of transnational linkages, which are themselves strongly interrelated (figure 1-1). The basic elements, underlying all the others, are *trade and investment flows*, which, as we show in chapter 2 below, have grown more rapidly

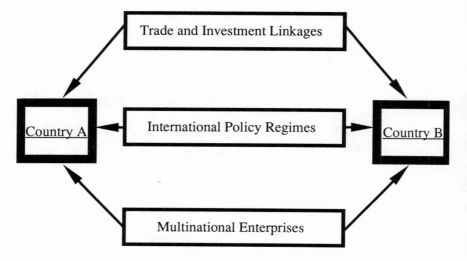

Figure 1-1.   Complex Linkages in the Global Economy.

than world gross domestic product (GDP) since the end of World War II. The growth of worldwide foreign investment is of particular importance, since investment leads to ownership links that persist over time and generate additional interactions, both economic and political. A second type of linkage arises from the activities of *multinational enterprises*, the managerial units created by foreign investment; operation of these firms in multiple national jurisdictions gives rise to economic and policy impacts that are beyond the purview of any individual government. These two major types of linkages give rise to a third, the *international policy regimes* that are the focus of this study. These regimes arise to facilitate and regulate the flows of trade and investment, as well as the activities of enterprises, whether multinational or domestic, participating in the growth of the global economy. It is particularly important to note that international policy regimes not only bring the *international* activities of various states, industries, and enterprises within a common framework but also penetrate *domestic* economies and policy structures as well.

The three basic forms of international economic and policy linkage are, of course, supported by a web of international communication and information, which is itself a major contributor to increased international interdependence. Transport and communication costs have fallen dramatically during the twentieth century. Measured in 1990 dollars, average ocean freight and port charges per short ton declined from $95 in 1920 to $29 in 1990; average air-transport revenue per passenger mile declined from 68 cents in 1930 to 11 cents in 1990; and the cost of a three-minute telephone call (New York to London) dropped from $244.65 in 1930 to $3.32 in 1990 (Hufbauer, 1991, p. 26).[1] In addition, there are many other kinds of transnational linkages—language and culture, religion, geographic proximity, strategic interests, etc.—that underlie and reinforce the economic, organizational, and policy connections that are emphasized here.

Global economic *interdependence* has two dimensions. One is *magnitude*—the number of contacts and volume of flows among the various participants in the global economy. The other is their mutual *sensitivity*, "the extent to which consumption patterns, production structures, money and capital markets [in any one country] are influenced significantly by policies and developments outside its borders" (Panic, 1988, p. 5; see also Cooper, 1985, chapter 1). The functional links among nations, industries, and enterprises are now more numerous, more diverse, and more complex than ever before; and the volumes of goods, services, financing, and communications flowing through these links are also larger than ever, even relative to the growth of the world economy. The speed with which knowledge of events spreads throughout the world is unprecedented. The result is that price changes, interest rate movements, stock market developments, and government policy actions taking place anywhere in the global economy reverberate almost instantaneously throughout the entire system, and produce simultaneous effects in widely separated locations.

Policymakers and executives in both governments and enterprises have responded to these developments by attempting to develop institutional arrangements and understandings that preserve and enlarge the benefits arising from these new global economic interconnections while reducing the costs and risks associated with increasing interdependence. In this process, the structures and agreements facilitating and governing international business operations have become increasingly numerous and important. These policy systems are necessarily multinational. They involve common understandings and mutually consistent behaviors among actors representing and operating within numerous and diverse political jurisdictions, and reflecting varied interests. Although some international business activities can still be handled bilaterally, activities of substantial size or continuity inevitably lead to consequences that require support, acceptance, or at least toleration by third parties or by the worldwide business and economic community. Moreover, in the contemporary era, no single hegemonic power or small group of like-minded actors can establish and enforce international economic arrangements inimical to the interests of other significant groups of participants. On the contrary, worldwide economic activity is increasingly governed by norms and behaviors established by the mutual consent of multiple and diverse entities—governments, enterprises, and other organizations—and therefore reflects their different and changing interests and objectives. According to a recent and penetrating analysis.

> The only way to achieve a stable system of international relationships under these conditions [i.e., interdependence] is for individual countries . . . either to agree formally on a mutually satisfactory code of behaviour or to accept one tacitly. In other words, stability of the international economic system depends now critically on the ability and willingness of individual countries to pursue policies which are compatible with their national economic objectives *and* with the objectives and policies of other countries. . . . This involves the acceptance of certain obligations and rules of behavior (Panic, 1988, p. 283).

The regulation of international business activity emerged as "a major new international economic problem" in the 1970s (Waldmann, 1980, p. 1; see also Coate, 1982). By the end of the 1980s, Bryant and Hodgkinson observed that "interdependence has become more intense and the need to cooperate more urgent. . . . There has been an increase in both the number and the significance of the problems that can be solved only through international agreement" (1989, in Cooper et al., eds., p. 1). Even analysts critical of some regime developments and proposals acknowledge their value in many areas: "Certainly not all international regulation is inimical to international business interests. . . . The US government and American industry continue to support and contribute to the beneficial international regulatory regimes [in a variety of areas]" (Adelman, ed., 1988, p. xvi).

1.1. The Concept of International Policy Regimes

In this study we refer to the arrangements and understandings among the numerous and diverse actors involved in international economic relationships as *international policy regimes*. The formal definition of such regimes developed by Krasner and generally accepted by leading international relations scholars is as follows:

> *A regime is composed of sets of explicit or implicit principles, norms, rules and decision-making procedures around which actor expectations converge in a given area of international relations* (Krasner, ed., 1983, p. 2 [emphasis added]).[2]

A critical feature of this definition, and of related formulations offered by others, is that regimes include not only 1) the formal *institutional arrangements* that embody and implement international agreements and understandings, but also 2) the *principles* (such as dominance, sovereignty, fairness, cooperation, or consistency of behavior) underlying and legitimizing such institutions, and 3) the expected *behavior patterns* associated with them. Cooper notes, with particular reference to monetary and financial arrangements, that the term *regime* "seems preferable to system or order . . . since it encompasses arrangements that are neither orderly nor systematic . . . [and includes] internal consistency and technical proficiency" (Cooper, 1987, p. 2).

The term *regime* is sometimes used as a synonym for *government*, but that meaning is not intended here. Following the usage in the international relations literature, we view regimes as sets of functional relationships and behaviors among diverse entities, and particularly among enterprises and other economic interests and the various governments and international organizations with which they come in contact. *National* policy regimes are those prevailing within individual countries; for example, there is a national regime for commercial banking within the US, with responsibilities and roles distributed among federal and state authorities, the Federal Reserve Board, and the banks themselves. *International* regimes, the subject of this study, involve relationships among actors and interests operating within, and sometimes on behalf of, diverse national jurisdictions.

It is important to emphasize that a *regime* consists primarily of functional and behavioral relationships, and that formal organizations and agreements are subsidiary or, occasionally, entirely absent. The international gold standard was a well-recognized and powerful regime that lacked any formal organizational base. (For an analysis of the gold standard as an international regime, see chapter 6 below.) Nor are all important international organizations key elements of significant regimes. The International Labour Organization (ILO) is a well-established agency, but there is no corresponding "regime" for international labor relations. The Organization for Economic Cooperation and Development (OECD) is an important forum for consultation and the exchange of information, but its influence on actual economic and business activity is at best indirect. Young emphasizes that, in analyzing regimes, "it is important not to conflate institutions and functions." Although the former may be essential to the latter, it is the functions themselves—or, more specifically, the "rules" and "behaviors"—that constitute the regime (Young, 1989, p. 13 and passim). Soroos observes, "Regimes are identified in terms of 'problem areas'; one or more international organizations are integral parts of most regimes, and many international organizations are involved in more than one regime" (1987, pp. 17–18). Cooper stresses that "the role of international organizations [is] derivative from the task to be performed. . . . [T]he presence and the appropriate form of international organization depends on the regime actually selected" (1987, p. 33).

A preliminary list of the major international regimes and related organizations affecting international business is shown in figure 1-2. We include here a number of organizations that lack regime status and one (the CMEA) that has recently disappeared. We refer to these regimes and organizations in various combinations and at various levels of detail in the course of our analysis. We acknowledge at the outset that any such list, or any selection of regimes for special study, is subject to critique; our selections and classifications are intended to be illustrative, not exhaustive. We believe, however, that the threefold classification of regimes shown here and reflected in our case studies is of particular significance:

Global and comprehensive regimes: Institutional and behavioral arrangements that are, at least in principle, unrestricted in both their geographic and functional scope. A genuine "world government" would, of course, constitute such a regime. The collection of regimes, both actual and proposed, evolving within the UN framework illustrates some features and problems of such a set of arrangements.

Regional or associative regimes: Arrangements involving groups of national states drawn together by locational or other common characteristics and interests. These arrangements might range from political union to common market, free trade area, or specific multinational agreement of more limited scope.

Functional regimes: Regimes limited in their coverage to specific industries, activities, or problems; within this category we further distinguish between "economic" and "environmental" regimes, because of their substantial differences in structure and character.

1.2. Historical Perspective

The evolution of policy regimes governing various aspects of international business is not a new phenomenon. Over the past two centuries, three distinct periods of regime development can be identified: nineteenth-century colonialism, vestiges of which persisted up until the end of World War II; the post-World War II transition decades; and the contemporary era of multipolar competition and interdependence.

Global and Comprehensive Regimes and Organizations
United Nations regime system, including:
  World Court
  Convention on International Sale of Goods
  Restrictive Business Practices Code
  Codex Alimentarius (WHO and FAO)
  Technology Transfer Code (UNCTAD)
  Code of Conduct on Transnational Corporations (UNCTC—in preparation)
  UN-based Consumer Protection Codes (e.g., Infant Formula)
  UN-based Environmental Regimes (e.g., Moon Treaty)

Regional and Associative Regimes and Organizations
European Community (EC), including:
  European Economic Community
  Euratom
  European Coal and Steel Community
  European Monetary System
US–Canada Free Trade Agreement (North American Free Trade Agreement—
  pending)
Latin American Free Trade Area, Andean Pact
Organization for Economic Cooperation and Development (OECD)
Council for Mutual Economic Assistance (CMEA, or "COMECON"—dissolved 1991)

Functional Regimes: Economic
Air Transport
  International Air Transport Association (IATA)
  International Civil Aviation Organization (ICAO)
Ocean Shipping
  UNCTAD Liner Conference Code
  International Maritime Organization (IMO)
Telecommunications
  International Telecommunications Union (ITU)
  INTELSAT
Trade
  General Agreement on Tariffs and Trade (GATT)
  Product and commodity agreements, GATT-related and otherwise
Money Exchange and Payments
  International Monetary Fund (IMF)
Investment
  World Bank
  International Finance Corporation (IFC)
  Multilateral Investment Guarantee Agency (MIGA)

Functional Regimes: Environmental
Air Pollution Agreements: Transboundary air pollution, sulfur, nitrogen oxides,
  chlorofluorocarbons (Vienna/Montreal Protocol)
Law of the Sea Treaty
Moon Treaty
Antarctic Treaty

Figure 1-2. Major Policy Regimes and Organizations Affecting International
Business. Although this list contains primarily the names of *organizations*, it is the
regimes and not the institutional forms that are of primary interest.

1.2.1.   Nineteenth-Century System

The roots of colonialism reach far back in time, but by the middle of the nineteenth century an elaborate system of worldwide power relations had evolved. Great Britain dominated this system because of its control of the seas and its relatively early industrial and financial development. Other European countries attempted to establish similar systems of colonial control and exploitation, and the US, Russia, and Japan also participated, although in somewhat different ways. The worldwide colonial system essentially collapsed during and immediately after World War I, but no new overarching system, either political or economic, appeared immediately to take its place. Protectionism and withdrawal from international economic contact were more characteristic of the chaotic interwar period. The last formal institutions of economic colonialism disappeared in the course of World War II.

1.2.2.   Postwar Transition

At the end of World War II, the global economy appeared to be composed of three different groups of national actors, often described as three "worlds":

The "First World" consisting of advanced industrial countries, initially dominated by the US and increasingly linked with each other by investment and trade, as well as by military and political considerations.

The "Second World" of the Communist bloc countries, headed by the Soviet Union (and for the early part of the period including China), within which an entirely different system of international linkages among state-operated industries and enterprises evolved.

The "Third World," a numerous and diverse collection of less developed countries (LDCs), many of which were closely linked to one or the other major blocs but which had in common only their lack of full membership within either.

This three-part division of the global economy generated two major forces: 1) bipolar competition between the two major economic and political power blocs, which were largely isolated from each other; and 2) strong pressures for development, sometimes collaborative and sometimes aggressively competitive, among the LDCs. These complex forces, operating within the context of the overall growth of the global economy and, in particular, the growth of multinational enterprises (MNEs) and global industries, stimulated and conditioned the evolution of most of the international policy regimes now in existence.

1.2.3. Contemporary Era

The "three worlds" conception was never particularly accurate and is now thoroughly obsolete. Diversity of interests and characteristics has always been great among countries in each of the groups. By the 1970s, the recovery of Europe and the rise of Japan led to both growth and stress within the First World, while aggressive regime development by some oil-producing countries, in the form of the Organization of Petroleum Exporting Countries (OPEC), produced shocks throughout the global economy. In the 1980s, a group of "newly industrialized countries" (NICs) emerged from Third World status; some of these countries built on a base of valuable natural resources (oil or other), while others such as South Korea and Taiwan emphasized cost control and aggressive international competition. At the end of the 1980s, the Second World economic and political system suddenly collapsed, opening up new possibilities for contacts among industries and entreprises that had long been foreclosed by political barriers.

The result of all these developments is a new global economy that is multipolar and increasingly interlinked. Kline comments, "Many new problems emerging in the international system are truly transnational in character, both in terms of their impact and the manner in which they must be managed" (1990, p. 5). Both collaborative and competitive forces are at work, and these forces arise from many different origins, push in different directions, and are subject to rapid change. Some of these developments strongly favor the evolution of policy regimes for international business, e.g., continuing worldwide economic growth and interdependence; growth of global industries and multinational enterprises; and identification of global problems involving resources and the environment. On the other hand, some features of the new global economy may significantly retard regime development, e.g., continuing differences in wealth and status among countries; political and military conflicts; and fundamental disagreements about relevant principles (property rights, sovereignty, etc.). The balance of forces seems to favor continued regime development, but the focus, speed, and character of regime evolution remains problematic.

1.3. A Final Issue: Active Economic Role of Governments

A final issue at the heart of multinational policy development is the role of national governments, individually and collectively, in the economic development process. The League of Nations tradition implicitly assumed that governments would play a restricted role, leaving the direction of economic

activity primarily in the hands of individual enterprises, most of which
would be privately owned and controlled. The post-World War II environment, however, presents an entirely different picture. Not only is the
number of governments participating in UN activities at least three times
greater than that ever involved in the League (45), and still growing, but
the differences among them with respect to economic structure and
internal policies are much greater as well (see relevant discussion below).
In both advanced and less developed countries, governments adopt broad
industrial policies or development strategies that lead them to take on
important partnership roles with independent enterprises and even to
assume primary initiative and operating responsibility in key industries.
And, in spite of recent changes in some formerly Communist countries, it
remains true that the economies of some important UN-regime participants are largely state owned or controlled. In addition, in some multinational arrangements such as the European Community (EC) and the
Andean Common Market, supragovernmental agencies are extensively
and actively involved in business and economic affairs.

This changed situation adds important new dimensions to the evolution of global policy regimes. In the first place, such fundamental policy
concepts as "national treatment" become ambiguous when some of the
entities involved are appendages, direct or indirect, of national states.
Subsidiaries of foreign MNEs can scarcely be treated like, and perhaps
not even equitably in relation to, state-owned enterprises in market-
oriented countries such as France, for example. Balancing the treatment
of foreign-owned units and state-controlled industries in post-Communist
countries is even more difficult. Increased emphasis on protectionist policies, selective industrial policies, direct and indirect subsidies, and other
forms of collaboration between governments and their domestic enterprises throughout the world economy suggest that the conditions of both
domestic and international policy evolution are becoming increasingly
complex.

Moreover, as Tharp (1976) emphasized, a number of important contemporary international policy developments concerning business have strong
elements of government activism at their core. Developments within the
EC offer multiple illustrations. The EC has a strong commitment to the
promotion of *European* MNEs, including the integration and rational-
ization of corporate activities *within* its constituent states. A comprehensive proposal for a Societas Europea (European Corporation) with
no national base and with special privileges throughout the Community
has also been developed (Scheenbaum, 1983, pp. 44–45). Multinational
consortia of businesses and governments have also evolved under North

Atlantic Treaty Organization (NATO) auspices to deal with large, strategically vital projects (e.g., aircraft, nuclear power) for which comprehensive planning is deemed to be a more important source of efficiency than competition. Each of these arrangements is unique and primarily focused on the special features of each situation rather than general patterns and standards. Hence, these developments do not appear to contribute to, and may actually work against, the evolution of more comprehensive multinational policies.

1.4. National and International Regimes

A major function of national governments is the creation and administration of policy regimes governing activities, particularly economic activities, within their borders. The growth of *international* regimes inevitably creates linkages among domestic systems that are fundamentally different from each other in character. Enterprises operating within competitive domestic environments become linked with national monopolies in other countries; privately owned enterprises from one jurisdiction engage in joint ventures with state-owned enterprises from another; market-based arrangements and administrative allocation mechanisms become subject to the same international policies and regulations.

Although any classification of national policy regimes is likely to be simplistic, and changes in particular countries are always in progress, we believe that it is helpful to recognize a spectrum of domestic policy systems ranging from market-oriented regimes at one extreme, through various degrees and forms of governmental direction, to extensive state control and planning. The principal elements of such a spectrum, with national examples as they appeared in the mid-1980s, are shown in figure 1-3. This spectrum of domestic policy regimes is shaped by two principal dimensions, which are partly (but only partly) overlapping. One dimension concerns the governmental choice between market-oriented and planning-oriented systems of state–enterprise interaction. The other dimension is the degree of state ownership of important enterprises and industries. Within the broad category of market-oriented systems, we note two types of distinctions:

1. The distinction among systems that emphasize governmental regulation (e.g., Switzerland, Hong Kong), and those that more heavily influence market activities through some variant of industrial policy (e.g., Japan, France); and

	Market-Oriented Systems		Planning-Oriented Systems	
	Regulatory Regimes	Industrial Policy Regimes	Development Regimes	Central Planning Regimes
Haphazard State Ownership				
Advanced Countries	Switzerland United States West Germany	Japan		
Newly Industrialized Countries	Chile Hong Kong	South Korea		
Developing Countries	Kenya		Nigeria	
State Domination of Basic Industries and Infrastructure				
Advanced Countries	Canada Italy	France Britain		
Newly Industrialized Countries	Singapore		India Mexico	
Developing Countries	Costa Rica		Egypt	
Predominantly State Ownership				
Advanced Countries				USSR
Newly Industrialized Countries				PRC
Developing Countries			Iraq	Cuba Mongolia

Figure 1-3. National Regimes Spectrum.

2. The distinction between systems where government ownership of
    enterprises is scattered and unsystematic (e.g., United States), and
    those in which a deliberate pattern of state ownership in basic indus-
    tries and infrastructure (e.g., France) can be discerned. Neither
    regulation nor industrial policy is necessarily associated with heavy
    state ownership. (The extreme of near universal state ownership
    is, of course, found in the nonmarket systems governed by formal
    state planning. The newly industrialized countries and developing
    countries are scattered all over the domestic policy spectrum in
    terms of whether development planning is associated with state
    ownership, and whether regulation or industrial policy is used.)

It was noted in the previous section that governments have, in both advanced and developing countries, adopted broad industrial policies or development strategies resulting in key economic roles for the government and state-owned enterprises. This general phenomenon of governmental intervention is characterized, however, by a tremendous range of domestic policy regimes. This range of domestic regimes results in a high degree of variation in both operating conditions for MNEs, and attitudes of specific governments toward multilateral collaboration. Nation-states character- ized by central planning and state-owned enterprise have tended to dis- courage MNE activities within their borders; the governments of some developing countries have tended to encourage foreign investment by MNEs, while the governments of other developing countries have tried to restrict or control foreign investment and the activities of MNEs; and the governments of industrial market economies have generally tried to secure free access for the trade and investment activities of their country's MNEs. These fundamental differences in policy orientation and enterprise owner- ship pattern, along with differences in wealth and level of development, thus strongly affect the objectives and behaviors of the participants in international regimes. The long period required for formulation of the UN Code of Conduct on Transnational Corporations (see the discussion in chapter 5 below) is due partly to profound disagreements among national governments about the precise principles and standards to be adopted. Other specific examples of these effects appear throughout the case studies, but the general point that truly diverse national systems are linked, and inevitably modified, through international arrangements is of critical importance.

There is a major dispute in the academic literature between two opposed viewpoints about the role of domestic policy regimes in the emerging global economy. These viewpoints have deep historical roots, one in the theory of mercantilism and the other in the theory of free trade. They are currently reflected in two widely discussed books, Michael Porter's *The Competitive Advantage of Nations* (1990) and Kenichi Ohmae's *The Borderless World* (1990).

Ohmae, taking the free trade view, argues that the functional efficiency of the global economy requires the replacement of the present collection of disparate national policy regimes by a truly international market system. Indeed, he argues that such a system is already well established among the "Triad" economies of the OECD community (North America, West- ern Europe, and the Pacific Rim countries Japan, Australia, and New Zealand). This argument is ultimately grounded in the classical free trade proposition that global economic welfare will be maximized by free mobility of resources and goods in response to worldwide demand. Within this perspective, integration of the developing nations into the free-trade global economy will hasten the process of worldwide economic development. Restrictive domestic policy regimes are barriers to development, and hence should be removed. Global industries and multinational enterprises, both based on economic rationality rather than political or ideological considerations, will provide primary direction for the development process.

Porter, by contrast, argues a modern version of the mercantilist theory that the wealth and power of a nation can be increased by systematic governmental intervention in the national economy in order to secure a favorable balance of foreign trade, internal development of agriculture and industry, and competitive advantage over other nations. Porter envisions a global economy composed of a set of powerful nation-state competitors, the government of each country pursuing some form of industrial policy in order to enhance its international comparative advantages. National governments are the critical actors in this system, and enterprises primarily the instruments of national policy.

Both these views have significant implications for the evolution of international policy regimes. According to Ohmae, enterprises and other forces of economic rationalism are the critical actors in the global economy; the interests of national states are subordinate, and gradually vanishing. International regimes would evolve only to the extent they were needed to facilitate economically rational activities. By contrast, a mercantilist or protectionist view would expect international regimes to develop only to the extent that they advanced the interests of national states, particularly those states that were able for whatever reason to dominate others.

This debate is critical to the future evolution and role of international policy regimes. The Ohmae perspective advocates that governments eliminate barriers to international economic activity of all types. International policy regimes would be restricted to those regimes that would facilitate MNE activities. The Porter perspective advocates (and expects) that governments will enter into partnership with enterprises for the purposes of enhancing national competitiveness. In this framework, international policy regimes would be the object of struggle among nation-states seeking competitive advantages. Our view is that elements of both perspectives will prove to be valid. There are strong economic forces making for international policy regimes that will in effect "liberalize" the global environment for MNE activities; MNEs will have strong incentives to push for such regimes. At the same time, there are strong economic and political forces making for "beggar-thy-neighbor" practices by nation-states; these forces will be felt in the evolution of international policy regimes. The balance of these various forces is difficult to forecast. As data in chapter 2 below indicate, world economic activity slowed substantially during the early 1980s; and there are continuing rumors of possible trade wars among the members of the OECD Triad. However, although it was widely feared in the US until recently that the implementation of EC 92 would lead to stronger import barriers, the EC is now moving toward a European Economic Association with the European Free Trade Area (EFTA) and will have important new investment opportunities in Eastern Europe. On balance, we expect the continuation of world economic growth and the collapse of the Cold War to provide an encouraging framework for international policy regimes that will tend to foster MNE activities.

1.5. Conclusion

The world economy is being integrated by three interrelated types of linkages: trade and investment flows, multinational enterprises, and international policy regimes. The sheer growth of the world economy—in the number and variety of participants, in global industries, and in the scope and activities of MNEs—has increased the recognition of common concerns among both governments and enterprises and given rise to an array of new problems and opportunities that are not amenable to unilateral solutions. The stage is therefore set for multinational policy development, and in fact a considerable amount of such development has already taken place. By analyzing the sources and patterns of these developments in some detail, we hope to illuminate both problems and potentials for future evolution.

Notes

1. Based on *Historical Statistics of the United States* (Washington, DC: US Department of Commerce) and *Statistical Abstract of the United States* (Washington, DC: US Department of Commerce), various years.

2. The international relations literature is filled with definitions, explications, and critiques of the "regime" concept; some salient issues raised in this literature are discussed in chapter 4 below.

References

Adelman, Carol C., ed. 1988. *International Regulation: New Rules in a Changing World Order*. San Francisco, CA: Institute for Contemporary Studies.

Bryant, Ralph C., and Edith Hodgkinson. 1989. "Problems of International Cooperation," in Richard N. Cooper, Barry Eichengreen, Gerard Holtham, Robert D. Putnam, and C. Randall Henning, eds., *Can Nations Agree?: Issues in International Economic Cooperation*. Washington, DC: Brookings Institution, pp. 1–11.

Coate, Roger A. 1982. *Global Issue Regimes*. New York: Praeger.

Cooper, Richard N. 1985. *Economic Policy in an Interdependent World*. Cambridge, MA: MIT Press.

Cooper, Richard N. 1987. *The International Monetary System: Essays in World Economics*. Cambridge, MA: MIT Press.

Hufbauer, Gary. 1991. "World Economic Integration: The Long View," *International Economic Insights*, vol. 2, no. 3 (May/June), pp. 26–27.

Kline, John M. 1990. "A New Environment for the Code," *The CTC Reporter*, no. 29 (Spring), pp. 2–6.

Krasner, Stephen D., ed. 1983. *International Regimes*. Ithaca, NY: Cornell University Press.

Ohmae, Kenichi. 1990. *The Borderless World: Power and Strategy in an Interlinked Economy*. New York: Harper Business.

Panic, M. 1988. *National Management of the International Economy*. New York: St. Martin's.

Porter, Michael E. 1990. *The Competitive Advantage of Nations*. New York: Free Press.

Scheenbaum, Steven M. 1983. "The Company Law Harmonization Program of the European Community," in Bart S. Fisher and Jeff Turner, eds., *Regulating the Multinational Enterprise: National and International Challenges*. New York: Praeger, pp. 26–58.

Soroos, Marvin S. 1987. *Beyond Sovereignty: The Challenge of Global Policy*. Columbia, SC: University of South Carolina Press.

Tharp, Paul A., Jr. 1976. "Transnational Enterprises and International Regulation: A Survey of Various Approaches to International Organizations," *International Organization*, vol. 30, no. 1 (Winter), pp. 47–73.

Waldmann, Raymond J. 1980. *Regulating International Business through Codes of Conduct*. Washington, DC: American Enterprise Institute.

Young, Oran R. 1989. *International Cooperation*. Ithaca, NY: Cornell University Press.

2 TRADE AND INVESTMENT LINKAGES

This chapter examines the way in which economic and financial linkages arising from conventional trade and investment activities are contributing to the creation of a truly global economy. These linkages establish the framework for the growth and operation of multinational enterprises, which will be examined in the following chapter. The present chapter is divided into three sections. The first briefly describes the basic structure of the global economy from contemporary data. The second section deals with trade linkages, the flows of imports and exports among countries. The third section deals with investment linkages, both in terms of annual flows (i.e., net *new* investment per time period) and the patterns of international ownership (i.e., aggregate investment *stocks*) that result from them. The multinational enterprises (MNEs) that account for a substantial portion of these international investment flows and stocks are analyzed in the following chapter. The international financial and monetary *regimes* that govern and facilitate trade and investment linkages are discussed in chapter 7 below.

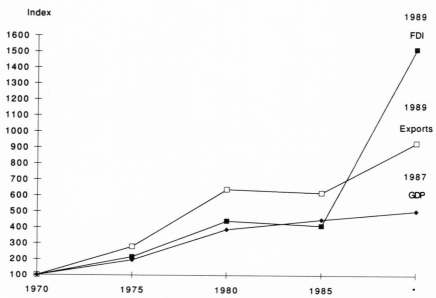

Sources: International Monetary Fund (IMF) and UNCTAD (see appendix table A-1 for data).

Figure 2-1.   Growth in World Economic Activity.

2.1.   The Global Economy

During the half century since World War II, economic activity has increased tremendously in almost every part of the world, and international economic activity—trade, investment, and foreign ownership —has expanded in both volume and importance. These worldwide trends are summarized in figure 2-1 (see data in appendix C, table A-1). Between 1970 and 1987 (the most recently available year), world gross domestic product (GDP), measured in current dollars, grew roughly fivefold. If we take account of inflation—estimated at 9% per year, GNP deflator, for 1972–1992 for the industrial countries, which account for the great bulk of total output (IMF, 1991, table A8)—the growth is still more than threefold. Over the same two decades, worldwide exports to 1989 increased ninefold, and foreign direct investment (FDI) to 1989 grew about fifteenfold in current dollars, or roughly six times and more than ten times, adjusted for inflation. The orders of magnitude involved in these important international economic flows are, of course, very different. The value of worldwide GDP in 1987 is estimated at $15 trillion; worldwide export value (1989) is almost $3 trillion; and total FDI (1989) is just under $200 billion. The most recent estimate of the total value of worldwide foreign capital stock is roughly $1.5 trillion, or about half the total value of exports (or imports) and between seven and eight times the value of annual FDI flows.[1]

Within this broad pattern of evolutionary growth, four major types of developments stand out. One is the trend toward increasing *interlinkage* among economically active nations and regions, both through trade and investment and through the operation of multinational enterprises. A second trend is the continuous appearance of *new economic actors* (national states, regions, industries, and enterprises) in the international arena. Both of these developments contribute to a third, the growth of *global industries* which operate within and among many different countries, creating new networks of international supplier–customer relationships and giving rise to new kinds of collaborative–competitive interactions. And a fourth trend is the persistence, and even increase, of *inequality and stress* between advanced and less developed countries and regions.

As the data presented below clearly demonstrate, direct economic interlinkage is most extensive within the so-called "Triad" (Ohmae, 1985) —the advanced industrial countries of North America, Western Europe, and the Pacific Rim. The Triad is roughly the membership of the Organization for Economic Cooperation and Development (OECD). The complex linkages among these economies have created the "borderless world" described by Ohmae (1990) and clearly evidenced by the almost instantaneous reverberation of major stock market movements, oil price changes, currency revaluations, etc., among these economies (cf. Panic, 1988, chapter 2).

The largest trade volume in the world is, by a better than 2:1 margin, intra-European Community (EC) trade (figure 2-2), followed by trade within the Asia/Pacific area (including Japan, Australia, and New Zealand). Trade among developing countries is relatively unimportant by comparison. The largest external trade flows are between the EC and the 'rest of the world' (excluding the Western Hemisphere and the Asia/Pacific region), and then between the Western Hemisphere and the Asia/Pacific countries. The most unbalanced external trade flow is from the Pacific Rim to the Western Hemisphere, reflecting the large trade surplus enjoyed by Japan and the newly industrialized countries (NICs) of Asia. The accuracy of present methods for calculating international trade balances between countries has been criticized recently by a panel of economists appointed

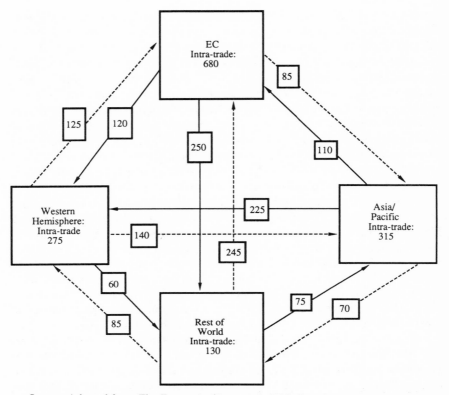

Source: Adapted from *The Economist* (January 5, 1991), based on International Monetary Fund (IMF) data.

Note: Numbers are rounded to the nearest $5 billion, so exact trade balances should not be computed without referring to original IMF data.

Figure 2-2.   World Trade Flows, 1989 ($ Billions).

by the US National Academy of Sciences. The panel concluded that US trade statistics do not incorporate intraenterprise sales, that is, exports from a US parent enterprise to its own foreign affiliates. Such sales account for more than 25% of US exports. Measured on this revised basis, the 1987 US trade deficit was $64 billion rather than the $148 billion officially reported (*Time*, February 10, 1992, p. 49). The importance of intra-enterprise sales is discussed further in section 3.3.2 below.

Expanding linkages between the Triad and other countries illustrate the second trend: increases in the number of significant actors and forces involved in the global economy. The members of the Organization of Petroleum Exporting Countries (OPEC) took on new importance during the 1970s. In the 1980s Japan, already an important participant in the global economy, became a major world economic power; at the same time, a number of NICs, particularly the four "Little Japans" or "Asian Tigers" of the Pacific Rim (Hong Kong, Singapore, South Korea and Taiwan), greatly increased their roles in the world economy. The most recent development is the opening up of Eastern Europe and the Soviet Union to worldwide economic contact. Both advanced and NIC economies are involved, and are increasingly integrated with each other, in the growth of global industries—automobiles, chemicals, electronics, pharmaceuticals, and petroleum and petrochemicals (Porter, 1986).

Finally, all three of these trends—increasing interlinkage, emergence of new actors, and growth of global industries—contribute to the fourth trend: the widening and increasingly conspicuous gap between incomes and living standards in the economies participating in these developments and the conditions that prevail in societies that remain, for whatever reason, outside the scope of the worldwide economic development process. These poorer countries, many with large populations, constitute challenges and opportunities for the global economy, and may threaten its continuing growth and prosperity.

All four aspects of globalization stimulate the development of international policy regimes. Interlinkage within the Triad, and between Triad countries and others, requires the creation of institutionalized systems of trade, monetary, and financial interaction. Increases in the number and variety of significant actors stimulate the need for explicit agreements and structures that reflect diverse, but mutually interdependent, interests. The growth of global industries would create new situations requiring multinational responses even if only domestic enterprises and import–export linkages were involved; the importance of MNEs in these industries adds further multinational complications and concerns. And the plight of the poorer countries becomes increasingly conspicuous and pressing within this context.

2.1.1. Data Classification and Statistical Profile

The several official data collections describing various aspects of the global economy have been constructed for different purposes and possess different strengths and limitations. (See appendix B for more detailed discussion.) In particular, different data sources use different classification systems for nations and economic systems, and assign countries to various categories according to somewhat different criteria. (The membership of various organized international economic groups—OECD, OPEC, EC, etc.—has also changed over time.) We rely here primarily on more or less comprehensive data published by the World Bank, the UN Conference on Trade and Development (UNCTAD), and the UN Centre on Transnational Corporations (UNCTC), but we group all these data according to the classification scheme of UNCTAD. All these data sources have significant gaps, errors, and omissions, and all the classification systems are problematic in one way or another. Fortunately, most of these discrepancies are not significant for our purposes, since our primary interest is in the *patterns* and *trends* in global economic relationships, and these are essentially the same in all major data sources.

International and comparative data on trade and investment, the focus of interest in this chapter, can be examined for geographic regions, for individual countries, or for countries grouped according to various criteria, such as income levels or types of economy. Our analysis relies primarily on the "type of economy" classification shown in table 2-1, which is based upon the system used by UNCTAD. Other groupings will be indicated in the text or exhibits as appropriate.

As table 2-1 indicates, UNCTAD recognizes five types of economies:

1. Industrial (or developed) market economies, often termed the advanced industrial countries or "Triad" countries. (The World Bank and UNCTAD include somewhat different sets of countries in this category, and we follow the World Bank grouping scheme in this instance.)
2. Eastern European economies, including the USSR. These countries are still described as "socialist," although they are changing rapidly and in diverse ways. These countries account for 8% of world population and, according to their official data, for 15% of world gross national product (GNP); however, their 8% share of world exports is probably a closer indication of their actual global economic position.
3. Asian "socialist" states, including the People's Republic of China (PRC). These countries are distinguished from those in the previous category by level of development, as well as location. They are poor by any standard, having 23% of world population and just 3% of world GNP; however, they contain pockets of development, such as the Chinese Special Economic Zones, that are of global economic significance.

Table 2-1. Basic Data by Type of Economy

Type of Economy	1989 Population (Millions)	% of World Population	1989 $ GNP (Billions)	% of World GNP	1989 $ GNP Per Capita	1988 $ Exports By Origin (Billions)	1988 % of World Exports (By Origin)	1985 % of Foreign-Owned World Capital Stock (By Origin)
World Total	5239	100	20,542	100	3921	2847	100	100.00
Industrial Market	754	14	14,505	71	19,239	1955	69	97.20
US	248	5	5208	25	21,000	322	11	35.10
EC10	305	6	4871	24	15,986	1037	36	
EFTA	32	1	715	3	22,492	178	6	
Japan	123	2	2929	14	23,810	265	9	11.70
Other	46	1	782	4	16,848	153	5	
USSR & Eastern Europe	402	8	3023	15	7521	223	8	0.10
USSR	289	6	2463	12	8521	111	4	
Asian Socialist	1200	23	430	2	358	51	2	
OPEC	438	8	629	3	1437	118	4	
Other	2445	47	1956	10	800	500	18	2.70
NIC7	335	6	987	5	2944	287	10	

Sources: World Bank, *World Tables* (Baltimore, MD: Johns Hopkins University Press, 1991) and UNCTAD, *Handbook of International Trade and Development Statistics* (New York: 1989), table 1. GNP data supplemented from *Statistical Abstract of the United States,* (Washington, DC: US Department of Commerce, 1990) for some Eastern European countries not reporting members of World Bank (1987 estimates).

Notes: $ GNP Per Capita is $360 for PRC, $330 for other "Asian Socialist" states (low-income developing countries). For definitions of the countries included in each type of economy, see appendix B "Note on Data and Sources."

4. Members of OPEC. A few of these countries rise out of the "less developed" category because of their high per capita incomes; however, their economies are not "advanced" overall, and many of them are relatively poor in spite of their export earnings. Also, the reader should note that some important countries (e.g., Bahrain, Brunei, Mexico, etc.) are not OPEC members; hence, this classification is more political than economic.

5. "Other" countries, including both developing and stagnant economies, have in common only their exclusion from the foregoing categories.

The added category of "newly industrialized countries" (NICs), included by most official data sources within "Other" countries, has come to be widely used in analyses of global economic change, although the specific characteristics and identity of the NICs are subject to debate. In general, NIC designation implies both a certain level of development —they are sometimes described as "*nearly* industrialized countries"— and an emphasis on global economic participation. Most references to NICs include at least the NIC7 identified in table 2-1:

East Asia: Hong Kong, Singapore, South Korea, Taiwan;

Latin America: Argentina, Brazil, Mexico.

Some analysts also include:

Israel—more than twice as rich per capita as South Korea, and comparable to Spain;

Venezuela—comparable to South Korea;

China and India—because of their aggregate size and the volume of their industrial exports.

We will refer to NIC7 as appropriate in connection with specific data. Reference to NICs in other than a statistical context connotes economies at an intermediate stage of development that are significantly engaged in international economic activity, rather than a specific list of countries.

Even a cursory examination of aggregate data on the world economy, such as are summarized in table 2-1, reveals one overwhelming fact: the dominant economic size and role of a relatively small group of advanced countries, variously referred to as the Triad, the First World, or "Industrial Market Economies." These economies include the US and Canada; most members of the European Community (here referred to as the EC 10, excluding Greece and Portugal, which are developing economies); members of the European Free Trade Area (EFTA); Japan; and Australia and New Zealand. These nations, which contained only 14% of the world's population in 1989, generated 71% of the world's GNP (1989), provided 69% of world exports (1988), and controlled 97% of world foreign-owned capital stock (1985). The US alone accounted for 5% of the world's population (about one third of the industrial countries' share), generated 25% of world GNP (just over one third of the industrial countries' share), and controlled over one third of world foreign-owned capital stock.

The great variations in global economic status and participation among various countries and groups indicated by these data are, of course, often associated with differences in their internal economic structures, particularly the relative importance of agriculture in the less developed countries (LDCs) (see appendix C, table A-2). In addition, there are significant differences in economic performance among the industrial market economies. During the entire period from 1958 to 1987, Japan had generally higher GNP growth and lower unemployment than the US and Western Europe. The EFTA countries also had somewhat higher GNP growth rates than the EC, and had unemployment rates comparable to those of Japan. Western Europe outperformed the US in terms of growth and unemployment until the 1980s, after which their relative positions were reversed (*Financial Times*, November 17, 1988).

2.2. Trade Linkages

Our analysis of trade linkages in the global economy involves levels and trends in three dimensions:

1. The volume of trade—the aggregate amount of trade taking place within the global system;
2. The structure of trade—the pattern of imports and exports among trading countries;
3. The content or composition of trade—the kinds and combinations of goods and services that are traded internationally.

Over the decades since World War II, the volume of world trade has increased enormously in absolute terms and also relative to national and world economic growth. This expansion has been a major force in the development of the contemporary global economy. The structure of world trade is dominated by the Triad economies; they account for some two thirds of the total volume, and they trade primarily with each other. Not surprisingly, however, in view of the growth of the NICs and other factors, the relative share of the industrial market economies in total world trade has been declining somewhat over time, even apart from the distorting short-term effects of fluctuations in international oil prices. (The statistical data presented here have been selected so as to bracket the effects of the OPEC-generated oil price increases of the 1970s.) The content of world trade has also changed somewhat over recent decades, particularly with respect to the growing importance of world trade in services.

2.2.1. The Volume of Trade

Between 1970 and 1988, the dollar value of world exports increased more than $2.5 trillion, or approximately 900% (see table 2-2). These changes in dollar values reflect, of course, effects of inflation and fluctuations in exchange rates, but the data nevertheless reveal an unprecedented growth in real export/import activity throughout the world. In particular, these increases are far in excess of both inflation rates and rates of GNP growth in the OECD countries, which dominate all of these trends. The only unusual features of the aggregate data tabulated in table 2-2 are 1) the re-latively small role of the industrial market economies in export growth during the 1980–1985 period, offset by exceptional growth during 1985–1988, and 2) the declining share of OPEC countries since 1980 due to fall-ing oil prices.

2.2.2. The Structure of Trade

The industrial market economies not only account for the largest part of world trade, but also they trade very largely with each other. The 1988 data reported in table 2-3 show that roughly two thirds of world exports originated in, and a similar proportion was received by, the industrial market economies; and nearly three quarters of this volume consisted of trade among themselves. (Data in appendix C, table A-3 show that most of these structural relationships have been fairly stable over the past two decades.)

In view of their role in total world trade, the industrial market econom-ies not surprisingly also accounted for major shares of trade with all other groups—more than half the imports of every group except the East European "socialist" countries, and more than half the exports of OPEC and "other" (developing) countries (again, chiefly NICs). The only other striking feature of this structural picture is the internal orientation of trade among the East European socialist countries. Even in 1988, however, their relative involvement with industrial market economies was substantial (22% of their exports and imports), and these figures are certain to increase as these countries become more integrated into the global system.

Within the industrial market or roughly OECD group of countries, trade (and all other forms of economic activity) is dominated by five nations —France, Germany (with East and West united in 1991), Japan, the UK, and the US. The other two members of the Group of Seven (G7), Canada and Italy, are important international actors, but Canada is tied largely to the US and Italy to the EC. A few other individual countries—particularly the Benelux states, Sweden, and Switzerland—also play significant international roles. Both EC and EFTA countries tend to trade heavily among themselves, but the EC countries are also strongly involved with the US, Japan, and the NICs; the US alone has accounted for 20% of EC imports and received nearly 25% of EC exports in recent years. The UK has important linkages with its former dominions (Australia, Canada, New Zealand, and South Africa) and colonies. Japan is the most isolated of the OECD members, followed by Australia and New Zealand, but all three of these Pacific states have important trade links with the countries of Southeast Asia. The EFTA countries (other than Sweden and Switzerland) tend to trade primarily with the EC and Eastern Europe (*Financial Times*, November 17, 1988).

The NICs and other developing countries also give rise to significant international trade, investment, and organizational activities, both among themselves and with more advanced countries. Longitudinal data (appendix C, table A-3) indicate a rise in the relative proportion of exports (from 19% in 1965 to 22.8% in 1985) going to the developing countries from the industrial market economies. The OECD countries are clearly dependent upon import of critical materials (especially oil, gas, minerals, and certain agricultural commodities) from the developing regions, which therefore cannot be viewed as "peripheral" elements of the international economic system. There is also some evidence to suggest that intra-Third World trade may be increasing (see appendix C, table A-3).

2.2.3. The Content of Trade

World exports and imports consist of both *services* and *merchandise*, the latter customarily subdivided into *manufactures* and *nonmanufactures*. Data at this level of detail are collected from a variety of sources and, for a

Table 2-2.   World Exports, 1970–1988 ($ Billion f.o.b.)

Origin of Exports		World Volume	% of World Volume	Period Growth in Volume	% Share of World Growth in Volume
World Total	1970	311.91	100.00		100.00
	1975	872.06	100.00	560.16	100.00
	1980	1994.29	100.00	1122.23	100.00
	1985	1929.54	100.00	85.94	100.00
	1988	2838.90	100.00	947.31	100.00
Industrial Market	1970	222.56	71.35		
	1975	573.11	65.72	350.55	62.58
	1980	1260.63	63.21	687.52	61.26
	1985	1262.10	65.41	1.46	1.70
	1988	1985.50	69.94	723.40	76.36
USSR & Eastern Europe	1970	30.53	9.79		
	1975	77.36	8.87	46.83	8.36
	1980	155.12	7.78	77.76	6.93
	1985	173.97	9.02	18.85	21.94
	1988	223.20	7.86	49.23	5.20

	Year				
Asian Socialist	1970	2.31	0.74		
	1975	7.26	0.83	4.95	0.88
	1980	19.96	1.00	12.70	1.13
	1985	30.06	1.56	10.10	11.75
	1988	51.10	1.80	21.04	2.22
OPEC	1970	17.99	5.77		
	1975	113.18	12.98	95.19	16.99
	1980	306.65	15.38	193.48	17.24
	1985	155.96	8.08	-150.69	-100.00
	1988	118.02	4.16	-37.95	-100.00
Other	1970	38.53	12.35		
	1975	101.16	11.60	62.63	11.18
	1980	251.93	12.63	150.77	13.43
	1985	307.45	15.93	55.52	64.61
	1988	461.08	16.24	153.64	16.22

Sources: UNCTAD *Handbook of International Trade and Development Statistics* (New York: 1989), table 1, and *Supplement* (1984, 1987), table A.1.

Notes: $ Billion f.o.b. ("free on board").

1985 and 1988 figures for "Period Growth in Volume" exclude the decline in dollar value reported for OPEC. Percentage shares for growth also exclude OPEC (which is 100% of decline). "Industrial Market" defined differently than in table 2-1: UNCTAD classifies Greece, Israel, Portugal, and South Africa as industrial economies; World Bank treats them as developing economies ("Other" in table 2-1).

Table 2-3. Origin and Destination of Exports by Type of Economy, 1988

Origin of Exports		World	Destination of Exports ($ Billion f.o.b.) Industrial Market	USSR & Eastern Europe	Asian Socialist	OPEC	Other
World Total	$ Volume	2824.02	1961.97	194.76	61.60	99.98	484.52
	% by Destination	99.25	69.47	6.90	2.18	3.54	17.16
	% by Origin	100.00	100.00	100.00	100.00	100.00	100.00
Industrial Market	$ Volume	1987.82	1536.71	43.76	26.45	68.38	298.82
	% by Destination	99.31	77.31	2.20	1.33	3.44	15.03
	% by Origin	70.39	78.32	22.47	42.94	68.40	61.67
USSR & Eastern Europe	$ Volume	226.88	50.74	126.46	11.51	5.20	32.28
	% by Destination	99.70	22.37	55.74	5.07	2.29	14.23
	% by Origin	8.03	2.59	64.93	18.69	5.21	6.66
Asian Socialist	$ Volume	50.82	18.05	5.29	0.54	1.24	25.58
	% by Destination	99.77	35.52	10.42	1.07	2.44	50.33
	% by Origin	1.80	0.92	2.72	0.88	1.24	5.28
OPEC	$ Volume	120.43	72.74	2.45	0.74	4.96	38.53
	% by Destination	99.16	60.40	2.04	0.62	4.12	31.99
	% by Origin	4.26	3.71	1.26	1.21	4.96	7.95
Other	$ Volume	438.07	283.73	16.80	22.35	20.19	89.32
	% by Destination	98.70	64.77	3.83	5.10	4.61	20.39
	% by Origin	15.51	14.46	8.62	36.28	20.19	18.43

Source: UNCTAD, Handbook of International Trade and Development Statistics (New York: 1989), table A.1.
Notes: $ Billion f.o.b. ("free on board").
"Industrial Market" defined differently by UNCTAD than World Bank (see table 2-2 notes).
% by Destination sums horizontally. May not sum to 100% due to minor data discrepancies.
% by Origin sums vertically. May not sum to 100% due to minor data discrepancies.

Table 2-4.   Content of World Exports, 1970–1988

	1970		1985		1988	
	$ Billions	Percentage Share	$ Billions	Percentage Share	$ Billions	Percentage Share
World Total	312	100	1930	100	1994	100
Services	35	11	344	18	368	18
Merchandise	277	89	1586	82	1627	82

Sources: Estimated from UNCTAD, *Handbook of International Trade and Development Statistics* (New York: 1989) and *Supplement* (1987); World Bank, *World Development Indicators*, 1987 diskette data set; World Bank, *World Tables 1991* (Baltimore, MD: Johns Hopkins University Press, 1991), various tables.

Notes: "Services" computed as the difference between "World Total" and "Merchandise."

In 1985, manufacturing (a subcategory of merchandise) was $1120 billion (58% of world total).

In 1985, "Oil Exporters" (a set of countries) was $156 billion (including services and merchandise) or 8% of world total.

Estimates approximate only due to use of different data series, but 1985 and 1988 percentage shares correspond almost exactly.

variety of reasons, the reported totals of exports and imports in these and other disaggregated categories (which should in principle be identical) do not coincide. Since our concern here, as elsewhere, is with broad patterns rather than with statistical detail, we focus on *export* data only and make no attempt at reconciliation.

In the late 1980s, merchandise constituted about 82% of world exports, and services the remaining 18% (table 2-4). The general trend since 1970, and probably over a much longer period, has been toward a relative increase in international trade in services. Manufactured goods account for about two thirds of all merchandise exports; the relative shares of manufactured and nonmanufactured exports within the merchandise export total are strongly affected by oil price fluctuations.

Manufacturing is of central importance in the process of economic development and particularly in the integration of new participants into the global economy. Hence, the level and growth of trade in manufactured goods is of particular interest. Table 2-5 shows the distribution of manufactured exports by origin and destination for 1965 and 1985. Since manufactured exports account for more than half of total exports, it is not surprising that the basic pattern is roughly the same as that shown in previous total-exports tables. The industrial market economies are about as important in manufactured exports as in total trade (70% as opposed to 69% in table 2-1); the oil exporting countries are essentially non-

Table 2-5. Origin and Destination of Manufactured Exports by Type of Economy in 1965 and 1985

	Origin of Exports		Industrial Market Economies		Nonmember Economies		High-Income Oil Exporters		Developing Economies	
	1965	1985	1965	1985	1965	1985	1965	1985	1965	1985
Destination of Exports in $ Millions										
World Total (calculated)	93,940	1,120,052	60,664	759,655	3037	32,333	1021	35,569	29,217	292,471
Industrial Market	86,876	946,968	57,338	662,878	1738	18,939	869	28,409	26,932	236,742
OPEC (calculated)	231	5749	114	3070	1	7	16	467	99	2182
Other Developing	6833	167,335	3212	93,708	1298	13,387	137	6693	2187	53,547
Percentage Distribution by Destination										
World Total (calculated)	100.00	100.00								
Industrial Market	92.48	84.55	66	70	2	2	1	3	31	25
OPEC (calculated)	0.25	0.51	49	53	0	0	7	8	43	38
Other Developing	7.27	14.94	47	56	19	8	2	4	32	32

Source: World Bank, World Development Indicators, 1987 diskette data set.
Notes: "World Total" is calculated from categorical data. World Bank does not report "OPEC," which is calculated from original data. "Other Economies" does not include nonreporting nonmembers in Eastern Europe and Asia. (See appendix B, "Note on Data and Sources," for details.)

participants. The change in world exports over the 1965–1985 period is analyzed in more detail in table 2-6, which makes the striking point that industrial market economy exports have increased at less than half the rate of those of all other global market participants. Such a difference might be expected for the oil-exporting countries because of relative price changes; however, the comparable increase for other less industrialized countries is a major factor in the transformation of the global economy over recent decades. Also notable from these data is the fact that, although non-OPEC developing countries have increased the share of their exports going to industrial market economies, the latter have become slightly more integrated with each other (intragroup exports increasing from 66% to 70%) during this period. (It should be remembered from table 2-2 that 1980–1985 was an unusual period of slowdown in world economic integration.)

Export patterns for individual countries, both OECD members and NICs, for 1965 and 1985 are shown in appendix C, table A-4. Among the OECD countries, the share of intragroup exports either rose or remained constant, while the share going to developing economies declined in every case but one (Scandinavia). South Korea is the classic NIC, with the dollar value of its manufactured exports increasing explosively over the period and the high share going to advanced countries remaining stable. By contrast, the great bulk of Chinese manufactured exports went in 1985 to developing countries—32% to industrial market economies and only 3% to other Communist states (UNCTAD, 1987, table A.1).

2.3. Investment Linkages

International investment, according to many analysts, has become more important than trade as a source of integration and interdependence of the global economy. In 1980, the US alone contributed about half of the total stock of outward FDI; in 1991, the EC accounts for almost as much outward stock of FDI, and it is predicted that Japan will catch up within the coming decade. These economies (which exclude Canada, Australia, New Zealand, and the EFTA) own some 81% of the total outward stock of FDI, compared to about 47% of world exports.[2] Julius comments:

> We are rapidly approaching a new level of economic integration through direct investment: a cascading of flows from more countries, into more sectors and involving more actors than ever before. Unlike trade, these FDI flows represent long-term commitments by companies to build viable businesses in one another's markets. They may be slowed, but they will not easily be reversed, by economic downturns or shifts in exchange rates (1990, p. 6).

Table 2-6.   Changes in Origin and Destination of Manufactured Exports by Type of Economy, 1965–1985

	World Exports by Origin	Destination of Exports in $ Millions			
		Industrial Market Economies	Nonmember Economies	High-Income Oil Exporters	Other Economies
1965–1985 $ Increase in Exports					
World Total	1,026,112	698,962	29,544	34,570	263,015
Industrial Market	860,092	605,539	17,202	27,540	209,810
Oil Exporters	5518	2956	6	782	2828
Other	160,502	90,466	12,342	6247	50,376
1965–1985 % Increase in Exports					
World Total	1092	1152	962	3395	901
Industrial Market	990	1056	990	3170	779
Oil Exporters	2389	2593	600	4890	2857
Other	2349	2817	951	4560	2303
1965–1985 Average Annual % Increase					
World Total	55	58	48	170	45
Industrial Market	50	53	50	159	39
Oil Exporters	119	130	30	245	143
Other	117	140.8	48	228	115

Source: World Bank, *World Development Indicators*, 1987 diskette data set.
Notes: "World Total" is calculated from categorical data. World Bank does not report OPEC. "Oil Exporters" includes both OPEC and other states. "Other Economies" does not include nonreporting nonmembers in Eastern Europe and Asia. (See appendix B, "Note on Data and Sources," for details.)

Trade and investment are, of course, intimately linked. At times they appear as alternatives: a producer in one country may export to another, or may establish a production facility there to serve the local market. In fact, however, through the dynamics of economic development, trade stimulates investment and investment correspondingly stimulates trade. The long-term relationships established through FDI are, however, as Julius emphasizes, quite different from those arising out of arm's–length trade transactions alone. (Wallace et al., 1990, present a stimulating overview of current FDI policy issues.)

Analysis of the role of international investment in the global economy involves two distinct concepts. One is the current *flow* of new investment among countries during any time period; data reflecting this flow are exactly comparable to trade data, although the magnitudes are quite different and the errors involved are more difficult to determine. The other is the accumulated *stock* of investment that enterprises and nationals from one country hold in another at any time period. Net investment flows from country A to country B during any time period add to the total stock of country A ownership in country B. Note, however, that even if no current flow takes place, the current stock of country A investment holdings in country B may be large as a result of investment flows during previous time periods.

The holding of investment stocks generates a third type of relationship, the flow of *earnings* from country B to investors located in country A. These earnings may be repatriated in the form of trade (exports from country B into country A) or as reverse capital flows (i.e., country B investors make investments in country A). They may also be reinvested, further expanding country A investors' ownership in country B. An additional complication is that investment, both stocks and flows, can take a variety of forms—"real" investment (facilities, equipment, etc.), financial investment (securities), and cash holdings.

For all these reasons, appropriate conceptualization and measurement of investment linkages among countries is extremely difficult, and there are significant differences between the reported values of theoretically identical magnitudes (country A's outbound investment in country B, and country B's record of inflows from country A). These differences, like differences in disaggregated import and export data, arise because the two sets of raw data are collected independently and from different sources. Outward stocks, outward investment flows, and inward earnings flows are reported by "home" countries (country A, in this example); inward stocks, inward investment flows, and outward earnings flows are reported by "host" countries (country B, in this example). Differences between

Table 2-7. Foreign-Owned Capital Stock by Type of Economy and Major Country, 1975 and 1985

Type of Economy	1975		1985	
	$ Value	% of Total	$ Value	% of Total
Outward Stocks (Origin) in $ Billions				
World Total	282	100	713.5	100
Industrial Market	275.4	97.7	693.3	97.2
US	124.2	44	250.7	35.1
UK	37	13.1	104.7	14.7
Japan	15.9	5.7	83.6	11.7
Other	98.3	34.9	254.3	35.7
Other	6.6	2.3	20.2	2.8
Inward Stocks (Destination) in $ Billions				
World Total	246.8	100	637.2	100
Industrial Market	185.3	75.1	478.2	75
US	27.7	11.2	184.6	29
Western Europe	100.6	40.8	184.3	28.9
Japan	1.5	0.6	6.1	1
Other	57	23.1	109.2	17.1
Other	61.5	24.9	159	25

Source: UN Centre on Transnational Corporations, *Transnational Corporations in World Development: Trends and Prospects* (New York: 1986).

Notes: For outward stocks, the UK is reported separately. The UK is a uniquely rentier economy holding abnormally large capital stocks overseas. "Other Industrial Market" includes Western Europe. For outward stocks, for inward stocks, "Western Europe" includes UK. USSR and Eastern Europe less than 0.1% in 1985 (origin). Asian Socialist negligible (origin).

reported figures for conceptually identical magnitudes may arise due to incomplete reporting, differences in definitions and source/destination information among countries, fluctuations in exchange rates, and even differences in the timing of transaction records and data collection activities. In any event, differences in inward and outward estimates of conceptually identical magnitudes may be quite substantial, as the data tables in this section reveal. Fortunately, as with the trade data, the general *pattern* of relationships appears to be about the same from both perspectives.

Examination of the available investment data, in spite of its inadequacies, reveals essentially the same picture found in the trade data. The OECD countries dominate global foreign investment, and intra-OECD investment is by far the most important element in the global total. According to the data shown in tables 2-7 and 2-8, about 97% to 98%

Table 2-8. Foreign Investment Flows by Type of Economy and Major Country, 1975 and 1985 ($ Billions)

Type of Economy	1975		1985	
	$ Value	% of Total	$ Value	% of Total
Outflows (Origin)				
World Total	27.60	100	59.90	100
Industrial Market	27.30	98.9	58.70	98
US	14.19	51.4	15.21	25.4
Western Europe	10.10	36.6	30.19	50.4
Japan	1.79	6.5	6.41	10.7
Other	15.40	55.8	22.10	36.9
Other	0.30	1.1	1.20	2
Inflows (Destination)				
World Total	21.50	100	49.30	100
Industrial Market	15.18	70.6	37.81	76.7
US	2.60	12.1	19.18	38.9
Western Europe	10.11	47	16.61	33.7
Japan	0.19	0.9	0.59	1.2
Other	2.19	10.2	1.38	2.8
Other	6.30	29.3	11.49	23.3

Source: UN Centre on Transnational Corporations, *Transnational Corporations in World Development: Trends and Prospects* (New York: 1986).

Notes: USSR, Eastern Europe, and Asian Socialist countries negligible. These data do not correspond exactly to revised data published in UNCTC, *World Investment Report 1991: The Triad in Foreign Direct Investment* (New York: UNCTC, August 1991). Since the 1991 data do not provide a corresponding breakdown of world totals by type of economy and major country, we continue to rely on the 1986 report.

of all foreign-owned investment, whether measured as stocks or flows, is accounted for by the industrial market economies; these countries are also the "hosts" of 75% of all foreign investment stocks. The emergence of Japan as a major international investor was one of the most important developments in the global economy during the 1980s.

The UK plays a considerably more important role in world investment than in trade, partially because its historic role in trade led to the accumulation of substantial foreign investments. The UK is almost uniquely a rentier economy. In 1985, it controlled 14.7% of world foreign-owned capital stock (table 2-7). By contrast, in 1985, its exports of $68.4 billion accounted for only 3.5% of world exports (appendix C, table A-4). With EC 92 rapidly approaching, Britain has become the world's second most popular location for FDI after the US. As outward investment flows have fallen somewhat (from 21 billion British pounds in 1988 to about 17 billion British pounds in 1990), inward investment flows have risen from about 3.5 billion British pounds in the early 1980s (1.5% of British GDP) to 22 billion British pounds (4.5% of GDP). Foreigners already own 20% of Birtish manufacturing production, a figure estimated to rise to 40% by 1995.[3]

2.3.1. Investment Stocks

The valuation of capital stock, even within a single economy, involves many complexities, and comparisons and accumulations among different economies over different time periods introduce further complications. Particular problems include estimation of depreciation rates, variations in inflation rates among countries, and variations in currency exchange rates over time. Our analysis relies primarily on data reported by the UNCTC.

According to the data summarized in table 2-7, the total value of foreign-owned capital stock, whether measured from origin or destination sources, increased about 2.5 times between 1975 and 1985. Virtually all (98%) of this investment was accounted for by the industrial market economies. US foreign holdings roughly doubled, and therefore declined relative to the total; Japan's holdings increased more than fivefold, and its relative share of the world total doubled. No other countries appear to have experienced substantial changes in relative share. The industrial market economies were also the principal site of foreign capital investment holdings, accounting for 75% of the total in both years. The major change over the period was the substantial increase in the share of total holdings located in the US (from 11% to 29%), and a corresponding decline in the share of other advanced countries. The relative share of foreign investment located in developing countries was essentially stable over the period.

The foreign holdings of the four major investor countries (Germany, Japan, the UK, and the US), shown in table 2-9, are distributed in diverse ways. Germany and the UK held 80% or more of their total foreign investments in industrial market economies, principally the US and Western Europe. US investments were slightly less concentrated in such economies, and its non-European holdings were roughly evenly disbursed among industrial and developing countries. Only about half of Japan's holdings were in advanced countries, and these were relatively concentrated in the US. Japan itself is not a significant recipient of foreign investment by others. Investments in developing countries are relatively greatest for Japan, although the US accounts for half again more total investment value in such countries.

Table 2-9. Location of Foreign-Owned Capital Stock for Leading Investor Countries, 1985: Outward Stock Reported by Home Country, Billions of Indicated Currencies

Investor Country	World Total	Type of Economy							
		Industrial Market					USSR & Eastern Europe	Other
		Total	US	Western Europe	Japan	Other		
Germany (DM)								
1985 Value	147.8	118.5	44.8	63.6	2.2	7.9	0.1	22
% 1985	100	80	30	43	1	5	0	20
Japan ($)								
1985 Value	83.6	42.4	25.4	10.8		6.2	0.2	41.1
% 1985	100	51	30	13		7	0	49
UK (BP)								
1984 Value	75.7	63.6	26.3	18.6	0.6	18	0	12.2
% 1984	100	84	35	25	1	24	0	16
US ($)								
1985 Value	250.7	184.5		105.1	9.2	70.1	0	60.9
% 1985	100	74		42	4	28	0	26

Source: UN Centre on Transnational Corporations, *Transnational Corporations in World Development: Trends and Prospects* 1986 (New York: 1986), annex tables A.5, A.6, pp. 518–526.

Notes: DM: Deutsch Marks. BP: British Pounds. Japan converted to US $. Percentages sum horizontally to approximately 100. "Other" calculated as a residual from "World Total," "Industrial Market," "USSR and Eastern Europe." Only 95% of German and 98% of US data reported.

Table 2-10.   Role of Foreign Direct Investment (FDI) in the US Economy, 1977 and 1986

Foreign Shares of Various US Aggregates	(1977)	(1986)
Capital Stock	2.1	6.3
Manufacturing Capital Stock	5.2	11.4
Employment	1.7	3.4
Manufacturing Employment	3.5	7.3
GNP (Total Value Added)	1.7	3.4
Manufacturing Value Added	3.7	8.3
Shares of Selected Countries in US FDI Stock	(1980)	(1988)
UK	16.6	31
Netherlands	25	14.9
Japan	6.2	16.2
Canada	14.4	8.3

Source: Edward M. Graham and Paul R. Krugman, *Foreign Direct Investment in the United States* (Washington, DC: Institute for International Economics, 1989), tables 1.2, 1.5, 2.2, pp. 13, 20, 34; based on Bureau of Economic Analysis, US Department of Commerce, various different reports cited.

Foreign investment is relatively more important in the Western European countries than in the US, and least important in Japan (see appendix C, table A-5). However, the increasing role of FDI in the US has been a major development of the past couple of decades and a major factor in increased integration among the industrial market economies. Several different perspectives on this development are reflected in table 2-10. The foreign-ownership share of US capital stock tripled during 1977–1986, and accounted for more than 10% of total capital stock in manufacturing industries by the end of the period. There has also been a significant shift in national origins of foreign capital stock holdings in the US. The Japanese share of FDI in the US more than doubled during the 1980s, and the UK share also increased substantially. The shares of other major investor countries decreased correspondingly.

2.3.2.   Investment Flows

Estimated annual foreign investment flows for 1975 and 1985 (table 2-8, above) show essentially the same pattern: nearly all of the investment flows originate in the industrial market economies, and these economies are also by far the largest investment recipients. In fact, the relative concentration of new FDI in the advanced countries has increased slightly over the period. There have also been internal changes in current investment patterns among the advanced countries. The relative share of US investors fell by about one half over the period, while the shares of all other industrial countries increased correspondingly. The share of annual FDI flowing into the US more than tripled over the period. From 1973 to 1988, for example, there was a dramatic increase in foreign banking assets located in the US. The foreign proportion of total US banking assets rose from 3.8% to 19.2% (Graham and Krugman, 1989, pp. 21–22, based on Federal Reserve Board data). In 1988, more than half of these foreign banking assets were held by Japan. Canada was a very distant second at 7.1%. Only the UK and Italy were even above 5% of foreign banking assets.

In 1984, the ten largest host countries for FDI were the US (27.3% of world FDI), Canada (10.3%, reflecting US investment there), the UK (7.8%), Germany (5.9%), Brazil (3.8%), Australia (2.8%), the Netherlands (2.7%), France (2.7%), South Africa (2.7%), and Switzerland (2.2%). All other countries together accounted for 32% of FDI (US Department of Commerce, 1988).

Table 2-11 compares US FDI abroad with FDI in the US by region and country, and also by industry, in 1988. US investment abroad was more diversified, since some 25% was outside the industrial market economies. Europe, Canada, and the rest of the Western Hemisphere were the most important locations. The largest industry group for US foreign investment was manufacturing, followed by banking and finance, and then by petroleum. FDI into the US came overwhelmingly from the industrial market economies, with two thirds coming from Europe, followed by Japan in importance. About one third of the investment flow was in manufacturing, followed in importance by banking and finance, and then by trade.

2.3.3. Earnings Flows

Successful investment in one period generates subsequent income, and international earnings flows are the revenue counterpart of FDI, after a time lag. Earnings flows are also an important aspect of international economic integration and interdependence. Relevant data by selected countries and regions of origin and destination for 1975 and 1985 are shown in table 2-12. The dollar value of total earnings outflows more than doubled over the decade. The effects of changes in the price and profitability of

Table 2-11. Direct Investment Into and Out of the US by Multinational Enterprises, 1988 ($ Millions)

	US Direct Investment Abroad		Foreign Direct Investment in US	
	$ Value	%	$ Value	%
All Countries	326,900	100.00	328,850	100.00
Industrial Market	245,498	75.10	302,757	92.07
Canada	61,244	18.73	27,361	8.32
Europe	152,232	46.57	216,418	65.81
Japan	16,868	5.16	53,354	16.22
Other	15,154	4.64	5624	1.71
Other Economies	76,837	23.50	26,093	7.93
Western Hemisphere	49,283	15.08	17,019	5.18
OPEC	10,229	3.13	6221	1.89
International Organizations	4565	1.40		
All Industries	326,900	100.00	328,850	100.00
Petroleum	59,658	18.25	34,704	10.55
Manufacturing	133,819	40.94	121,434	36.93
Trade	34,401	10.52	64,929	19.74
Banking and Finance	83,854	25.65	71,758	21.82
Services	15,168	4.64	36,024	10.95

Source: US Department of Commerce, Bureau of Economic Analysis, *Survey of Current Business*, vol. 69, no. 6 (June 1989), Russell B. Scholl, "The International Position of the United States in 1988," pp. 41–49.

Note: "Banking and Finance" includes insurance and real estate.

oil exports dominate the percentage shifts during 1975–1985; the 1985 percentage distributions probably should be taken as representative. The key observation is that the US is the major net recipient of foreign earnings flows (with inflow more than five times outflow in 1985). For all developing countries, and even for Japan, outflows exceed inflows by substantial amounts.

2.4. Conclusion

The world economy has expanded rapidly during the last two decades through the growth of trade and investment, both of which have increased much more rapidly than world production. This pattern of growth has greatly increased the scope and variety of international linkages, which

Table 2-12. Earnings Flow Data by Type of Economy and Major Country, 1975 and 1985 ($ Millions)

Type of Economy	1975		1985	
	$ Value	% of Total	$ Value	% of Total
Outflows (Origin)				
World Total	20.43	100.00	43.06	100.00
Industrial Market	10.53	51.54	29.37	68.21
US	2.25	11.01	6.30	14.63
Western Europe	4.81	23.54	16.93	39.32
Japan	0.29	1.42	0.83	1.93
Other	3.18	15.57	5.30	12.31
Oil Exporters	8.02	39.26	9.14	21.23
Other	1.87	9.15	4.56	10.59
Inflows (Destination)				
World Total	25.11	100.00	53.67	100.00
Industrial Market	24.99	99.52	53.03	98.81
US	16.65	66.31	32.32	60.22
Western Europe	7.01	27.92	15.62	29.10
Japan	0.51	2.03	2.56	4.77
Other	0.82	3.27	2.54	4.73
Other	0.13	0.52	0.64	1.19

Source: UN Centre on Transnational Corporations, *Transnational Corporations in World Development: Trends and Prospects* (New York: 1986).

Notes: "Oil Exporters" includes OPEC plus other states. USSR, Eastern Europe, and Asian Socialist countries negligible.

in turn are creating a complex economic system that is truly "global" in character. At the present time, these linkages are dominated by and occur largely within the Triad economies of the OECD. The principal changes in recent years have been the relative growth in the size and importance of Japan and the appearance and impact of certain smaller countries commonly described as NICs. The rise and decline of oil prices over the past two decades produced distorting effects, both in the real economy and in its statistical descriptors, but little substantial long-term change in the relative importance of oil-exporting countries. The advent of EC 92 and the impending economic integration of the EC and EFTA are most likely to reinforce the domination of global trade and investment linkages by industrial market economies; however, continued growth for some other participants in the global economy should also be anticipated.

Notes

1. This figure comes from UNCTC, August 1991, table 10, p. 32. Intra-EC FDI is included in this figure (intra-EC exports are counted in worldwide exports).
2. "Foreign Investment and the Triad," *The Economist*, August 24, 1991, p. 57.
3. "A Rentier Economy in Reverse," *The Economist*, September 22, 1990, pp. 63–64.

References

Graham, Edward M., and Paul R. Krugman. 1989. *Foreign Direct Investment in the United States*. Washington, DC: Institute for International Economics.

International Monetary Fund (IMF). 1991. *World Economic Outlook: October 1991*, Washington, DC: IMF.

Julius, DeAnne. 1990. *Global Companies and Public Policy: The Growing Challenge of Foreign Direct Investment*. New York: Council on Foreign Relations Press for Royal Institute of International Affairs.

Ohmae, Kenichi. 1985. *Triad Power: The Coming Shape of Global Competition*. New York: Free Press.

Ohmae, Kenichi. 1990. *The Borderless World: Power and Strategy in an Interlinked Economy*. New York: Harper Business.

Organization for Economic Cooperation and Development (OECD). 1987. *International Investment and Multinational Enterprises: Recent Trends in International Direct Investment*. Paris: OECD.

Panic, M. 1988. *National Management of the International Economy*. New York: St. Martin's.

Porter, Michael E., ed. 1986. *Competition in Global Industries*. Boston, MA: Harvard Business School Press.

UN Centre on Transnational Corporations (UNCTC). 1986. *Transnational Corporations in World Development: Trends and Prospects*. New York: UNCTC.

UN Centre on Transnational Corporations (UNCTC). 1991. *World Investment Report 1991: The Triad in Foreign Direct Investment*. New York: UNCTC (August).

UN Conference on Trade and Development (UNCTAD). 1987. *Handbook of International Trade and Development Statistics: Supplement*. New York: UNCTAD.

US Department of Commerce. 1988. *International Direct Investment: Global Trends and the U.S. Role*. Washington, DC: US Department of Commerce.

Wallace, Cynthia Day, et al. 1990. *Foreign Direct Investment in the 1990s: A New Climate in the Third World*. Dordrecht, Netherlands: Martinus Nijhoff.

3 MULTINATIONAL ENTERPRISES IN THE GLOBAL ECONOMY

The international trade and investment linkages that have evolved since World War II have been importantly influenced by, and have in turn greatly influenced, the growth of multinational enterprises (MNEs). We use the term *enterprise* rather than any more restrictive term, such as *corporation*, to refer to organizations engaged in business activities such as production, service, and sales, regardless of their legal form or type of ownership. In particular, both investor-owned entities and state-owned entities are included, along with various hybrid combinations. The appearance and growth of hybrids—both private–government partnerships and multinational joint ventures and strategic alliances—is a particularly significant feature of the contemporary international business environment. We follow Dunning in defining a *multinational* enterprise as one that "owns and controls income-generating assets in more than one country" (Dunning, ed., 1974, p. 13), or more recently as "a coordinator of value added in two or more countries" (Dunning, 1991, p. 3; see also Dunning, 1979). More elaborate terminological distinctions among such enterprises, such as those suggested by Porter (1986, 1990), Bartlett and Ghoshal (1989), and others (see Hoogvelt, 1987, for a comprehensive compilation) are useful for some purposes, and are introduced as relevant below.

It is important to emphasize that international economic linkages can and do arise without the involvement of MNEs. Trade can take place among enterprises in different jurisdictions, each of which is purely domestic in its own operations; and international capital movements can occur without any integration of management and policy among the capital-sending and capital-receiving organizations. In fact, however, the management and operations of most MNEs are significantly integrated across countries, and substantial and increasing proportions of total world trade and investment take place within the MNE framework. Hence, over the past half century the growth and evolution of MNEs have been intimately involved in both the growth of international trade and investment and in the process of economic development and integration throughout the world. In some instances, initial trade and investment flows stimulated by independent economic forces led to the formation and growth of MNEs. On other occasions, MNEs are created when successful domestic firms move into new markets or production locations. In either case, once established, MNEs in turn generate (or impede) new trade and investment flows, and create (or prevent) new forms of international coordination, in the light of their own organizational structures and objectives.

The growth and evolution of MNEs is closely related to the development of international policy regimes. MNEs form important links within the global economy that go beyond, and sometimes supersede, the relationships established by governments. They create new structures of international economic integration; and the flows of managerial and technical knowledge and control that occur within MNE structures are significantly different from product and capital flows that occur through market channels. MNE structures and activities may be either welcomed or resisted by various national governments and other economic and political actors, and a major concern in both advanced and developing countries over the postwar decades has been the harmonization of MNE operations with national economic and social goals. Many international policy regimes include enterprises (both domestic firms and MNEs) as active participants for purposes of policy-making and/or implementation.

MNEs for their own part are steadily evolving new types of collaborative relationships in response to the opportunities and problems arising in the global economy. The opportunities lie in the product-market and geographic diversification and expansion possibilities arising from the globalization process. The problems lie both in interfirm relationships and in the difficulties caused by tremendous variations in national operating conditions and national policy treatment of foreign-owned enterprises.

One stimulus for international regime development is the need to shape a more stable and less risky global environment for MNEs.

The first section of this chapter examines the nature of the multinational enterprise, a topic that is the subject of a very large literature (cf. Slomanson's extensive bibliography, 1989). The second section presents a schematic framework for analyzing the various types of enterprises participating in the global economy on the basis of their ownership-control structures and geographic bases. The third section examines the patterns of international linkage that have evolved as a result of growth in the numbers, size, and importance of MNEs in the global economy; the increasingly important roles of global industries and MNE networks are emphasized. The final section discusses some aspects of international policy regimes that focus specifically on the existence and operation of MNEs.

3.1. The Nature of the Multinational Enterprise

The increasing number and size of MNEs over the postwar decades, and their increasing importance within the global economy, have attracted considerable attention to the theory of the MNE and the evolution of global business structures. The contemporary literature has focused on several interrelated issues: Why do MNEs emerge? In what ways are they different from purely domestic enterprises? How does their appearance and growth affect the development of individual industries and national economies?[1]

Porter (1986, 1990) points out that international industries can be configured in either "multidomestic" or "global" patterns, with many mixed structures possible between these extremes. In a multidomestic industry, competition takes place within national or regional markets that are essentially independent of each other; the industry is "international" only in the sense that it exists in parallel form in many different countries. Some multidomestic industries are the exclusive province of purely domestic firms within each national environment; in other cases, MNEs from various countries may also be active, along with local competitors. In any event, in a multidomestic industry, competitive interaction takes place on a national/regional basis, and products and operating practices may be quite different from country to country.

By contrast, in a global industry, the competitive environment itself is defined in international terms. The key feature, according to Porter, is that "a firm's competitive position in one nation significantly affects (and is affected by) its position in other nations;" the competitive enterprises in such an industry, which are necessarily MNEs, interact "on a truly world-wide basis, drawing on competitive advantages that grow out of their entire network of worldwide activities" (Porter, 1990, p. 53).

The post-World War II expansion of MNEs can be seen as an essentially "natural" market and resource expansion of technologies, including management technology, already in existence (initially) in the US and (subsequently) in Western Europe and Japan. However, evolution from earlier colonialist and international trade models is also important. Current worldwide growth of MNEs—including those emerging in the newly industrialized countries (NICs) and the less developed countries (LDCs), as well as state-owned/supported enterprises—has a rationale and dynamic of its own that is not necessarily consistent with conventional notions of comparative advantage and protectionism.

Explanations for the evolution of MNEs include a number of factors: exploitation of scale and scope advantages; relative ease of *intra*-organizational (as compared to *inter*organizational or "market") transfers of management skills, technology, and capital across borders; "early mover" advantages in extending domestic innovations into new markets; and so forth (Buckley, 1990). The scale-economy argument holds that larger markets create cost and market power advantages; the scope-economy argument explains diversification of products and services along related lines (Teece, 1986). Reduction of transaction costs through improvements in transportation and communication technologies has been instrumental in generating the opportunities to exploit such scale and scope economies (Williamson, 1975, 1985).

The distinctive characteristics of MNEs include their need to operate across diverse national cultures and their complex governance structures, which are strongly affected by differences among national policies and by international policy developments. While MNE expansion may arise in economic rent seeking and transaction cost reductions, organizational structure and culture are stressed by multinational operations. "Managers of today's multinationals are not so much economic decision makers as they are governors of a social and political strategic management process" (Bower and Doz, 1979, p. 165). The *governance* of enterprises involves both 1) formal legal arrangements (ownership and internal control) and 2) external relationships, both transactional and stakeholder. National governments are inevitably stakeholders in major enterprises operating within their jurisdictions, and this stakeholder relationship is strengthened and formalized by policy attention, regulation, and (in the most extreme case) partial or total government ownership. The MNE is inevitably a sociopolitical institution, and MNE management involves greater problems of governance than those of the typical purely domestic enterprise. Combining local autonomy and conformity to domestic conditions with global strategic integration presents both internal and external governance problems.

The impact of MNEs on the growth and development of individual economies, particularly in the LDCs, has been a matter of considerable debate, and differences of opinion about this matter have been highly significant in the evolution of international policy regimes during the postwar decades (see Adams and Whalley, 1977; Committee for Economic Development, 1981). Most contemporary literature treats the MNE as an economic actor with significant social impacts (Caves, 1982; Hymer, 1976); but, according to Boddewyn, "Political behavior by MNEs has usually been ignored, downplayed or passively treated in dominant economic models of the multinational enterprise" (1988, p. 341). In fact, however, there are important political dimensions to the ownership, activity internalization, and geographic location advantages associated with MNEs, and their social and political role may be as important as their economic impact. The nonmarket environment of the MNE, including its political dimensions, interacts with the market environment and with the character of the enterprise itself to yield complex results for which no single element is responsible; and political expertise may be as important as managerial and technological skill in accounting for MNE success or failure (Boddewyn, 1988; see also Behrman and Grosse, 1990; Mahini, 1988; Poynter, 1985; Safarian, 1983).

3.2. Types of Multinational Enterprise

Many different types of firms, both domestic and MNE, are active participants in the global economy, and the differences in their structure and ownership have a significant impact on their status and treatment under national and international policies. Figure 3-1 presents a classification system for enterprise types designed to highlight these important features, with illustrative examples. The vertical dimension of the figure differentiates enterprises by type of ownership: enterprises with private-investor ownership; enterprises jointly controlled by two or more parent organizations (which may include partial state ownership); and state-owned enterprises (SOEs).[2] The horizontal dimension of figure 3-1 differentiates enterprises according to their national/international status:

| | Multinational Enterprises | | |
Purely Domestic Enterprises	National-Base Enterprises	Joint Ventures, Strategic Alliances, Enterprise Networks	Stateless Global Enterprises
Investor-Owned Enterprises Ansett Australian National Airways (Ansett ANA) Canadian Pacific	Nestle (Switzerland) Union Carbide (US)	Caltex (US) Auto Companies ⟶	BCCI Likely ➤
Jointly-Controlled Enterprises and Private-Government Combinations Conrail (US)	British Petroleum (BP)	Union Carbide India , Ltd. (UCIL) SAS (Sweden, Norway, Denmark) ⟶	Possible ➤
State-Owned Enterprises Trans Australian Airlines (TAA) Amtrak (US) Canadian National	Quantas (Australia)	Renault (France) ⟶	Unlikely ➤

Figure 3-1.   Classification of Enterprises.

domestic enterprises; national-base organizations with operations in other parts of the world; networks of national-base enterprises such as joint ventures and strategic alliances; and (presently only a theoretical possibility) "stateless" global corporations.

Before turning to the various MNE forms suggested by this framework, the variety of domestic enterprises depicted is worth brief attention. It is particularly notable that enterprises of various ownership types may exist within the same national economic setting, and indeed may be engaged in active competition with each other. For example, in Australia two principal domestic airlines compete: Trans Australian Airline (TAA) is state owned; Ansett Australian National Airways (Ansett ANA) is owned by private investors. (Qantas, a national-base state-owned enterprise, competes with foreign firms in the overseas travel market.) A similar situation is found in the Canadian railroad industry, where Canadian National (state owned) and Canadian Pacific (investor owned) are competitors in transcontinental service. In the US, Conrail (originally a government corporation formed out of pre-existing private firms) is a government–private joint venture for intercity rail freight; Amtrak is a government corporation offering intercity rail passenger service. None of these domestic enterprises has any significant international role, but their existence illustrates the fact that, even in highly market-oriented countries, various combinations of investor-owned and state-owned firms are engaged in providing goods and services in the marketplace. Varied ownership-control patterns within the same industry are very common in socialist states, where nationally controlled and provincially controlled enterprises (both state owned) may interact with various kinds of cooperatives, foreign MNEs, and joint ventures.

Among MNEs, the national-base enterprise operating through foreign subsidiaries or affiliates is by far the most common type. These enterprises are chartered and headquartered in a particular country, which is also the primary source of their managerial staff; hence, they tend to reflect that country's culture, standards, and values. Nestle (Switzerland) and Union Carbide (US) are investor-owned national-base MNEs that have gained recent and unfavorable notice in connection with their operations in LDCs. (Nestle's involvement in the international infant formula controversy of the 1980s is discussed in chapter 5 below.) British Petroleum (BP) originated as a private–government combination; BP supplied oil to the Royal Navy, and government representatives on the BP board possessed veto power. Renault (France) is a state-owned enterprise, a diversified conglomerate making and selling a variety of products (including, of course, automobiles) throughout the world.

Between such national-base enterprises and the "stateless" corporations that may appear in the future, there are many different hybrid combinations. These may take the form of informal cooperation, consortia, strategic alliances, contractual agreements, equity joint ventures, mergers and acquisitions of various types, and so forth. Participants may be investor owned, state owned, or both. According to Reich (1991), MNEs are increasingly operating through "global nets" in which more or less formal relationships among specific organizations are maintained on a relatively permanent basis (see also Auster, 1987).[3] Reich (1991) argues that national products, technologies, and enterprises are disappearing; what will matter in the twenty-first century will be national origin of value added in global products or services sold by global nets.

These hybrid arrangements are alternatives to both arm's-length market transactions and the establishment of wholly owned foreign subsidiaries. Joint ventures typically involve equity participation, and thus represent a form of foreign direct investment (FDI). Contractual relationships such as licensing, management contracts, franchising, turnkey operations, sub-contracting, and so forth "are more akin to sales transactions than to investment, since they usually do not involve a long-term ownership interest by one entity in another" (UNCTC, 1983, p. 40).

Caltex, headquartered in Dallas, Texas, and jointly owned by Standard Oil of California and Texaco, is a good example of an equity joint venture between two investor-owned MNEs; the firm markets petroleum products in LDCs. In 1987, Corning Glass Works participated in at least 20 strategic alliances in other countries, including Australia, China, France, Germany, and the UK; these activities contributed half of its net income (Kanter, 1983, p. 192). General Electric had over 100 cooperative ventures with other enterprises in 1986 (Kanter, 1989, p. 183).

The special situations that may arise as a result of combined investor and state ownership are well illustrated by the case of Union Carbide India Ltd. (UCIL), owner of the Bhopal chemical plant that caused death and injury to thousands of people in 1984. Union Carbide (US) held a majority interest (51%) in UCIL, and Indian investors, including a state government, held the remainder. Under government pressure, UCIL had turned all plant operations over to Indian nationals, although the parent company retained primary operating responsibility. After the disaster, both the locus of responsibility for the accident and the jurisdiction (India or the US) in which the matter was to be adjudicated became subjects of widespread international debate (for a concise summary, see Steiner and Steiner, 1985, pp. 180–195).

The Scandinavian Airlines System (SAS) is a classic example of a private–government joint venture involving multiple countries. Denmark, Norway, and Sweden each have domestic airlines owned half by private investors and half by the national government. SAS is a combination of these three airlines for international travel. It also operates various other enterprises and owns a substantial share of Continental Airlines in the US. In spite of this diversity, however, SAS is not likely to become a "stateless" enterprise, because of its strong focus on Scandinavia.

The auto industry, however, may be moving toward a truly "stateless" character, as a result of joint ventures and strategic alliances among US, Japanese, and European firms. It is now difficult to identify readily the national origin of autos being sold in the US (Mitchell, 1992). The network of interenterprise and international relationships is summarized in figure 3-2. General Motors has a US joint venture with Toyota, plus ownership positions in Suzuki and Isuzu in Japan, and in Saab in Europe. Ford has complex links with three European and two Japanese companies, and Chrysler is primarily linked with Mitsubushi. Isuzu, Fuji Heavy Industries, and Nissan (all of Japan) are interlinked, and both Nissan and Toyota are

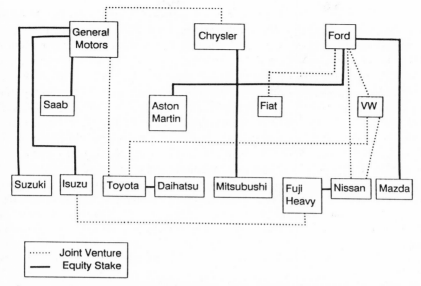

Source: Murray Weidenbaum and Mark Jensen, *Threats and Opportunities in the International Economy*. St. Louis, MO: Washington University, Center for the Study of American Business, July 1990, Formal Publication No. 100, figure 1, "The Complex World of the Automobile Industry," p. 12.

Figure 3-2.   International Linkages in the Automobile Industry.

linked with Volkswagen, which is in turn linked with Ford (Weidenbaum and Jensen, 1990).

In the extreme logical case, not yet observed in practice but implicit in proposals for European Community (EC) or United Nations (UN) corporate chartering, an MNE would no longer be tied to a particular national base, but would become a truly "stateless" global corporation without national identity or interests. Such an enterprise might be a kind of organizational chameleon, taking on local camouflage as appropriate in each jurisdiction. For example, its headquarters (staffed on a multinational basis) might be located in Liechtenstein or in the Caribbean. Its national affiliates or subsidiaries, scattered around the world to optimize costs and market access, might be staffed entirely with local personnel. Its ownership might be dispersed among individuals, other corporations, and governments throughout the globe. Although such an entity is beyond the range of current experience, proposals for the establishment of pan-European enterprises after 1992 ("European Corporations"), and even for "United Nations Corporations," may be harbingers of things to come (Schelpe, 1991). The international legal and financial problems arising in connection with the operations of the Bank of Credit and Commerce International (BCCI), officially controlled by BCCI Holdings (Luxembourg) S.A. but operating throughout the world, illustrate the difficulty in regulatory and legal oversight of MNEs in the absence of any kind of comprehensive international system. It has been alleged that BCCI units engaged in laundering criminal funds and in supporting terrorist activities around the world; and, in July 1991, in a move headed by the Bank of England, the assets of BCCI were seized by bank regulators of several countries. The ultimate outcome in this case is unknown at the time of this writing. However, it seems likely that some large MNEs and MNE networks will evolve into "stateless" entities over the coming decades, and that some kind of international regulatory arrangements will evolve to deal with these entities.

3.3. Enterprise Linkages

The data presented in chapter 2 above clearly show that international economic activity is dominated by relatively few advanced industrial countries that are increasingly linked with each other through trade, investment, and policy coordination. These countries also are the home bases for the great majority of the world's largest enterprises (see table 3-1).

Available data on MNEs are subject to a number of limitations with respect to both coverage and classification procedures. In the first place, every one of the giant enterprises enumerated in table 3-1 may not be an MNE in the strictest sense; however, most of them clearly are, and no more selective compilation of data is currently available. In addition, some large and internationally important entities, particularly state-owned enterprises and alliance/network arrangements, may escape coverage in these compilations. In spite of these discrepancies, there is little doubt that the industrial market economies are home to well over 90% of all large MNEs, and the US alone to between one third and one half of them. Gradual decline in the relative role of the US—which accounted for well over half of all MNEs during the early postwar decades—has been due to the postwar recovery of Europe and, more recently, to the rapid growth of MNEs based in Japan and, to a much lesser extent, in NICs and other less advanced countries. The recent UNCTC study of 600 large industrial and agricultural MNEs with $1 billion or more in sales (the "billion dollar club"), reported

Table 3-1. National Base of the World's Largest Enterprises, Selected Years

	Fortune Industrial Firms 1980 (Composite "Global 500")		Fortune Industrial Firms 1990 (Reported "Global 500")		UNCTC Industrial and Agricultural Firms 1985 ("Billion Dollar Club")		Business Week All Types of Firms 1990 (Reported "Global 1000")	
	Number	%	Number	%	Number	%	Number	%
Total	500	100.0	500	100.0	600	100.0	1045	100.0
Industrial Market	477	95.4	469	93.8	577	96.2	980	93.8
US	219	43.8	167	33.4	273	45.5	329	31.8
EC 4	125	25.0	114	22.8	130	21.7	196	18.7
Other EC 8	20	4.0	16	3.2	16	2.7	43	4.1
EFTA	21	4.2	34	6.8	33	5.5	38	3.6
Japan	71	14.2	111	22.2	98	16.3	333	31.9
Other	21	4.2	27	5.4	27	4.5	41	3.9
Other	23	4.6	31	6.2	23	3.8	65	6.2
NICs	18	3.6	25	5.0	18	3.0	64	6.1
OPEC	2	0.4	3	0.6	3	0.5		
LDCs	3	0.6	3	0.6	2	0.3	1	0.1

Sources: Fortune, Business Week, UN Centre on Transnational Corporations, Transnational Corporations in World Development: Trends and Prospects (New York: 1988).

Notes: UNCTC "Billion Dollar Club" defined as firms with sales above $1 billion. 1980 Business Week report excluded US firms. 1980 Fortune "Composite Global 500" was prepared by authors from 1980 Fortune "Foreign 500" and "US 500" reports.

A few firms owned jointly by two EC countries (either UK or Italy) have been assigned to the "EC 4" (France, Germany, Italy, UK).

Fortune ranks the joint firm; Business Week reports the separate partners unranked.

"Other Industrial Market": Canada, Australia, New Zealand.

NICs: Argentina, Brazil, Chile, Hong Kong, India, Israel, Mexico, Singapore, South Africa, South Korea, Taiwan, Turkey.

Business Week excludes countries where stock markets are largely closed to foreigners and major firms are often privately owned. Brazil, Mexico, South Korea, Taiwan (reported as addendum data for annual revenues over $1 billion) included here together with unranked jointly owned firms, bringing "Global 1000" to a count of 1045.

that US-based MNEs accounted for 51% of the total sales of this group of enterprises; Japan-based firms for 14%; and firms from other industrial market economies for 32%. These figures leave only 3% of giant MNE sales to be accounted for by enterprises based in the NICs and elsewhere (UNCTC, 1986, p. 36).

These data, which focus on the largest MNEs in the world, give an incomplete indication of the important and growing role played by smaller MNEs from less advanced countries, which are shown in more detail in table 3-2. The *Business Week* "global" survey is conducted on a broader scale than the *Fortune* industrial or UNCTC industrial/agricultural surveys. *Business Week* includes more firms in all industries, and better captures the effects of increasing enterprise size in the NICs. The most notable change over the 1980–1990 period, according to the *Business Week* data, is the dramatic decline in LDC-based enterprises—which includes the Organization of Petroleum Exporting Countries (OPEC)—and the increasing number of MNEs based in South Korea. (The importance of "nonconventional" MNEs—whether smaller or LDC-based—is also emphasized in the 1990 UNCTC report on this topic and in Kahn, ed., 1986.)

3.3.1. MNE Linkages in Global Industries

The emergence of global industries—that is, industries operating in many parts of the world and often dominated by MNEs that operate in many countries and markets—is a major feature of worldwide economic evolution during the past half century (Porter, 1990). Indeed, Porter argues that the explanation for the competitive advantage/disadvantage of various economies is to be found in the status of industries, industry clusters, and firms, not in national aggregates and attributes. He emphasizes that it is firms, not nations, that compete in international markets, and that "the leaders in particular industries and segments of industries tend to be concentrated in a few nations and sustain competitive advantage for many decades" (1990, p. 19). Industry "clustering" involves the development of related groups of industries within individual nations, and often within very restricted subnational locations.

The global status of particular industries can be gauged to some extent from the activities of the world's largest industrial firms, summarized for the 1990 *Fortune* "Global 500" in table 3-3. The three largest industries, each accounting for more than 10% of total "Global 500" sales—petroleum refining, motor vehicles and parts, and electronics—accounted

Table 3-2. Largest Enterprises by Home Country, Selected Years

| | Fortune "Foreign 500" Industrial Firms | | | | UNCTC Industrial and Agricultural Firms ("Billion Dollar Club") | | Business Week All Types of Firms | | | |
| | 1980 | | 1990 | | 1985 | | 1980 | | 1990 | |
	No.	%	No.	%	No.	%	No.	%	No.	%
Total	500	100.0	500	100.0	327	100	777	100.0	718	100.0
Newly Industrialized Countries (NICs)										
Total	33	6.6	41	8.2	18	6	98	12.6	64	8.9
Argentina	1	0.2	1	0.2	1	0	2	0.3	—	—
Brazil	7	1.4	5	1.0	2	1	14	1.8	5	0.7
Chile	1	0.2	1	0.2	1	0	2	0.3	—	—
Hong Kong							8	1.0	13	1.8
India	2	0.4	7	1.4	—	—	6	0.8	—	—
Israel	1	0.2	1	0.2	1	0	9	1.2	—	—
Mexico	3	0.6	2	0.4	2	1	4	0.5	7	1.0
Singapore							10	1.3	3	0.4
South Africa	5	1.0	6	1.2	2	1	17	2.2	5	0.7
South Korea	10	2.0	11	2.2	6	2	6	0.8	23	3.2
Taiwan	1	0.2	4	0.8	—	—	17	2.2	8	1.1
Turkey	2	0.4	3	0.6	3	1	3	0.4	—	—
Organization of Petroleum Exporting Countries (OPEC)										
Total	2	0.4	4	0.8	3	1	10	1.3	—	—
Less Developed Countries (LDCs)										
Total	4	0.8	4	0.8	2	1	55	7.1	1	0.1

Sources: Fortune, Business Week, UN Centre on Transnational Corporations, Transnational Corporations in World Development: Trends and Prospects (New York: 1988). UNCTC "Billion Dollar Club" includes firms earning over $1 billion. Business Week and UNCTC surveys adjusted to exclude US firms.

Notes: All percentages calculated from global totals. Business Week excludes countries where stock markets are largely closed to foreigners and major firms are often privately owned.

Table 3-3. Industry Composition of the *Fortune* Industrial "Global 500", 1990

Industry	Number of Enterprises	Sales ($ Billions)	% of Total Sales	Employees (Thousands)	% of Total Employees
Petroleum Refining	52	759	16.53	1658	6.22
Motor Vehicles and Parts	42	745	16.23	3823	14.35
Electronics	46	589	12.83	4162	15.62
Food	46	379	8.26	2201	8.26
Chemicals	49	375	8.17	2009	7.54
Metals and Metal Products	56	307	6.69	1959	7.35
Computers and Office Equipment	18	261	5.69	1674	6.28
Industrial and Farm Equipment	24	166	3.62	1144	4.29
Aerospace	17	157	3.42	1363	5.12
Forest Products	26	139	3.03	752	2.82
Pharmaceuticals	17	94	2.05	632	2.37
Beverages	17	92	2.00	725	2.72
Building Materials	16	81	1.76	621	2.33
Mining and Crude Oil	12	74	1.61	1267	4.76
Scientific and Photographic Equipment	7	71	1.55	488	1.83
Publishing and Printing	12	61	1.33	357	1.34
Textiles	12	53	1.15	291	1.09
Rubber and Plastics	8	53	1.15	502	1.88
Soaps and Cosmetics	9	52	1.13	273	1.02
Tobacco	5	44	0.96	414	1.55
Transportation Equipment	4	21	0.46	141	0.53
Furniture	2	7	0.15	90	0.34
Apparel	2	6	0.13	76	0.29
Toys and Sporting Goods	1	4	0.09	17	0.06
Total	500	4591	99.98	26,638	100.00

Source: Fortune "Global 500" (July 30, 1990).

Notes: Industries ordered by volume of sales. US enterprises are included.

for about 45% of total sales and 36% of employees for the entire group. The next three industries, each with 4% to 9% of total sales—food, chemicals, and metals—accounted for 23% of both sales and employment. No other industry accounted for more than 4% of sales.

The role of giant firms, based in various countries, in major global industries is shown in table 3-4. US-based MNEs are clearly the most numerous in food, chemicals, computers, aerospace, forest products, and pharmaceuticals. Japanese firms dominate the motor vehicle industry, followed by Western Europe, combining the EC and the European Free Trade Area (EFTA). The EC dominates beverages, as well as metals and metal products combined. The US and Western Europe are about equal in numbers in petroleum refining, and the US and Japan in electronics. Chemicals and industrial/farm equipment are about equally divided among the US, Japan, and Western Europe. (Western Europe also dominates building materials, as well as mining and crude oil.) Otherwise, the sources of international competition are widely distributed, with the only other important grouping being NIC-based enterprises in petroleum refining.

The comprehensive UNCTC study of national participation in industrial, agricultural, and service industries in 1985 (summarized in table 3-5) shows that although the US accounts for almost half of all large industrial or agricultural firms, Japan and Europe are home to three fourths of the world's largest banks. European organizations are also relatively numerous among the largest enterprises in insurance/reinsurance, retailing, and other areas. The relative importance of US-based firms in the major service industries listed in this table indicates that US dominance in worldwide service activities may offset to some extent its relative decline in leadership in manufacturing.

The relative importance of foreign affiliate operations in total MNE activity certainly varies from firm to firm, and even among groups of MNEs based in various countries. Some indication of this variation is suggested by UNCTC data covering the operations of the world's largest industrial MNEs during the period 1971–1980 (UNCTC, 1983, p. 48). Foreign operations accounted for 40% of the aggregate sales of all included enterprises in 1980, and 53% of their aggregate net earnings; both of these figures are increases from 1971 levels. By country, the foreign share of sales was above 50% for MNEs based in France and Germany, and above 40% for Japan and the UK. The share of foreign affiliate sales for US-based MNEs (31%) was by far the lowest in the group. All these figures reflect substantial increases over the preceding decade.

Table 3-4. Fortune "Global 500" Enterprises by Industry and National Base, 1990 (Percent and Total of "Global 500" Sales in Each Industry in Parenthesis)

Sales in $ Billions % of Sales	Petroleum Refining ($759) (16.53%)	Motor Vehicles and Parts ($745) (16.23%)	Electronics ($589) (12.83%)	Food ($379) (8.26%)	Chemicals ($375) (8.17%)	Metals and Metal Products ($307) (6.69%)
US	15	7	16	20	16	11
EC	11	12	8	10	17	20
Japan	7	18	15	10	9	13
EFTA	3	2	3	2	5	6
Other Market	2	1	1	3	1	3
NIC	11	2	3	1	—	3
OPEC/LDC	3	—	—	—	1	—
Total	52	42	46	46	49	56

Sales in $ Billions % of Sales	Computers and Office Equip. ($261) (5.69%)	Industrial and Farm Equip. ($166) (3.62%)	Aerospace ($157) (3.42%)	Forest Products ($139) (3.03%)	Pharmaceuticals ($94) (2.05%)	Beverages ($92) (2.00%)
US	10	8	11	12	10	4
EC	4	6	6	1	3	8
Japan	3	6	—	5	2	2
EFTA	1	—	—	4	2	—
Other Market	—	3	—	4	—	2
NIC	—	—	—	—	—	1
OPEC/LDC	—	1	—	—	—	—
Total	18	24	17	26	17	17

Sales in $ Billions % of Sales	Building Materials ($81) (1.76%)	Mining and Crude Oil ($74) (1.61%)	Scientific and Photo. Equip. ($71) (1.55%)	Publishing and Printing ($61) (1.33%)	Textiles ($53) (1.15%)	Rubber and Plastics ($53) (1.15%)
US	3	—	4	4	3	2
EC	6	5	1	3	1	3
Japan	3	—	2	2	6	3
EFTA	2	2	—	—	—	—
Other Market	2	4	—	3	1	—
NIC	—	1	—	—	1	—
OPEC/LDC	—	—	—	—	—	—
Total	16	12	7	12	12	8

Sales in $ Billions % of Sales	Soaps and Cosmetics ($52) (1.13%)	Tobacco ($44) (0.96%)	Transportation Equipment ($21) (0.46%)	Apparel, Toys, Sporting Goods ($10) (0.22%)	Furniture ($7) (0.15%)
US	4	2	1	2	2
EC	2	2	1	—	—
Japan	2	1	1	1	—
EFTA	1	—	—	—	—
Other Market	—	—	1	—	—
NIC	—	—	—	—	—
OPEC/LDC	—	—	—	—	—
Total	9	5	4	3	2

Source: Fortune "Global 500" (July 30, 1990).
Note: Industries ordered by volume of sales (see table 3-3).

Table 3-5. National Base of Largest Enterprises in Selected Industries Reported by UNCTC, 1985

	Industrial and Agricultural	Banking	Financial Services	Insurance	Reinsurers
US	273	5	10	14	5
EC	172	17	1	7	8
Japan	98	21	8	7	1
EFTA	7	4		2	1
Other Market	27	1	1		
NICs	12	2			
OPEC/LDC	11				
Eastern Europe					
Total	600	50	20	30	15

	Trading	Retailing	Accounting	Advertising	Market Research
US		18	13	12	8
EC	2	9	7	6	2
Japan	13	2		2	
EFTA	1				
Other Market	1	1			
NICs	3				
OPEC/LDC					
Eastern Europe					
Total	20	30	20	20	10

	Law	Construction	Publishing	Transportation	Airlines
US	7	6	8	11	12
EC	6	6	5	9	6
Japan		8		6	2
EFTA				2	2
Other Market	2		2	1	1
NICs				1	1
OPEC/LDC					1
Eastern Europe					
Total	15	20	15	30	25

	Hotels	Restaurants
US	17	20
EC	6	
Japan		
EFTA		
Other Market		
NICs		
OPEC/LDC		
Eastern Europe	2	
Total	25	20

Source: UN Centre on Transnational Corporations, *Transnational Corporations in World Development: Trends and Prospects* (New York: 1988).

Notes: "Total" is the number of largest enterprises in each industry.
"Other Market": Australia, Canada, New Zealand.
"Eastern Europe": USSR and East European members of CMEA.

3.3.2. MNE Networks[4]

The structure and function of individual MNE networks are difficult to grasp from aggregate data. In fact, several different kinds of network linkages are involved. At any point in time, an MNE is a *structure* of business units located in various national jurisdictions and linked by ownership patterns and control arrangements. Such a structure can be described in static terms, e.g., assets, employment, and sales at each location, or production and marketing links among them. However, the activities of MNEs must also be described in terms of the *flows*, both those that take place *within* the structure and those that take place *between* it and the outside world. Some of these flows, such as investment flows, initially create and then expand the structure itself; others simply utilize the existing structure in order to perform MNE functions.

To analyze the functional character of MNEs, Gupta and Govindarajan (1991) identify three types of flows: 1) capital and revenue flows, including investment, sales (both interaffiliate and external), and repatriation of profits; 2) product-service flows (again, both interaffiliate and external); and 3) communication flows, both managerial and technological. Attempts to map these flows within an individual MNE generally produce diagrams that look much like a ball of string, with overlapping lines running in all directions. Nevertheless, these flows are the true essence of MNE operations.

Aggregate data may improperly convey a mistaken impression that foreign trade is largely a matter of arm's-length transactions between unrelated buyers and sellers in different countries (Helleiner and Lavergne, 1979). In fact, transactions *among* the affiliated units of single enterprises compose a large and growing segment of all international commerce. Reliable data on intraenterprise trade are available only for the US, where the Department of Commerce (Bureau of Economic Analysis) collects such information as part of its periodic surveys of MNE activities. It was noted in section 2.1 earlier that such intraenterprise trade may not be properly reflected in the US trade balance. Using this source, Hipple (1990) has estimated intraenterprise trade into/out of the US for both US-based and foreign-based MNEs through their affiliates for 1977 and 1982 (see table 3-6). As might be expected, exports are relatively more important for the US units of US-based MNEs, and imports more important for the US units for foreign firms. In 1988, intraenterprise merchandise exports amounted to 39% of the total value of US merchandise exports; the proportion for merchandise imports was 43.7% (Hipple, 1990).

Only very limited aggregate data are available concerning the structure of worldwide MNE affiliate networks. Historical data on the affiliates of

Table 3-6. Percentage Share of US Foreign Trade Handled Through MNE Intraenterprise Shipments, 1977 and 1982

	1977 % of Total Value	1982 % of Total Value
All Multinational Enterprises (MNEs)		
Total US Merchandise Trade		
Share of Exports	39.0	31.8
Share of Imports	43.7	38.3
US Trade in Manufactured Goods		
Share of Exports	40.1	34.3
Share of Imports	50.3	45.2
US Trade in Nonmanufactured Goods		
Share of Exports	36.7	26.5
Share of Imports	36.5	28.2
US-Based Multinational Enterprises (MNEs)		
Total US Merchandise Trade		
Share of Exports	27.8	22.4
Share of Imports	23.0	17.6
US Trade in Manufactured Goods		
Share of Exports	36.6	29.8
Share of Imports	21.8	18.1
US Trade in Nonmanufactured Goods		
Share of Exports	8.8	6.9
Share of Imports	24.3	16.9
Foreign-Based Multinational Enterprises (MNEs)		
Total US Merchandise Trade		
Share of Exports	11.3	9.3
Share of Imports	20.7	20.7
US Trade in Manufactured Goods		
Share of Exports	3.5	4.5
Share of Imports	28.5	27.1
US Trade in Nonmanufactured Goods		
Share of Exports	27.8	19.6
Share of Imports	12.1	11.3

Source: F. Steb Hipple, "Multinational Companies and International Trade: The Impact of Intrafirm Shipments on U.S. Foreign Trade 1977–1982," *Journal of International Business Studies*, vol. 21, no. 3 (Fall 1990), pp. 495–504, tables 1, 2, and 3, based on US Department of Commerce (Bureau of Economic Analysis) surveys.

Note: Percentages rounded to nearest tenth.

Table 3-7.   Distribution of US-Owned Foreign Affiliates by Location, 1950–1980

	1950		1966		1980	
	Number	%	Number	%	Number	%
Total	7417	100.0	23,282	100.0	33,647	100.0
Industrial Market Economies	4657	62.8	15,128	65.0	21,959	65.0
Other Economies	2760	37.2	7718	33.2	11,688	35.0
Africa	175	2.4	683	2.9	765	2.27
Asia	524	7.1	1599	6.9	3707	11.02
Western Hemisphere	2061	27.8	5436	23.3	7216	21.45

Sources: UN Centre on Transnational Corporations, *Transnational Corporations in World Development: Trends and Prospects* (New York: 1973 and 1983 editions).

Notes: All types of enterprises are included.

Asia includes Turkey and Oceania (other than Australia and New Zealand).

Difference between total and subcategories in 1966 is due to unallocated affiliates (less than 2%). UNCTC data provided a geographical breakdown within Industrial Market Economies in 1950 and 1966, but not in 1980.

US-based MNEs are available for selected years 1950–1980; all types of enterprises are included (see table 3-7). The tremendous growth in the number of affiliates—more than fourfold over three decades—is striking evidence of the expansion of MNE networks. Affiliates located in industrial market economies dominate throughout the entire period; however, the continuing importance of Latin American affiliates and the growth of Asian contacts are evident.

The UNCTC has published some limited information on the affiliates of 243 service-industry MNEs for 1988 (see table 3-8). Only large companies were included in the study, and all parent companies included were headquartered in the industrial market economies. The distribution of companies among major service industries is shown in the table; the principal activities represented are business services and finance. More than 60% of all service-MNE affiliates covered by this study were located in industrial market economies; only Japan-based MNEs had fewer than half of their affiliates in these locations.

As noted above, the best available information on global parent–affiliate linkages covers US-based MNEs and foreign MNE affiliates operating in the US. Those data provide the best overall picture of the network of international linkages formed by MNEs and their affiliates, although the picture is far from complete (see table 3-9). These data, which include only nonbank entities, show that MNEs based in industrial market economies

Table 3-8. Regional and Industry Distribution of Foreign Affiliates of Industrial Market Economy Parents, Service Industries, 1987

	Number of Enterprises			Location of Affiliates			
	Parents	Foreign Affiliates	% of Affiliates by Region or Industry	Industrial Market Economies	% of Affiliates by Region or Industry	Other Economies	% of Affiliates by Region or Industry
Region							
US	95	6185	45	3788	61	2383	39
Japan	65	2540	19	1077	42	1427	58
Europe	75	4356	32	3197	73	1131	27
Other	8	590	4	378	64	212	36
Total	243	13,671	100	8440	62	5153	38
Industry							
Finance	87	3439	25	2041	59	1398	41
Wholesale Trade	19	2329	17	978	42	1351	58
Retail Trade	22	253	2	195	77	58	23
Business Services	57	6004	44	4059	68	1945	32
Construction	20	321	2	167	52	154	48
Other Services	41	1351	10	1030	76	321	24
Total	246	13,697	100	8492	62	5205	38

Source: UN Centre on Transnational Corporations, *Transnational Corporations in World Development: Trends and Prospects* (New York: 1988), table XXII.6, p. 411; table XXII.7, p. 412.

Notes: Minor rounding errors due to calculation methods for estimating region by industry breakdowns.

Data exclude airlines, hotels, fast-food, and restaurant chains due to lack of information.

Affiliates include a small number operating in centrally planned economies (14 for US, 36 for Japan, 28 for Europe). South Korea removed from total figures for home countries.

Finance (banking, securities and financial services, insurance, reinsurance), trade (wholesale and retail), business services (accounting, advertising, market research, legal), other (publishing, nonair transportation). Industry data include three Korean parents with 26 affiliates (19 in developed, 7 in developing countries). Affiliate data include 78 in centrally planned economies (64 of which are in banking).

Table 3-9. Comparison of US Foreign Affiliates and US Affiliates of Foreign-Owned MNEs, 1987

	Total Assets ($ Millions)	% of Total Assets	Total Sales ($ Millions)	% of Total Sales	Number of Employees (Thousands)	% of Employees
Nonbank US Affiliates of Foreign-Based Parent Enterprises (Operating in US)						
Country of Ultimate Beneficial Ownership						
All Countries	926,042	100	731,392	100	3159.7	100
Industrial Market	832,118	90	675,263	92	2904.5	92
Canada	140,822	15	89,303	12	590.5	19
Europe	467,607	50	387,010	53	1903.5	60
Japan	195,773	21	182,327	25	284.6	9
Other	27,916	3	16,623	2	125.7	4
US	24,189	3	10,145	1	35.5	1
Other	69,735	8	45,985	6	219.8	7
Western Hemisphere	32,180	3	27,150	4	143.6	5
OPEC	23,003	2	13,404	2	41.7	1

Nonbank Foreign Affiliates of US Parent Enterprises (Operating Outside US)

Location of US Affiliate						
All Countries	1,098,166	100	1,052,260	100	6234.6	100
Industrial Market	831,548	76	872,104	83	4272.7	69
Canada	151,061	14	145,215	14	912.4	15
Europe	527,422	48	562,448	53	2569.0	41
Japan	105,978	10	114,717	11	345.5	6
Other	47,086	4	49,724	5	445.8	7
Other	252,911	23	174,829	17	1933.8	31
Western Hemisphere	161,164	15	89,245	8	1228.8	20
International	13,707	1	5327	1	28.1	0

Sources: US affiliates of foreign parents from Ned G. Howenstine, "U.S. Affiliates of Foreign Companies: 1987 Benchmark Survey Results," Survey of Current Business, vol. 69, no. 7 (July 1989), pp. 116–140, at p. 121 (US Department of Commerce, Bureau of Economic Analysis), estimated from survey results.

Foreign affiliates of US parents from Obie G. Whichard, "U.S. Multinational Companies: Operations in 1987," Survey of Current Business, vol. 69, no. 6 (June 1989), pp. 27–39, at p. 32 (US Department of Commerce, Bureau of Economic Analysis), estimated from survey results.

Notes: Foreign "parent" defined as foreign direct investment (FDI) in US owned 10% or more by a foreign person and with assets, sales, or net income of more than $1 million. Data are classified in terms of ultimate beneficial ownership (UBO), so that a foreign-based enterprise can have a US owner. Such enterprises are classified under US ownership. US "parent" defined as US person owning 10% or more of a foreign affiliate.

The category "International" means that some activities not classified as to a specific location.

"Other Industrial Market": Australia, New Zealand, South Africa due to classification used in Whichard.

account for more than 90% of all foreign MNE affiliate sales and employees in the US; and affiliates of US-based MNEs are only slightly less concentrated in those same economies (83% sales and 69% employees).

The foreign activities of US-based MNEs occur primarily through majority-owned affiliates (see data in table 3-10). In 1987, majority-owned affiliates accounted for 77% of all US affiliate sales, and for the great majority of sales in all industries and in all host countries except for Japan.

Foreign acquisitions are an important means of creating and enlarging MNE networks, and the 1980s witnessed a boom in international mergers and acquisitions by both US and foreign firms. According to a study by Smith and Walter (1991), the dominant flow of transnational acquisitions was *into* the US. During the period 1985–1989, US firms completed an estimated 305 cross-border transactions (defined as mergers, tender mergers and offers, purchases of stakes, divestitures, recapitalizations, exchange offers, and leveraged buyouts), with an aggregate disclosed value of $38.8 billion. During the same period, there were 941 foreign transactions involving US companies, for a total disclosed value of $178 billion. (As a basis for comparison, there were 6195 comparable domestic transactions within the US, valued at just over $1 trillion, during the same period.) Outside the US, there were a total of 3098 domestic and cross-border transactions, valued at $328.8 billion.

The merger and acquisition boom spread to Western Europe in the late 1980s, in anticipation of EC 92. In July 1990, France, Japan, and the US were the three leading sources of announced cross-border acquisitions in Europe. Each country's enterprises disclosed European acquisitions valued in excess of one billion ECUs, followed by the UK with a total of 743 million ECUs. Overall, cross-border acquisitions in Europe have tended to focus on the UK.[5]

3.4. Policy Regimes for Multinational Enterprises

The growth of MNEs has stimulated the development of policy regimes, both national and international, specifically focused on this type of enterprise. Increased competition within global industries, expanded service and information links in finance, and other factors enlarging the scope and importance of international economic contacts would, of course, have led to new policy initiatives even in the absence of MNEs. However, the size, growth, and prominence of MNEs have been additional and specific stimuli. Indeed, the MNEs themselves, both individually and collectively, have been active participants in the evolution of regimes, since

Table 3-10. Foreign Affiliates of US Parent Enterprises, 1987

	All US Nonbank Affiliates		Majority-Owned US Nonbank Affiliates	
	Total Affiliate Sales ($ Millions)	% of Total Parent Enterprise Sales	Majority-Owned Affiliate Sales ($ Millions)	% of Total Affiliate Sales
By Area of Affiliate Operation				
All Countries	1,052,260	100	813,467	77
Industrial Market	872,104	83	674,537	77
Canada	145,215	14	135,788	94
Europe	562,448	53	462,501	82
Japan	114,717	11	42,416	37
Other	49,724	5	33,832	68
Other	174,829	17	134,757	77
Western Hemisphere	89,245	8	72,466	81
International	5327	1	4174	78
By Industry of Affiliate				
All Industries	1,052,260	28	813,467	77
Petroleum	213,857	43	168,435	79
Manufacturing	522,311	28	389,156	75
Wholesale	172,583	50	156,841	91
Finance	44,337	11	36,911	83
Services	30,497	26	26,400	87
Other	68,675	14	35,725	52

Source: Obie G. Whichard, "U.S. Multinational Companies: Operations in 1987," *Survey of Current Business*, vol. 69, no. 6 (June 1989), pp. 27–39 (US Department of Commerce, Bureau of Economic Analysis), estimated from survey results.

Notes: "Other Industrial Market": Australia, New Zealand, South Africa due to classification used by Whichard.

The category "International" means some activities are not classified as to a specific location.

Finance includes insurance and real estate, but not banking.

"Other Industries" includes agriculture, forestry, fishing, mining, construction, transportation, communication, public utilities, and retail trade.

Breakdown of affiliate sales as % of parent sales not available by country.

many of their activities require authorization or support from multiple sources and jurisdictions.

Two distinct views of the relative strength of MNEs vis-a-vis national and international policies and institutions are found in the contemporary literature. One view, succinctly captured in the title of Vernon's classic study *Sovereignty at Bay* (1971) and reflected in many other well-known publications (e.g., Barnet and Muller, *Global Reach*, 1974; Vernon, *Storm over the Multinationals*, 1977), holds that large MNEs are more powerful than the governments of the various jurisdictions within which they operate. By playing one interest off against another, and by optimizing their operations in relation to national and international policies as well as in relation to resources, costs, and markets, they may select and control their environments in their own interest. The opposite view, associated with C.D. Wallace (1982, 1990), Weidenbaum and Jensen (1990), and others, and dramatized by reference to such celebrated international business incidents as the Dresser Industries case (Sethi, 1982) and the Barcelona Traction case (C.D. Wallace, 1982, pp. 281–292), holds that MNEs are victims, rather than masters, of national and international policies, and are more likely to suffer than benefit from differences in national policies and objectives. In addition, the growth of state-owned and state-sponsored/ protected MNEs from both Third World and post-Communist countries in recent years adds to the ranks of enterprises that are more controlled by, rather than in control of, their own policy environments.

Whatever the relative balance of power between MNEs and governments, either individually or collectively, MNEs are inevitably sociopolitical institutions, and MNE management is conspicuously a problem of *governance* and balance among multiple, and often competing, interests (Bower and Doz, 1979). National states are inevitably "stakeholders" in the enterprises operating within their respective jurisdictions (and particularly so in the case of state-owned or state-sponsored enterprises), and the relationship is always symbiotic; that is, MNEs are also "stakeholders" in their host environments. The distinctive feature of MNEs, however, is that they are involved in several, possibly many, such relationships, an involvement that automatically creates new links—and not necessarily welcome or consistent ones—among the various jurisdictions themselves.

3.4.1. National Regulation of MNEs[6]

In both advanced and developing countries, potential conflict between MNE activities and national interests has been a major policy concern for

half a century. MNE "home" countries fear the export of jobs and industries; "host" countries fear domination and exploitation. In nearly all countries, MNEs are encouraged to engage in certain types of activity (e.g., exports) and are restricted or entirely foreclosed from others. (Indeed, even foreign portfolio investment is restricted in some instances, cf. Eun and Janakiramanan, 1986.) Behrman and Grosse contend that relationships between MNEs and governments generally follow a "bargaining pattern.... That is, both government and company seek to pursue their own goals, and each is constrained by the other . . . ; therefore, negotiation is required" (1990, p. 7). In addition, of course, MNEs and governments (both home and host) share many common goals, and the distinction between them may become blurred, either through the "capture" of one side by the other or through the growth of state-owned MNEs, joint ventures, and other intermediate arrangements.

Taxation is a particularly important focus of government-MNE conflict, although the net impact of specific tax policies is often unclear. For example, the US is generally perceived to have higher corporate tax rates than Germany, but the US defers taxes on foreign subsidiary income until it is remitted to the US parent. Germany requires consolidation of domestic and foreign earnings and does not permit deferrals. (Both countries grant domestic credit for foreign taxes paid.) With such differences in both tax rates and methods of tax calculation, it is not clear which country offers more stimulus (or less handicap) to the growth of home-based MNEs through these policies. Comparable differences occur in the treatment of MNE subsidiaries in host environments as well; it is widely believed that the US subsidiaries of foreign MNEs do not pay their "fair share" of US taxes (Levinsohn and Slemrod, 1990).

Taxation is a difficult issue from both government and MNE perspectives. MNEs inevitably fall under the jurisdiction of more than one tax authority; the policies of these various authorities will inevitably differ, and these differences will influence MNE behavior, both operating and strategic. On the government side, as Adams and Whalley point out, there is no particular reason that subsidiaries of foreign MNEs should receive "the most favorable of the domestic tax treatments, the least favorable, some form of average, or a completely separate treatment;" moreover, in spite of the international network of tax treaties and related practices, there is no general agreement on the principles that should govern the "total taxation" of MNEs (Adams and Whalley, 1977, p. 5).

In addition to broad policies, such as taxation, that affect similarly situated MNE units within a particular jurisdiction in a similar manner, governments engage in a wide variety of "microinterventions" with respect to foreign subsidiaries. Important examples are 1) reservation of market shares or product lines to "home" country enterprises; 2) domestic content requirements; 3) partial domestic ownership or joint venture requirements; 4) export requirements; and 5) specific activity (e.g., research and development) requirements. Poynter (1985) analyzes the reasons for various types and levels of microinterventions by host governments. He attempts to identify enterprise characteristics, such as subsidiary size and strategic importance, and management tactics that may reduce or avoid such specific controls on MNE activities.

3.4.2. International Regimes for MNEs[7]

In view of the large volume and great variety of national policy actions directed toward MNEs over the past half century, it is not surprising that a number of attempts have been made to establish a broader multinational framework of norms and understandings about the relations among MNEs and their major clients and stakeholders, particularly including national governments. C.D. Wallace emphasizes that national and international policy developments are not mutually exclusive; instead, both elements are involved in the actual process of "international control," which "is not necessarily synonymous with a single international regulatory system or agency . . ." (C.D. Wallace, 1982, p. 23). None of the proposals for comprehensive international surveillance or control of MNEs has achieved the status of a formal regime, and legally binding international regulation of MNEs does not currently exist or appear likely. In fact, the activities and impacts of MNEs, joint ventures, and domestic enterprises are now so closely intertwined that the rationale for developing a special policy framework for MNEs may be gradually disappearing. Most of the critical policy issues of international business arise from the *activities* being carried out, not from the type of enterprise (MNE or other) involved.

The earliest attempt to set forth a code of conduct for MNEs was made by the International Chamber of Commerce (1974); the only other substantial statement arising outside the UN agency framework is due to the OECD. The most ambitious proposal, long under discussion but not yet formally adopted, is the UN Code of Conduct on Transnational Corporations; the principal policy issues involved and the several other international codes dealing with technology transfer, restrictive practices, etc., evolving under UN auspices are discussed in chapter 5 below.

3.4.2.1. International Chamber of Commerce. It is of some significance that the first attempt to set forth a group of international policy standards that were specifically focused on MNEs arose from the business community rather than from governments. In the late 1940s, the International Chamber of Commerce (ICC), an organization composed of large, investor-owned MNEs, issued an "International Code of Fair Treatment for Foreign Investments," a document addressed entirely to the practices of host governments. Proposals for a parallel set of principles addressed to investing enterprises (i.e., MNEs) were discussed off and on thereafter, and eventually, in 1972, the "ICC Guidelines for International Investment" were adopted, with recommendations directed toward both foreign investors (i.e., enterprises operating outside their home jurisdictions) and home and host governments. This document had, of course, no official legal or government policy status but, according to Kline, who uses "MNCs" to denote MNEs, "sought to offer practical guidance for improving the dialogue between MNCs and governments across a series of issues including ownership and management, finance, employment, technology, and commercial policies" (1985, pp. 44–45). The ICC has over the years issued several sets of more narrowly focused guidelines: advertising (1937, updated 1973 and 1986), marketing research (1971), and sales promotion (1973), all three combined into an "International Code of Marketing Practice" in 1974; environmental protection (1974); extortion and bribery (1977); and direct mail and direct sales practices (1978) (Kline, 1985, pp. 90–92). A distinctive feature of all this ICC activity is its emphasis on parallel and mutually reinforcing policies and practices on the part of both enterprises and governments. All the recommendations, of course, involve only "voluntary" actions by all parties.[8]

3.4.2.2. OECD Guidelines.

The second major set of general international guidelines for MNEs, again addressed to both enterprises and governments, arose from discussions within the Organization for Economic Cooperation and Development (OECD). The OECD evolved out of an earlier entity, the Organization for European Economic Cooperation (OEEC), that was designed to promote coordinated use of Marshall Plan aid among the nations of Western Europe after the Second World War. After the formation of the European Community (1957), the OEEC was broadened to include the US and Canada, and eventually Australia, New Zealand, and Japan; it became, in effect, the collective economic policy forum for the advanced industrial countries, the First World's official Economic Club. The OECD, however, has not evolved into a formal international policy regime. Although its members share many common policy concerns and perspectives, they tend to break up into smaller subgroups (the EC itself, the G5 and G7 groups, etc.) for some purposes, and/or to become involved with numerous other and diverse nations in other forums—e.g., the UN, the General Agreement on Tariffs and Trade (GATT), the International Monetary Fund (IMF)—to address broader international issues (Safarian, 1983).

Nevertheless, the attempt by OECD members to produce a common set of principles concerning the relations between and among MNEs and national governments (both home and host) is of some interest. The OECD *Declaration on International Investment and Multinational Enterprise*, adopted in 1976 and reissued periodically with refinements and interpretations, contains a set of guidelines jointly addressed by the member countries to each other and to MNEs operating within their borders.

Like the International Chamber of Commerce code, the OECD Guidelines are entirely voluntary for both enterprises and governments. The recommendations to enterprises cover such areas as disclosure of information, tax payments, transfer pricing, competition, and so forth; the emphasis throughout is cooperation in both letter and spirit with national standards in every operating jurisdiction. On the government side, the OECD Guidelines endorse the principle of "national treatment," that is, the idea that all enterprises within a national jurisdiction are to be treated equitably, without regard to their "home" (i.e., domestic) or "guest" (i.e., foreign subsidiary) status. Clarifying the meaning of this principle and detecting and resolving departures from it have been major concerns since the initial policy statement was adopted (cf. Aranda, 1988). The OECD Guidelines become operative only insofar as they are adopted and enforced by individual governments, and even there the impact is problematic; the OECD itself does not have access to any kind of sanctions to ensure compliance (see Aranda, 1988).

3.5. Conclusions on MNE Regulation

Publication of the OECD Guidelines was followed shortly by the development of the International Labour Organization (ILO) *Tripartite Declaration of Principles Concerning Multinational Enterprises and Social Policy* (1977), and the underlying context for both of these documents was an atmosphere of concern and criticism about MNE operations and impact that was most clearly expressed in UN debates and LDC political statements (see further discussion in chapter 5 below). More than a decade later, the international atmosphere has changed rather dramatically. For one thing, as the preceding discussion of *national* regulation makes clear, both home and host governments have become more sophisticated in their dealings with MNEs, and better able to pursue their own interests in government–business negotiations. Both government officials and the general public have also come to recognize the benefits of MNE activity, including technological transfer and economic development as well as short-run employment and income opportunities. In addition, MNEs themselves may have realized that their operations could be carried out in ways that would be less disruptive of national cultures and norms. Finally, although the long-evolving UN document still bears the title "Code of Conduct on Transnational Corporations," most knowledgeable authorities seem to agree that many problems initially perceived as uniquely associated with MNEs, and particularly with the operations of MNEs in LDC environments, are in fact results of expanding international economic contact, regardless of the particular forms of enterprise or type of economic and cultural setting involved. In the light of this revised perception, it seems most likely that policy initiatives will be focused on problems embracing diverse types of organizations and environments.

Notes

1. For a comprehensive historical perspective on these issues, see Teichova, Levy-Leboyer, and Nussbaum, eds., 1986, particularly the paper by Fieldhouse. Other major references include Casson, ed., 1983; Dunning, ed. 1974; Grou, 1986; OECD, 1987; Rugman, ed., 1982; Taylor and Thrift, 1983; and Clegg, 1987. Some of the classic contributions to this literature are collected in Casson, ed., 1990.

2. On the international activities of state-owned enterprises, see Anastassopoulos, Blanc, and Dussauge, 1987; Lewin, ed., 1981; Mazzolini, 1983; and Walters and Monsen, 1979.

3. Important current references to these developments include. Badaracco, 1991; Fennema, 1982; Gerlach, 1987; Ghemawat, Porter, and Rawlinson, 1986; Harrigan, 1987; Kanter, 1989; Morris and Hergert, 1987; Ohmae, 1989; and Porter and Fuller, 1986.

4. We are indebted to Professor Anil K. Gupta, University of Maryland, College Park, for assistance in the development of this section; see also OECD, 1987, and references cited therein.

5. *Translink's 1992 M&A Monthly*, August 30-September 29, 1990.

6. This section is based primarily on Behrman and Grosse, 1990; Fisher and Turner, 1983; Poynter, 1985; Safarian, 1983; and C.D. Wallace, 1990. A comprehensive reference on MNE tax issues is Adams and Whalley, 1977.

7. Out of a large literature, the most helpful recent reference on the evolution of international policies directed specifically to MNEs is Kline, 1985; earlier contributions of particular value are Horn, 1980; Keohane and Ooms, 1975; Sanders, 1982; Tharp, 1976; D. Wallace, 1976; and Waldmann, 1980 (see also Frederick, 1991). For a variety of contemporary issues and perspectives, see Adelman, 1988, particularly the papers by Waldmann, Kline, and Weidenbaum.

8. Another comprehensive and thoughtful set of guidelines for MNEs and governments, with special emphasis on LDC concerns, was published by the Committee for Economic Development, 1981.

References

Adams, J.D.R., and J. Whalley. 1977. *The International Taxation of Multinational Enterprises in Developed Countries*. Westport, CT: Greenwood.

Adelman, Carol C., ed. 1988. *International Regulation*. San Francisco, CA: Institute for Contemporary Studies.

Anastassopoulos, Jean-Pierre, Georges Blanc, and Pierre Dussauge. 1987. *State-Owned Multinationals*. Chichester, England: Wiley.

Aranda, Victoria. 1988. "Experience with the OECD Guidelines: The Clarifications," *The CTC Reporter*, no. 25, pp. 34–37.

Auster, Ellen R., ed. 1987. "International Corporate Linkages: Dynamic Forms in Changing Environments," *Columbia Journal of World Business*, vol. 22, no. 2 (Summer), entire issue.

Badaracco, Joseph L. 1991. *The Knowledge Link: How Firms Compete through Strategic Alliances*. Boston, MA: Harvard Business School Press.

Bartlett, Christopher A., and Sumantra Ghoshal. 1989. *Managing Across Borders: The Transnational Solution*. Boston, MA: Harvard Business School Press.

Barnet, Richard J., and Ronald E. Muller, 1974. *Global Reach: The Power of the Multinational Corporations*. New York: Simon and Schuster.

Behrman, Jack N., and Robert E. Grosse. 1990. *International Business and Governments*. Columbia, SC: University of South Carolina Press.

Boddewyn, Jean J. 1988. "Political Aspects of MNE Theory," *Journal of International Business Studies*, vol. 19, no. 3 (Fall), pp. 341–363.

Bower, Joseph, and Yves Doz. 1979. "Strategy Formulation: A Social and Political Process," in Dan E. Schendel and Charles W. Hofer, eds., *Strategic Management*. Boston, MA: Little and Brown, pp. 152–179.

Buckley, Peter J. 1990. "Problems and Developments in the Core Theory of International Business," *Journal of International Business Studies*, vol. 21, no. 4 (Winter), pp. 657–665.

Casson, Michael, ed. 1983. *The Growth of International Business*. London: George Allen & Unwin.

Casson, Michael, ed. 1990. *Multinational Corporations*. Brookfield, VT: Gower.

Caves, Richard E. 1982. *Multinational Enterprise and Economic Analysis*. Cambridge, England: Cambridge University Press.

Clegg, Jeremy. 1987. *Multinational Enterprise and World Competition*. London: Macmillan.

Committee for Economic Development (CED). 1981. *Transnational Corporations and Developing Countries*. New York: CED.

Dunning, J.H., ed. 1974. *Economic Analysis and the Multinational Enterprise.* London: George Allen & Unwin.

Dunning, J.H. 1979. "Explaining Changing Patterns of International Production: In Defence of the Eclectic Theory," *Oxford Bulletin of Economics and Statistics,* vol. 41, no. 4 (November), pp. 269–295.

Dunning, J.H. 1991. "Governments–Markets–Firms: Towards a New Balance," *The CTC Reporter,* no. 31 (Spring), pp. 2–7.

Eun, C.S., and S. Janakiramanan. 1986. "A Model of International Asset Pricing with a Constraint on the Foreign Equity Ownership," *Journal of Finance,* vol. 41, no. 4 (September), pp. 897–914.

Fennema, M. 1982. *International Networks of Banks and Industry.* The Hague, Netherlands: Martinus Nijhoff.

Fieldhouse, D.K. 1986. "The Multinational: A Critique of a Concept," in Alice Teichova, Maurice Levy-Leboyer, and Helga Nussbaum, eds. *Multinational Enterprise in Historical Perspective.* New York: Cambridge University Press, pp. 9–29.

Fisher, Bart S., and Jeff Turner. 1983. *Regulating the Multinational Enterprise: National and International Challenges.* New York: Praeger.

Frederick, William C. 1991. "The Moral Authority of Transnational Corporate Codes," *Journal of Business Ethics,* vol. 10, no. 2 (February), pp. 165–177.

Gerlach, Michael. 1987. "Business Alliances and the Strategy of the Japanese Firm," in Glenn Carroll and David Vogel, eds., *Organizational Approaches to Strategy.* Cambridge, MA: Ballinger, pp. 127–143.

Ghemawat, Pankaj, Michael E. Porter, and Richard A. Rawlinson. 1986. "Patterns of International Coalition Activity," in Michael E. Porter, ed. *Competition in Global Industries.* Boston, MA: Harvard Business School Press, pp. 345–365.

Grou, Pierre. 1986. *The Financial Structure of Multinational Capitalism.* New York: St. Martin's.

Gupta, A.K., and V. Govindarajan. 1991. "Alternative Value-Chain Configurations for Foreign Subsidiaries," working paper, College of Business and Management, University of Maryland, College Park, MD.

Harrigan, Kathryn R. 1987. "Strategic Alliances: Their New Role in Global Competition," *Columbia Journal of World Business,* vol. 22, no. 2 (Summer), pp. 67–70.

Helleiner, G.K., and Real Lavergne. 1979. "Intra-Firm Trade and Industrial Exports to the United States," *Oxford Bulletin of Economics and Statistics,* vol. 41, no. 4 (November), pp. 297–311.

Hipple, F. Steb. 1990. "Multinational Companies and International Trade: The Impact of Intrafirm Shipments on U.S. Foreign Trade 1977–1982," *Journal of International Business Studies,* vol. 21, no. 3 (Fall), pp. 495–504.

Hoogvelt, Ankie. 1987. *Multinational Enterprise: An Encyclopedic Dictionary of Concepts and Terms.* New York: Macmillan.

Horn, Norbert, ed. 1980. *Legal Problems of Codes of Conduct for Multinational Enterprises.* Deventer, Netherlands: Kluwer.

Hymer, Stephen E. 1976. *The International Operations of National Firms: A Study of Direct Investment*. Cambridge, MA: MIT Press.

Kahn, Khushi M., ed. 1986. *Multinationals of the South: New Actors in the International Economy*. New York: St. Martin's.

Kanter, Rosabeth M. 1989. "Becoming PALs: Pooling, Allying, and Linking Across Companies," *The Academy of Management Executive*, vol. 3, no. 3 (August), pp. 183–193.

Keohane, Robert O., and Van Doorn Ooms. 1975. "The Multinational Firm and International Regulation," *International Organization*, vol. 29, no. 2 (Winter), pp. 169–209.

Kline, John M. 1985. *International Codes and Multinational Business: Setting Guidelines for International Business Operations*. Westport, CT: Quorum.

Levinsohn, J.A., and J.B. Slemrod. 1990. "Taxes, Tariffs, and the Global Corporation," Working Paper No. 3500, National Bureau of Economic Research, Cambridge, MA.

Lewin, Arie Y., ed. 1981. "Research on State-Owned Enterprises," *Management Science*, vol. 27, no. 11 (November), pp. 1324–1347.

Mahini, Amir. 1988. *Making Decisions in Multinational Corporations: Managing Relations With Sovereign Governments*. New York: Wiley.

Mazzolini, Renato. 1983. "The International Strategies of Government-Controlled Enterprises," in Robert Lamb, ed. *Advances in Strategic Management*, vol. 1, pp. 183–201. Greenwich, CT: JAI.

Morris, Deigan, and Michael Hergert. 1987. "Trends in International Collaborative Agreements," *Columbia Journal of World Business*, vol. 22, no. 2 (Summer), pp. 15–22.

Ohmae, Kenichi. 1989. "The Global Logic of Strategic Alliances," *Harvard Business Review*, vol. 67, no. 2 (March-April), pp. 143–154.

Organization for Economic Cooperation and Development (OECD). 1987. *Structure and Organization of Multinational Enterprises*. Paris: OECD.

Porter, Michael E., ed. 1986. *Competition in Global Industries*. Boston, MA: Harvard Business School Press.

Porter, Michael E. 1990. *The Competitive Advantage of Nations*. New York: Free Press.

Porter, Michael E., and Mark Fuller. 1986. "Coalitions in Global Strategy," in Michael E. Porter, ed. *Competition in Global Industries*. Boston, MA: Harvard Business School Press, pp. 315–343.

Poynter, Thomas A. 1985. *Multinational Enterprises and Government Intervention*. New York: St. Martin's.

Reich, Robert B. 1991. *The Work of Nations: Preparing Ourselves for 21st Century Capitalism*. New York: Knopf.

Rugman, A.M., ed. 1982. *New Theories of the Multinational Enterprise*. London: Croom Helm.

Safarian, A.E. 1983. *Governments and Multinationals: Policies in the Developed Countries*. Washington, DC: British–North American Committee.

Sanders, Pieter. 1982. "Implementing International Codes of Conduct for Multinational Enterprises," *The American Journal of Comparative Law*, vol. 30, no. 2, pp. 241–254.

Schelpe, Dirk. 1991. "A Statute for a European Company," *The CTC Reporter*, no. 31 (Spring), pp. 17–19.

Sethi, S. Prakash. 1982. "Dresser Industries, Inc.," in *Up Against the Corporate Wall: Modern Corporations and Social Issues of the Eighties*. Englewood Cliffs, NJ: Prentice-Hall, pp. 3–28.

Slomanson, W.R. 1989. *International Business Bibliography*. Buffalo, NY: William S. Hein.

Smith, Roy C., and Ingo Walter. 1991. *The First European Merger Boom Has Begun*, Formal Publication No. 103, Washington University, Center for the Study of American Business, St. Louis, MO.

Steiner, G.A., and J.F. Steiner. 1985. *Business, Government and Society*, 6th edition. New York: McGraw-Hill.

Taylor, Michael, and Nigel Thrift. 1986. *Multinationals and the Restructuring of the World Economy*. London: Croom Helm.

Teece, David. 1986. "Transactions Cost Economics and the Multinational Enterprise: An Assessment," *Journal of Economic Behavior and Organization*, vol. 7, no. 1 (March), pp. 21–46.

Teichova, Alice, Maurice Levy-Leboyer, and Helga Nussbaum, eds. 1986. *Multinational Enterprise in Historical Perspective*. New York: Cambridge University Press.

Tharp, Paul A., Jr. 1976. "Transnational Enterprises and International Regulation: A Survey of Various Approaches to International Organizations," *International Organization*, vol. 30, no. 1 (Winter), pp. 47–73.

UN Centre on Transnational Corporations (UNCTC). 1983. *Transnational Corporations in World Development: Trends and Prospects*. New York: UNCTC.

UN Centre on Transnational Corporations (UNCTC). 1986. *Transnational Corporations in World Development: Trends and Prospects*. New York: UNCTC.

UN Centre on Transnational Corporations (UNCTC). 1988. *Transnational Corporations in World Development: Trends and Prospects*. New York: UNCTC.

UN Centre on Transnational Corporations (UNCTC). 1990. "Non-Conventional TNCs," *The CTC Reporter*, no. 30 (Autumn), pp. 37–45.

Vernon, Raymond. 1971. *Sovereignty at Bay: The Multinational Spread of U.S. Enterprises*. New York: Basic Books.

Vernon, Raymond. 1977. *Storm over the Multinationals*. Cambridge, MA: Harvard University Press.

Waldmann, R.J. 1980. *Regulating International Business through Codes of Conduct*. Washington, DC: American Enterprise Institute.

Wallace, Cynthia Day. 1982. *Legal Control of the Multinational Enterprise*. The Hague, Netherlands: Martinus Nijhoff.

Wallace, Cynthia Day. 1990. *Foreign Direct Investment in the 1990s*. Dordrecht, Netherlands: Martinus Nijhoff.

Wallace, Don. 1976. *International Regulation of Multinational Corporations*. New York: Praeger.

Walters, Kenneth D., and Joseph Monsen. 1979. "State-Owned Business Abroad: New Competitive Threat," *Harvard Business Review*, vol. 57, no. 2 (March–April), pp. 160–170.

Weidenbaum, Murray, and Mark Jensen. 1990. *Threats and Opportunities in the International Economy*, Formal Publication No. 100, Washington University, Center for the Study of Business, St Louis, MO.

Williamson, Oliver E. 1975. *Markets and Hierarchies*. New York: Free Press.

Williamson, Oliver E. 1985. *The Economic Institutions of Capitalism: Firms, Markets, Relational Contracting*. New York: Free Press.

4 INTERNATIONAL REGIMES: ISSUES AND ANALYSIS

The concept of international policy regimes has come into widespread use over the last two decades, but this usage has also involved significant controversy. Some analysts have challenged the validity of the regimes concept itself. Others have debated the origins of regimes and their connections with underlying forces such as economic and military power, national or group interests, and social values. And others have questioned the importance of regimes, raising the ultimate analytical question: Do regimes matter?

In this chapter we review some of the issues raised in this discussion and offer our own responses to them. We explain our intended use of the regimes concept and illustrate our intent with a brief case study of the earliest formal regime for international business functions, the still evolving regime for international telecommunications.

4.1. Definitions and Controversies

According to the standard definition quoted in chapter 1 above, international policy regimes consist of the collection of "principles, norms, rules and decision-making procedures" mutually accepted and anticipated by the principal actors in some area of international relations (Krasner, 1983, chapter 1). Young stresses the importance of "recognized roles linked together by clusters of rules or conventions;" the "cluster of rights and rules" is the "core" of the regime (Young, 1989, pp. 12–17). The term *right* may be excessively legalistic in a functional analysis, particularly since all commentators recognize that most rights are not absolute, and that even broadly recognized rights cannot necessarily be exercised in all circumstances. Kratochwil refers to rights as "socially protected claims;" he bases his analysis of regimes, however, on "norms," which may be either explicit (i.e., embodied in formal rules) or implicit (i.e., evidenced only in behavior) (Kratochwil, 1989, pp. 6–12).

In any event, it is generally agreed that international policy regimes embody the normative, as well as the institutional, underpinnings for the conduct of economic and business activity among both governments and enterprises in an international setting. The central idea is that participants in regimes behave in accordance with a "rule of anticipated reactions" by others (Friedrich, 1963, chapter 11); so long as most participants behave in mutually anticipated ways (including ways for resolving disputes and modifying the regime itself), the regime continues in force. Few contemporary international regimes possess, or are willing to exercise, the power to compel appropriate behavior from their participants; compliance is obtained more on the basis of benefits received, in relation to costs, than on the threat of sanctions.

Kratochwil views international regimes, which he terms *soft law*, as a supplement to the conventional dichotomy between domestic *order* based on formal government power and the international *anarchy* that might be expected to prevail because of the absence of a formal power system. He notes that international relations are not, in the main, anarchical, and observes: "Markets are probably *the* social institution most dependent on normative underpinnings" (1989, p. 47, emphasis in the original). Kratchowil's treatise probes the philosophical and legal bases for the regimes concept, which he considers poorly developed in the mainstream literature. In their 1989 volume *Rediscovering Institutions*, March and Olsen essentially equate *institution* and *regime*, both terms referring to well-established and continuing social relationships involving "roles, procedures and arrangements" within society.

The strongest attack on the validity and usefulness of the regimes concept has come from Susan Strange. In a 1983 exchange with Krasner, she criticizes it as faddish, imprecise, value biased, static, and overly state centered (cf. Strange, in Krasner, ed., 1983, pp. 337–354, and response by

Krasner, pp. 355–368). In her own comprehensive 1988 study, she identifies a set of basic "structures of power"—national security, production, finance and "knowledge"—and shows how these lead to the development of "secondary structures" governing international transport, trade, energy, and "welfare" (e.g., foreign aid). Her discussion of "structures" tends to conflate underlying conditions, such as historical developments and resource endowments, with arrangements deliberately established in response to these conditions. However, she is right to stress the roles of nongovernmental actors, too frequently neglected in the mainstream regimes literature, which has primarily emphasized the roles of states. Strange offers a rich discussion of the actual evolution and impact of several important international economic regimes, in spite of her resistance to actual use of the term.

Our own view is that some concept very similar to the generally accepted meaning of "international regimes" is useful, and probably unavoidable, for analyzing the contemporary policy environment of international business and economic affairs. The various major types of international economic contact—trade, investment, services, and communications—are carried out according to "rules of the game," which generate and depend upon mutually reinforcing expectations and behaviors among the participants involved. Such rules, some of which are quite elaborate, are often embodied in organizations or institutions that then become additional actors in the international business environment. It is, in fact, difficult even to talk about the kind of continuous coordination and harmonization that goes on in the international economy without reference, either explicit or implicit, to something like the regimes concept.

4.1.1. Regime Origins and Impacts

The two major substantive controversies about the regimes concept in the international relations literature involve 1) the *origins* of regimes and 2) the *impact* of regimes on actual processes and outcomes in international affairs.

International relations scholars have attempted to explain the origins, stability, growth, and decline of regimes in both structural and functional terms. The structural ("realist") thesis holds that regimes reflect the underlying power and interests of international actors, chiefly national states. Its strongest contention is that regimes are established by (and hence reflect the goals of) dominant hegemonic states or state coalitions; from this perspective, regimes are extensions of state-based power, and should be expected to decline when and if the underlying power base erodes. By contrast, functional analysts argue that regimes come into being in order to achieve the common objectives of member participants; they place a strong emphasis on the importance of information sharing, reducing transaction costs, and the general benefits arising from cooperative behavior.

Our own view is that both types of explanations of the origins and evolution of regimes have some validity. International economic relations involve both conflict and cooperation; mixed games are usually being played. Structural effects may be more important where hegemonic power is strong; functional considerations are probably more important in multipolar situations—and therefore, in general, for the future. Like many other contributors to this literature, we adopt the term *complex interdependence* to refer to the multiple forces and relationships that contribute to the creation and evolution of regimes. We believe that the provision of information, reduction of uncertainty, and reduction of transaction costs are critical features. We also believe that many different arrangements might contribute to these broad goals; hence—and this is a significant point—no single *optimal*, and thus no unambiguously *predictable*, regime can be specified in any particular industry or area of international business. Young notes that regimes may be "spontaneous," "imposed," or "negotiated;" but in all cases they are responses to "collective-action problems" in which cooperation among the parties involved is otherwise "problematic" (Young, 1989, p. 5).

The second controversy, concerning the substantive impact of regimes, raises more difficult questions. How, if at all, are the relationships among states, enterprises, and other entities different from what they would be otherwise because a particular regime is in place? In short: *Do regimes matter?* A negative response to this question rests on the view that, although any substantial area of international economic activity requires some set of operating arrangements and understandings, the specific features of any particular regime are of little significance. (Analogously, some standardized system of automobile traffic control is essential for efficiency and safety, but whether driving is on the left or the right, parking is parallel or diagonal, etc., is of little significance; the main concern is that there be general adherence to a common practice.) The mainstream view, by contrast, is that regime characteristics and changes therein have significant impacts on both processes and outcomes in the global economy. As March and Olsen put it: "Institutions affect the flow of history.... [T]hey not only respond to their environments but create those environments at the same time" (1989, pp. 159–162).

We believe that our analysis supports the conclusion of the mainstream international relations literature: *Regimes do matter.* The many original research studies that we have surveyed in the course of work on this volume document in detail the impact of specific regimes and regime changes on the character and content of international affairs. We must, of course, avoid the assumption that some regime must be present in every international activity, or that institutional arrangements, where present, inevitably have significant (either intended or unintended) effects. In particular, we must avoid the value-bias for which some of the mainstream literature has been justly criticized. Young (1989), among others, cautions against the belief that the development of regimes is inherently desirable, or that their effects are uniformly benign. He notes that the mere existence of a regime may lend an element of "orderliness" to some area of international affairs, but "there is no reason to assume that institutional arrangements will guide human activities toward well-defined substantive goals" (Young, 1989, p. 14). In particular, there is no guarantee that operating procedures developed within any specific regime will be fair or open, or that the results achieved will be equitable or efficient. The most that can be said, in general, is that explicit attention to the development and functioning of regimes may increase the likelihood that problems of mutual concern will be recognized and addressed. Criteria that might be used to determine the specific effects of particular regimes are further discussed below.

4.2. Principles Influencing Regime Development

The literature suggests that a number of different *fundamental principles*, such as power, efficiency, and equity, have influenced the establishment and evolution of various regimes at various times. Relevant principles may involve the *processes* of regime establishment and operation as well as their ultimate *substance* and *impact*. Some of the most important principles involved in regime development are discussed in the following paragraphs.

1. *Power and interests.* Hegemonic power has unquestionably been a critical element in the establishment of many regimes. But power alone is insufficient. As Kindleberger notes, the momentum of regime development "tends to run down pretty quickly unless it is sustained by a powerful commitment.... There needs to be positive leadership, backed by resources and a readiness to make some sacrifice in the international interest" (1988, p. 137). Power in various forms may also be used to *prevent* certain types of regime evolution, but even this use need not be successful, as recent developments in telecommunications illustrate.

2. *Efficiency.* The efficiency aspects of international regimes may be of two different types: 1) *technical efficiency*, lowering operating and transactions costs and reducing risks for regime participants; and 2) *allocative efficiency*, in the technical economic sense that the most valuable of all viable transactions are accomplished. Technical efficiency can be very important factor in regime success, since it provides benefits to participants. Allocative efficiency is a measure of the regime's contribution to increasing global welfare.

3. *Equity or fairness.* Some acknowledgment of a principle of equal treatment, or at least equal opportunity to participate in some sphere of economic activity, has been a major element of many contemporary regime debates. Specifics often involve equal access to information and to natural resources (particularly new and unexploited ones). The notion that equal *outcomes* might be obtained by all regime participants, however, is not widely accepted.

4. *Sovereignty.* National sovereignty is an essential element of all regimes that require any kind of endorsement or support by governments; yet most regimes involve some reduction in sovereign authority as a means of obtaining other desirable benefits. The dilemma of choice between freedom of individual national action on one side, and the attainment of mutually beneficial results on the other, is an inherent aspect of regime evolution.

5. *Economic development/protection.* Many contemporary regimes have as an explicit purpose the economic modernization of LDCs and/or some modification of processes of change that are already underway. Although some critics argue that the LDCs are occasionally willing to sacrifice economic gains for status and control, it is unquestionably true that the liberal trade regimes of the postwar period have contributed greatly to the development and growth of the poorer regions of the world. (For a detailed discussion of the role of LDCs in major international regimes, see Krasner, 1985.)

These and other fundamental principles may be operative, in various combinations and relative strengths, in any particular regime. They may also be sources of intra- or interregime conflict and/or compatibility and reinforcement. The role of these principles in the evolution of specific regimes will become obvious in the case studies presented in part II of this volume.

4.3. Regime Characteristics and Research Issues

To guide our research on the evolution and impact of specific regimes, we adapt an analytical framework originally proposed by Haggard and Simmons (1987), modifying and supplementing their analysis with other

Scope—Sphere of international economic/business activity covered by the regime; specific aspects involved (e.g., market participation; access to resources; price; output).

Purpose—Specific objectives to be achieved by the regime (e.g., harmonization, coordination or competition; stabilization, redistribution, development, etc.).

Organizational Form—Institutional structure of the regime; base in government, private, or other organizational structures and collaborative agreements; membership requirements and restrictions.

Decision and Allocation Modes—Role of voting; distribution of costs and benefits in equal or weighted proportions; relative scope of market and administrative processes.

Strength—Extent to which members conform to the norms and guidelines of the regime; forces making for change.

Figure 4-1. Basic Regime Characteristics. This exhibit establishes the format to be used for descriptive summary exhibits in each of the case studies.

ideas from the literature and from our own research. The resulting generalized set of regime characteristics, summarized in figure 4-1, is used throughout this research and particularly in our case studies. The elements of this framework are explained in the following paragraphs.

Scope defines the range of business and economic activity over which the regime is intended to have influence. The intended range may be, at least in principle, unlimited as to both industries/functions and geographic reach, as in the case of the United Nations (UN), which we describe as the source of a "global and comprehensive" system of regimes (figure 4-2). Most regimes are limited geographically, as in the case of the European Community (EC) and other regional systems, and/or according to specific industries and functions, as in the case of the General Agreement on Tariffs and Trade (GATT) or the Canada–US free trade agreement. The concept of *scope* also includes the particular features or activities of relevant actors that the regime intends to influence, such as market access, price, output, or technology.

Purpose identifies the objectives of the regime, within the given scope. Among the broad purposes to be accomplished by regimes, we distinguish at least three critical differences:

1. Harmonization. Participants intend to behave *alike*, often because of technical or economic considerations (e.g., international transport).

FUNCTIONAL SCOPE
OF REGIME

		Specific	Comprehensive
	Regional	Canada-US Free Trade Area	EC
GEOGRAPHIC SCOPE OF REGIME			
	Global	GATT	UN

Figure 4-2. Classification of International Regimes.

2. Coordination. Participants intend to make mutually acceptable
   moves, which may be quite different from each other depending
   upon the situation (e.g., monetary adjustments).
3. Competition. Participants agree to abide by the rules of a competitive market game (e.g., GATT).

These broad procedural purposes may, of course, be used to accomplish
many different specific goals—stabilization, redistribution, economic development, and so forth.

Organizational form is the most conspicuous aspect of most regimes,
and the most convenient means of quick reference to many of them, but it
must be reemphasized that it is the functional activity, not the formal structure, that constitutes the regime. As previously noted, there is at least one
instance of an important international regime that lacked any formal
organizational element (the gold standard regime for international payments), and there are conspicuous international organizations, such as
the International Labour Organization (ILO) and the Organization for
Economic Cooperation and Development (OECD), about which identifiable functions and behaviors sufficient to constitute a "regime" have
not evolved. Many functional–behavioral regimes arise within the context of preexisting organizations. The UN system, which continues to
generate proposals for new regimes, is the obvious case, but there are
others. The current international payments regime administered through
the International Monetary Fund (IMF) is quite different from the
arrangement conceived at the time that organization was created. Like
many other social institutions, the organizational elements of international

regimes are initially established to accomplish the purposes agreed upon among original regime participants. With the passage of time, the organizations change and adapt in response to changes in the identities and interests of regime participants. Within any particular organizational form, we note that membership or participation in regimes may be limited (i.e., named entities only, with specific admissions criteria) or open, and may be based on commonalities among participants (e.g., the regional regimes) or diversity among them. Both the "closed" colonial regimes (mother country plus colonies) and the essentially "open" UN regime system are structured in ways that emphasize diversity among participants, although for very different purposes.

Decision and allocation modes include both the one-participant/ one-vote option (where the participants may be either governments or enterprises) and arrangements in which decision-influencing power is related to size, resource endowments, volume of regime activity, and so forth. Benefits and costs may also be distributed equally and/or by weighted formula. Young notes that the rules of decision and allocation within regimes include 1) procedural rules governing regime operations and the handling of disputes; 2) use rules, which often limit access to regime resources; and 3) liability rules, which deal with the "locus and extent of responsibility" in the event of injuries or violations among regime participants (Young, 1989, pp. 16–17).

Strength is fundamentally the ability of the regime to influence the behavior of the involved participants (and perhaps of others as well). However, it is important that regime strength not be tested solely by evidence of choice of less preferred over more preferred alternatives. Many regimes facilitate, and reduce the cost and riskiness of, *preferred* behaviors. (I drive on the right side of the road in the US and on the left side in the UK because I prefer to avoid the oncoming traffic. The traffic regime is only superficially restraining; in fact, it enables me to achieve my fundamental objective—completion of a safe trip.) The analysis of strength necessarily involves the identification and impact of forces making for change, since these forces provide empirical evidence of the regime's strength or weakness.

4.4. Do Regimes Matter?

Once the existence and operations of a particular regime have been examined within this framework, we come to the ultimate analytical issue:

Do regimes matter? Again building upon the work of Haggard and Simmons (1987), we pose two more specific questions:

1. Have regimes altered the situations within which relevant actors function, so that collaboration (conflict) among them is more (less) likely than it would be otherwise?
2. Have regimes altered the preferences and interests of relevant actors, so that new strategies and actions emerge, with results that would not otherwise occur?

These questions, in many different specific forms and contexts, are repeatedly addressed in the course of our analysis. At this point, we simply repeat our overall conclusion, noted above, that *regimes do matter*. Indeed, the entire history of international economic relations involves an evolution from anarchy, based on the primitive rule of capture, to a system of regimes that both facilitate and constrain international economic contact.

The development of regimes necessarily involves an increased role for governments (including very possibly subnational governments and multistate organizations such as the EC) within the international economic system. However, as Panic strongly emphasizes, the "spontaneous integration" of the world economy through enterprise-level decisions and actions has often *preceded*, rather than *followed*, "institutional integration" through intergovernmental policies (1988, pp. 6–7). Moreover, an expanded role for government *policy*, through international agreements and understandings, need not involve an increase in government *economic activity* or in the use of political, rather than economic, allocations within the international economy. For example, a commitment to adhere to basic free trade principles, rather than ad hoc protectionism, constitutes explicit government *policy*; such commitment enlarges, rather than constricts, the scope of *market forces* in international trade. Lenway (1985) argues that the US policy commitment to the General Agreement on Tariffs and Trade (GATT) has had precisely this effect in a number of specific industries. Similarly, Haas concludes that "the Mediterranean Action Plan (Med Plan), a regime for marine pollution control, . . . played a key role in . . . the development of convergent state policies" in its area of activity (1989, p. 377).

We now turn to an illustrative case study of the formal international regime with the longest evolutionary history—the regime for telecommunications. The telecommunications regime is, of course, substantively important in itself. It also serves as a model of regime formation, structure, and evolution, and as an illustration of the approach and method employed in the larger case-study chapters in part II.

4.5. Case Study: The International Telecommunications Regime[1]

The international telecommunications regime is one of the oldest formal multilateral policy systems affecting business; it is also one of the most clearly "global" (figure 4-3). The International Telegraph Union (ITU) was organized, under the sponsorship of the French Emperor Napoleon III, in 1865. "Telecommunications" replaced "Telegraph" in the ITU name in 1932, and it became a specialized agency of the UN in 1947. Yet, as a result of changing technology, exploding levels of utilization, and changing political circumstances, there is at the present time no set of coherent international policies in place governing interconnections, access, investment, or trade in this important arena of business and technology (Aronson and Cowhey, 1988). A century-old system based on techno-logical standardization, national monopoly, and international cartel arrangements is collapsing in the fact of technological change, changing national regulatory policies, and the emergence of new forms and forces of competition (Noam, 1989).

4.5.1. Background and Regime Characteristics

Telecommunications involves an interwoven system of equipment, ser-vices, and information content. Two distinct technologies—telephone and broadcast—are utilized, often in combination, to produce both transient contacts (conversations, broadcasts) and permanent records (facsimile copies, data records). And, with a combination of telecommunications and computer services, there are also possibilities for qualitative change (data processing and other forms of value-added service in the transmitted material occurring in the course of the transmission process). International and domestic communications services are indissolubly interlinked, and domestic services are universally regulated and frequently state owned. Efficient international telecommunications requires technological com-patibility among systems; indeed, compatibility, plus the avoidance of interference, was the major principle of the telecommunications policy regime during its first century. However, technological compatibility facilitates contacts that may be in conflict with other national policies—control of national security information, censorship of political and cultural viewpoints, etc. Hence, even at a technical level, the concerns of the international telecommunications regime expand to include issues of system utilization and communications content as well as equipment and channels (Dizard, 1988).

Description	Cable	Satellite	All Modes
Institutional identification	Joint operating agreements	INTELSAT	ITU/CCITT
Technology	Point-to-point	Network	All technologies
Purpose and Scope			
Purpose	Market access to monopoly facility	Administer access	Set technical standards; resolve increasingly complex issues
Scope	Entry, rates, technology	Entry, rates, technology	Expanding to include all issues
Organizational Form			
Structure	Private (no government aspect)	Enterprise-level (US COMSAT and national PTTs), multipartite, under government auspices	Multilateral (governments)
Power/concentration	Companies/countries with critical locations and capabilities	US technology initially assured control	Political; uncertain
Decision and Allocation Modes	Market, with government approval	Administrative	Administrative, negotiated
Strength and Change			
Peak strength	1800s–present	1965–1980	ITU: 1900s–1960s
Current	High	Medium, declining	ITU/CCITT strong but new institutions emerging (e.g., GATT)
Why change?	Satellite technology did not eliminate cable; new competition is developing in satellites; increasingly complex issues emerging.		

4.5.2. Purpose, Form, and Allocation Modes

From its nineteenth-century origins up to the present, the primary focus of the ITU has been on technological cooperation, including standardization of both procedures and equipment. Emphasis shifted from telegraph to radio in 1906, and spectrum allocations under ITU auspices began in 1927. The ITU has been for many decades the administrative authority for the "global commons" of worldwide communications space. (The evolution and structure of the ITU are exhaustively described in White and White, 1988.) Major policy decisions of the ITU are made at periodic World Administrative Radio Conferences (WARCs) attended by several thousand delegates from more than 100 countries. WARC decisions are made on a "one-nation, one-vote" basis and require national ratification and enforcement. The most significant operating body of the ITU is the Consultative Committee for International Telephone and Telegraph (CCITT) which, according to Aronson and Cowhey, has evolved from a purely technical body into "a virtual telephone cartel for PTTs" (1988, p. 14). Compliance with ITU regulations has been very high because of the common interests among the national PTTs (post, telephone, telegraph providers), and also because any nation had to conform to international standards in order to participate in the worldwide communications system. However, the circumstances that favored voluntary compliance are now being altered by changes in technology and national policies.

As with air transport at a later date, the North Atlantic region was a major focus of international telecommunications development from the beginning. The first undersea telegraph cable linking North America and Europe was laid in 1866, and the number of such cables increased steadily for several decades. These undersea cables were owned and operated by private firms that controlled the entire communications circuit and negotiated connections with domestic carriers at either end. Two-way radio (voice) transmission across the Atlantic was initiated by AT&T in 1915 and offered commercially in 1927. Although this technology ultimately proved unreliable, it introduced a new policy feature of permanent importance. For national security and spectrum scarcity reasons, both the US and European nations were unwilling to grant broadcast licenses to foreign enterprises. Therefore, radio links were based on operating agreements between domestic carriers in each country, with each carrier formally in control of only a half circuit of the international communications link. When later technology permitted the laying of transatlantic telephone cables, the principle of half-circuit joint operation was maintained.[2]

Development of satellite technology in the 1960s opened an entirely new phase of international telecommunications. The vast potential capacity of satellite systems appeared just as world economic integration was greatly increasing the demand for communications services and computerization was generating enormous new collections of material available for transmission. In addition, satellite technology permitted the creation of global networks, within which multiple stations send and receive information simultaneously. However, because satellite communication involves conventional broadcast technology for the up–down links, the issue of national control arose here just as it had with radio a half century earlier.

In light of all these considerations, the concept evolved of an internationally owned and operated satellite system with nationally owned earth stations in each participating country. The US was at the time the only country other than the USSR able to launch satellites, and a leader in other aspects of satellite technology as well. Hence, US leadership was critical in the formation of INTELSAT, an arrangement for joint ownership and management of space communications technology by the authorized agencies of the cooperating governments, COMSAT for the US, and national PTTs for most of the others.

4.5.3. Strength and Change

The first century of the international telecommunications regime was dominated by considerations of technical efficiency, including the introduction of improved technologies as they became available. During the 1970–1990 decades, however, increased congestion in the communications environment, and increased concern with the economic and political implications of international communications, generated pressures for change that will necessarily involve other fundamental principles.

In the 1960s it was generally believed that satellite technology would displace cable and that INTELSAT's structure and service capacity would make it the global monopolist of satellite operations; both of these beliefs, however, proved unfounded. Fiber optic technology has revitalized cable operations; and, although considerable excess capacity remains in the INTELSAT system, a number of competitive alternatives and proposals have arisen. Some of these alternatives entirely bypass common carrier communications channels. Orion, a private US satellite firm, has established direct linkages among users in various countries (usually units of a single multinational entity) who install their own transponders for direct contact with the satellite; a similar arrangement for a firm specializing in service to international financial institutions has been approved by the FCC. In addition, various groups of nations have proposed new systems targeted toward their special needs: Arabsat (Arab countries consortium); the European Communications System (ECS); and Palapa-B (Indonesia and neighboring countries). In addition, many developing countries believe that both broadcast frequencies and orbital locations should be allocated without regard to immediate use considerations in order to break the pattern of communications dominance by the advanced countries and to preserve their own possibilities for future development (Soroos, 1982, p. 157). Such proposals call into question the traditional "first come, first served" approach to space allocation within the world communications environment and favor an alternative principle based on national jurisdiction and interest—the same kind of principle that applies to overflight airspace and territorial waters. The ongoing "Space-WARC" taking place under ITU auspices over the past decade is addressing these issues as they relate to satellite communications.

In the midst of all these developments, the fundamental jurisdictional concept of international communications law has also been challenged. From the very beginning of international communication among persons (which took place, of course, by post), it has been assumed that each sovereign state had the right to control the flow of communications into and out of its territory, and most states have in fact exercised such control at one time or another. In recent years, however, the concept of a basic human right to communicate, including contact across national boundaries, which was enunciated in the 1948 UN Universal Declaration on Human Rights, has gained a certain amount of general support. The ITU formally recognized such a right in 1973, and comparable ideas are included in numerous bilateral treaties and conventions. Although these declarations are primarily aimed at freedom of personal communication and open access to public news and information, the principle of unrestricted communication almost necessarily implies the disregard of content, particularly since the same facilities and systems are used for all purposes. On the other hand, the concern of various governments and enterprises with the control of transborder data flows and with the maintenance of cultural independence creates a strong set of offsetting pressures.[3]

The important point with respect to policy about the content–data aspects of communications is that one set of forces is pressing for greater freedom and openness, while another is pressing for greater control and restriction. Both sets of forces, however, increase the pressure for further regime development, since the issues involved cannot be resolved by national policies or bilateral agreements alone. The complex interlinkage of government and organizational interests and concerns involved in these issues—particularly the functional needs of multinational enterprises and financial institutions—demands their resolution through multiparty negotiations. The likely outcome would seem to be the gradual evolution of an communications policy regime of increasing openness.

Under what institutional auspices will the new international communications regime evolve? It seems clear that INTELSAT will evolve as a competitive player, not as a global communications monopoly and still less as a vehicle for international policymaking. The future roles of ITU and CCITT are equally problematic, although no one expects them to go out of business. One problem is that international telecommunications issues are becoming increasingly politicized, and the ITU is not an ideal forum for political debate. Most authorities on international communications policy are shifting attention to other institutions—GATT, the UN Conference on Trade and Development (UNCTAD), OECD—in which combinations of economic and political concerns are normally debated. Although, as Aronson and Cowhey (1988) emphasize, the GATT process was not initially designed to cover services, the growing importance of international service industries has placed them on the current (Uruguay Round) GATT agenda. This development may be highly appropriate for telecommunications, since unlike other important service activities (e.g., finance), in telecommunications there is an intimate link between equipment—a conventional GATT concern—and service performance. Hence, although both ITU and INTELSAT will continue to perform significant roles, it seems likely that GATT will provide an integrating focus for the international telecommunications regime over the coming decades. (See further discussion of the evolving service industries regime in the epilogue.)

4.6. Conclusion: Do Regimes Matter?

This concluding section examines the question of whether or not the international telecommunications regime "matters" in the sense that it has (or has not) influenced the actions of enterprises and governments, and hence the character of business activity and technological performance, within its functional sphere. It is, of course, impossible to imagine that international communication could have taken place without any sort of supportive institutional setting. The relevant analytical question therefore is this: Does the particular regime actually observed appear to have had discernable direct consequences?

The answer to this question is clearly affirmative. From the very beginning, the ITU created both a cooperative technological environment and a price-fixing, market-limiting cartel. However, increasingly sophisticated and complex institutions such as the ITU also increase the possibilities for conflict among the participating governments and enterprises. The most important point may be that, because of increased government involvement, such multinational regimes tend to shift the focus of both cooperation and conflict from the economic to the political arena.

Within this arena, the evolution of the telecommunications regime has both increased and decreased the strength of national, as opposed to international, forces. Both ITU and INTELSAT, being organizations sponsored by governments, affirm the importance of national boundaries; however, both have fostered new international interests (an interference-free radio spectrum and satellite communication) as well. Both organizations were formed as coalitions, but forces outside these coalitions remain significant and may grow stronger.

Notes

1. Important general references on the international telecommunications regime include Aronson and Cowhey, 1988; Branscomb, ed., 1986; Dizard, 1988; Noam, 1989; Rein et al., 1985; and Soroos, 1982.

2. International one-way broadcast communication is limited, of course, only by the power of transmitters and receivers, and by overt interference in broadcast signals ("jamming") to prevent their reception. The right of sovereign governments to engage in such interference is not seriously questioned, although their success is often limited.

3. Space does not permit significant discussion of these issues here. Important references include UNESCO, 1978; Blatherwick, 1987; and Taishoff, 1987.

References

Aronson, J.D., and Peter F. Cowhey. 1988. *When Nations Talk*. Cambridge, MA: Ballinger.

Blatherwick, David E.S. 1987. *The International Politics of Telecommunications*. Berkeley and Los Angeles, CA: University of California, Institute of International Studies.

Branscomb, Anne W., ed., 1986. *Toward a Law of Global Communications Networks*. New York: Longman. See especially articles by Branscomb, Herzstein, and Glasner.

Dizard, Wilson P. 1988. "International Regulation: Telecommunications and Information," in Carol C. Adelman, ed., *International Regulation: New Rules in a*

Changing World Order. San Francisco, CA: Institute for Contemporary Studies, pp. 115–136.

Friedrich, Carl J. 1963. "Influence and the Rule of Anticipated Reactions," in *Man and His Government: An Empirical Theory of Politics*. New York: McGraw-Hill, pp. 199–215.

Haas, Peter M. 1989. "Do Regimes Matter? Epistemic Communities and Mediterranean Pollution Control," *International Organization*, vol. 43, no. 3 (Summer), pp. 377–403.

Haggard, Stephan, and Beth A. Simmons. 1987. "Theories of International Regimes," *International Organization*, vol. 41, no. 3 (Summer), pp. 491–517.

Kindleberger, Charles P. 1988. *The International Economic Order*. Cambridge, MA: MIT Press.

Krasner, Stephen D., ed. 1983. *International Regimes*. Ithaca, NY: Cornell University Press.

Krasner, Stephen D. 1985. *Structural Conflict: The Third World Against Global Liberalism*. Berkeley and Los Angeles, CA: University of California Press.

Kratochwil, Friedrich V. 1989. *Rules, Norms and Decisions: On the Conditions of Practical and Legal Reasoning in International Relations and Domestic Affairs*. New York: Cambridge University Press.

Lenway, Stefanie A. 1985. *The Politics of U.S. International Trade: Protection, Expansion and Escape*. Boston, MA: Pitman.

March, James G., and Johan P. Olsen. 1989. *Rediscovering Institutions: The Organizational Basis of Politics*. New York: Free Press.

Mitchell, Jacqueline. 1992. "Growing Movement to 'Buy American' Debates the Term," *Wall Street Journal* (January 24), pp. A1 and A9 (Southwest Edition).

Noam, Eli M. 1989. "International Telecommunications in Transition," in Robert W. Crandall and Kenneth Flamm, eds., *Changing the Rules: Technological Change, International Competition, and Regulation in Communications*. Washington, DC: Brookings Institution, pp. 257–297.

Panic, M. 1988. *National Management of the International Economy*. New York: St. Martin's.

Rein, Bert W., Bruce L. McDonald, Danny E. Adams, Carl R. Frank, and Robert E. Neilsen. 1985. "Implementation of a U.S. 'Free Entry' Initiative for Transatlantic Satellite Facilities: Problems, Pitfalls, and Possibilities," *George Washington Journal of International Law and Economics*, vol. 18, pp. 459–536.

Soroos, Marvin S. 1982. "The Commons in the Sky: The Radio Spectrum and Geosynchronous Orbit as Issues in Global Policy," *International Organization*, vol. 36, no. 3 (Summer), pp. 665–677.

Strange, Susan. 1983. "*Cave! Hic Dragones*: A Critique of Regime Analysis," in Stephen D. Krasner, ed., *International Regimes*. Ithaca, NY: Cornell University Press, pp. 337–354.

Strange, Susan. 1988. *States and Markets*. New York: Basil Blackwell.

Taishoff, Marika N. 1987. *State Responsibility and the Direct Broadcast Satellite*. London: Frances Pinter.

UN Educational, Scientific, and Cultural Organization (UNESCO), International Commission for the Study of Communications Problems. 1978. *Interim Report on Communication Problems in Modern Society*. Paris: UNESCO.

White, Rita L., and Harold M. White, Jr. 1988. *The Law and Regulation of International Space Communication*. Boston, MA: Artech House.

Young, Oran R. 1989. *International Cooperation*. Ithaca, NY: Cornell University Press.

II INTERNATIONAL REGIMES: CASE STUDIES

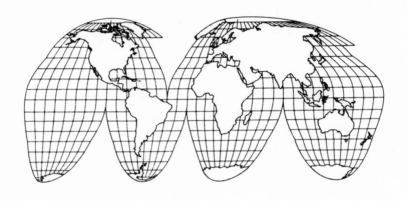

5 GLOBAL AND COMPREHENSIVE REGIMES: THE UN SYSTEM

As explained in chapter 1 above, the scope of multinational policy regimes must be defined in at least two different dimensions: 1) *geographic* or *political scope*, referring to spatial and/or other jurisdictional dimensions of the regime; and 2) *functional scope*, referring to the kinds of activities over which the regime is intended to have some influence. The geographic/political scope of the European Community (EC), for example, is limited to certain countries in Europe that have opted and been accepted for membership. The functional scope of most multinational regimes is also typically limited; they deal only with the specific set of concerns—trade, air travel, environmental issues—agreed upon among their participants. A regime that is (at least in principle) open to all participants that might have an interest in its activities, or that takes actions intended to affect all parts of the world, may be termed *global*. A regime that may (again, at least in principle) address any and all concerns that might arise among its participants, without regard to specific prior agreement as to the appropriateness of the inquiry, may be termed *comprehensive*. (It might be noted that national political regimes, i.e., governments, are functionally comprehensive within their individual borders.)

The United Nations is the only contemporary source of regime initiatives that, taken together, are both global and comprehensive. The UN is clearly *global*, since it involves nations and interests from all parts of the world, and it takes actions intended to have worldwide effects, even among nonmember countries and in international waters and air spaces. It is also, at least in principle, *comprehensive* with respect to functional coverage. Its original Charter and its broad concern with issues of peace and human welfare throughout the world permit the UN and its various agencies to direct attention to any aspect of international life that may be of interest to a significant number of its members. The so-called General Debate with which each General Assembly session opens is precisely that; speakers raise an incredible range of issues, none of which (except the internal affairs of member countries) can be arbitrarily declared off limits. The UN does not constitute a regime in itself, and most UN-based regime initiatives are limited in functional scope and discussed elsewhere in this study. This chapter stresses the overall scope—*global and comprehensive*—of the UN system and discusses some significant issues that have arisen within that setting that have general implications for regime development. The final section of the chapter examines some UN-based regime initiatives specifically concerned with the worldwide status and activities of multinational enterprises (MNEs).

5.1. Key Elements of the UN System

The United Nations was formed in 1945 as an organization of governments devoted to world peace and economic and social development. Its structure and activities have been strongly influenced by prior experience with the League of Nations, which was created by the Treaty of Versailles (1919) and dissolved in 1946. Membership in the UN has expanded from the original 51 founding states to a 1990 level of 159. The central organ of the UN is the General Assembly, in which all participating states are represented. The Security Council, consisting of five permanent members with veto power (US, UK, USSR, People's Republic of China, and France) plus ten rotating members elected by the General Assembly, has a limited range of functions, primarily involving international peace and security.

The UN inherited from the League of Nations, and subsequently created on its own, a group of agencies and organizations with diverse scopes and functions. Some of these are subunits of the UN itself, such as the Economic Commissions for various regions of the world, the UN Conference on Trade and Development (UNCTAD), and the UN Economic and Social Council (formerly known as ECOSOC, but now referred to as UNECOSOC), which itself embraces many subsidiary units, including the UN Commission on Transnational Corporations. The UN system also includes affiliated organizations with somewhat independent status, such as the International Court of Justice (World Court), International Labour Organization (ILO), World Health Orgnaization (WHO), Food and Agriculture Organization (FAO), World Bank, and International Monetary Fund (IMF). The broad range of UN concerns, both procedural and substantive, is evident from these titles alone.

5.1.1. The UN and International Business Activity

The conduct of business activity was not a major concern of the League of Nations, and there was little indication in 1945 that the UN would develop a major role in this area. However, as UN activities have expanded in both scale and scope, its potential impact on international business has inevitably increased. (For an overview of these developments, as observed from within the UN structure, see Dell, 1990.) Like the broad scope of certain clauses of the US Constitution that have provided the basis for pervasive federal government policies and programs, the general framework of the UN creates a setting for consideration of any international issue that may be of concern to a substantial number of members. As Weidenbaum states, "Few areas of private business decisionmaking escape the attention of one or another agency" (1985, p. 350).

The UN's expansion into business-related areas is welcomed by some and opposed by others. Weidenbaum (1985), for example, notes a shift of emphasis from "a desire to improve business performance" to "redistribution of economic power, and especially of income and wealth;" he believes that the UN is becoming "an economic body involved in radically changing the performance and character of private economies throughout the world" (Weidenbaum, 1985, pp. 349 and 362). Others, however, stress the limited power and influence of the UN and other international organizations, and believe that their impact is derived from "moral" rather than "legal" considerations (Frederick, 1991). Development of a broad multinational policy regime for international economic and business activity was conceived as the initial task of the proposed UN International Trade Organization (ITO), as described in the Havana Charter of 1948. Although this initiative was abandoned, its surviving elements became the framework for the General Agreement on Tariffs and Trade (GATT), which is primarily an arrangement for mutual consultation and negotiation rather than a formal organization with well-defined authority (see further discussion in chapter 7 below).

The broadest attempt to convert the UN into an agency of worldwide economic reorganization occurred during the mid-1970s when the Group of 77, the organized body of developing countries sometimes termed the "proletariat . . . within the world political system," demanded the establishment of a "New International Economic Order" (NIEO) (Luard, 1977, p. 4; see also Ghosh, 1984; de Rivero, 1980). The NIEO proposal, formalized by UN resolution in 1974, was based on a perception by many Third World countries that neither they nor their predecessor constituencies had played significant roles in the establishment of the present system of international ownership, finance, and trade—including the framework of "international law" intended to govern this system—and that the resulting arrangements were therefore seriously biased against their interests. They proposed a wholesale overhaul of international economic arrangements, including much wider use of commodity agreements, increased aid from rich to poor countries, debt relief, and other measures that, taken together, came to be known as NIEO. These proposals produced considerable discussion, but very little action, and are no longer prominent on the international agenda. Indeed, the most important UN policy initiatives concerning business specifically assume the continuation of existing international economic arrangements and work toward modification of business and government behavior within the established framework. The NIEO proposal itself, however, suggests the potential *scope* of a truly global and comprehensive policy regime; and some of the issues raised in the NIEO discussions remain significant for the future (Krasner, 1985).

5.2. Critical Issues in Regime Evolution

Before turning to a discussion of some examples of actual UN policy initiatives, it is appropriate to examine some conceptual issues that have arisen in the context of UN debates. These issues, in various forms, arise in many other contexts and have pervasive implications for the evolution of multinational regimes of both broad and narrow scope, and under various organizational auspices.[1]

5.2.1. International vs. Supranational: The Power Issue

As noted above, both the general concept of the UN and some of its most important characteristics and functions can properly be regarded as vestiges of the League of Nations. In particular, the UN shares one of the League's critical characteristics: lack of sufficient power, either military or economic, to compel compliance with its decisions. The UN and its various constituent and affiliated agencies are thus *international* organizations but not *supranational* organizations. (By contrast, the EC is, in principle, a *supranational* organization, with authority to override national policy decisions, at least to a limited extent, through qualified majority voting.) Lacking the power to compel compliance with its authority, the UN, like the League before it, cannot be described as a "government." However, as Luard (1977) emphasizes, compulsion actually plays a limited role in government, even at the national level:

> The citizen in a national state does not obey this government mainly because he is afraid of the buffets of the policeman's truncheon or the threat of imprisonment. He obeys because he is usually aware, if only unconsciously, that the effective functioning of his society would be impossible without some co-operation among its citizens; because he wishes, through such co-operation, to enjoy its benefits; above all because he is *conditioned* to conform with those behaviour patterns widely expected within his community (Luard, 1977, p. 1).

Compliance with authority is of course the product of complex forces, including the threat or use of compulsion. The recent ethnic turmoil in the USSR illustrates the reality that even a totalitarian state may face grave difficulties when the habit of conformity is abandoned. What Luard says about the individual citizen within a national state is probably even more true of a sovereign nation within the international system. Military action by an international coalition was necessary in early 1991 to eject Iraq from its August 1990 occupation of Kuwait, but the coalition limited its subsequent intervention in Iraq's internal affairs.

In any event, the "power" issue may be least significant with respect to the UN's influence on economic and business activities. The most effective power that any international business and economic regime possesses derives from an ability to exclude nonconformists from the regime's activities and benefits. However, since acceptability to actors in other jurisdictions is a critical necessity for most international business operations, the ability to deny access is uniquely important in this area. Moreover, since every possible eventuality cannot be covered by law or contract, "markets are probably *the* social institution . . . most dependent on normative underpinnings" (Kratochwil, 1989, p. 47, previously cited in chapter 4 above).

5.2.2. Temporal Orientation: Ex Post vs. Ex Ante

Two of the League's surviving entities, the World Court and the International Labour Organization (ILO), both of which reflect broadly shared goals and concerns among diverse constituencies, constitute foundation elements of the UN system. Neither of these institutions forms the core of a distinct policy regime, but the characteristics of these two institutions, including the differences between them, reflect many of the current features and controversies about international policy development. One of these characteristics is the difference between 1) dealing with problems on an *ex post* basis, attempting to redress grievances and rectify objectionable situations after they arise, and 2) anticipating problems and developing guidelines and standards on an *ex ante* basis (in advance).

The World Court, located at The Hague, in The Netherlands, was founded as the Permanent Court of World Justice in 1921 and reestablished under UN auspices in 1946 as the International Court of Justice. By the nature of its mandate, the World Court takes an ex post approach to policy problems. Problematic situations arise and are subsequently brought before the Court for resolution; all but the most basic principles are established by the accumulation of precedents in a series of individual case decisions. In the World Court, specific complaints are brought by national governments acting on their own or in the interests of some of their constituents.

The ILO was founded as an autonomous agency of the League in 1919 and converted to a UN agency in 1946. This organization illustrates the ex ante approach. The 150 member countries of the ILO are represented by teams of government, labor, and employer delegates. The ILO's principal policy actions take the form of Conventions and Recommendations that become operational only when, and to the extent that, they are subsequently ratified by individual member states. In effect, the ILO develops standards and principles that become *multinational* through a process of state-by-state ratification. The ILO has adopted over the years more than 300 Conventions and Recommendations, which are supported by more than 5000 national ratifications (ILO, 1986).

In contrast to the World Court, the ILO and similar organizations aim to establish norms and standards governing broad sets of activities that will take place in the future. Past experience is relevant for diagnosis of problems and design of responses, but the basic orientation is anticipatory and aimed at problem avoidance rather than at subsequent corrective action.

The choice of one or the other of these alternative approaches to policy formation is a major step in the evolution of all policy regimes. Regimes taking an ex post approach tend to focus on the development of reporting systems and procedures for dispute resolution; those emphasizing an ex ante approach tend to stress the development of substantive rules and formal guidelines. Although these two types of activities necessarily overlap and interact in actual practice, the two fundamental orientations are quite different. (This distinction between ex post and ex ante regulation, with specific reference to MNEs, is particularly stressed by Tharp, 1976.)

5.2.3. International Law vs. Obligations

A major issue underlying both the past and future development of international policy regimes has been identified in the UN debates as a conflict between the concepts of *international law* and *international obligations*. (This issue is comprehensively developed in Robinson, 1986, and Vagts, 1986; see also Dell, 1990, pp. 87–90.) In the context of this debate, *international law* refers not only to formal agreements and treaties among nations that take on the authority of law within their respective borders, but also to customary doctrines that have evolved over past decades (largely at the initiative of the advanced industrial countries) with respect to the responsibilities of national states for the persons and property of aliens, including the local subsidiaries of foreign-owned MNEs. Oversimplifying somewhat, the "international law" perspective holds that alien entities are entitled to all of the rights/protections of domestic entities, and, moreover, are protected by an "international" standard, which may be more demanding. According to this view, for example, although the confiscation of domestically owned property without compensation is entirely an internal matter, foreign owners of confiscated property are entitled to restitution or compensation according to "customary international procedures." Thus, such persons should have legitimate recourse, through their governments, to international tribunals and negotiations—all avenues unavailable to domestic parties in comparable circumstances—in order to obtain satisfaction. The existence and activities of the World Court embody the concept that relations among countries and their nationals are regulated by international law in this procedural sense.

The contrasting concept, identified as *international obligations* by some parties to this debate, holds that only obligations specifically accepted by a national government can be legitimately enforced upon it. The notion that foreign interests are somehow protected by a "higher" international standard is specifically rejected; indeed, it is argued that the whole concept of "customary" standards and practices is largely illusory. One version of this idea is the "Calvo doctrine," named for the Argentinian jurist and diplomat Carlos Calvo (1824–1906), which holds that each sovereign state is entitled to complete freedom from any form of interference, whether by diplomacy or force, by others; that foreign interests are entitled to the same, but no better, treatment as domestic ones; and that dispute redress can be obtained only within national courts. Some variant of this position is typically put forward by most socialist states, as well as by many less developed countries (LDCs), and is reflected in many UN documents and statements. Both the emergence of new states and the evolution of new concepts of sovereignty within pre–existing ones has favored the idea that prior arrangements—particularly control by foreigners over natural resources—may be altered without recourse to "customary" principles, whatever they might be, toward which current governments feel little commitment or sympathy (see Dell, 1990, chapter 2 and passim).

5.2.4.   Binding vs. Voluntary Standards

A closely related issue at the heart of international policy development is whether agreements and understandings reached through negotiations are or should be legally binding on the parties (as they would be if they were considered elements of international law), or whether they are merely statements of intention that become binding only upon those jurisdictions that specifically ratify and attempt to enforce them. The latter is clearly the case with respect to the ILO Conventions and Recommendations.

In the early 1960s, the Organization for Economic Cooperation and Development (OECD) members agreed to a "Code of Liberalization of Capital Movements" that encouraged free capital movement through foreign direct investment (FDI) and national treatment of foreign affiliates by host countries. In the mid-1970s, the OECD members agreed to a "Declaration on International Investment and Multinational Enterprises," including voluntary "Guidelines for Multinational Enterprises," together with three other decisions on intergovernmental dispute-resolution procedures for the guidelines, national treatment for foreign investors, and reports on international investment incentives and disincentives. The actual purpose of these various guidelines was to discourage the developing countries from restricting multinational enterprises based in the OECD countries. A Committee on International Investment and Multinational Enterprises (CIME) was created to review guideline experiences periodically and to receive recommendations from both a Business and Industry

Advisory Committee (BIAC) and a Trade Union Advisory Committee (TUAC).

In spite of some evidence of the effectiveness of such voluntary approaches, and in spite of the virtual absence of international enforcement mechanisms, pressures for the development of binding agreements remain strong. Labor representatives strongly urged that the OECD "Guidelines for Multinational Enterprises," issued in 1976, be presented in binding form. (Evolution of the OECD Guidelines is extensively discussed in Horn, 1980.) Although specific language to this effect was not adopted, several attempts were made in the late 1970s to bring possible Guidelines violations to official OECD (and ILO) attention and to stimulate enforcement responses. The key case was brought before OECD by the Belgian government and the International Federation of Commercial, Clerical, Professional and Technical Employees. Badger Corporation (US) decided to close its Belgian subsidiary and declared that it did not have sufficient funds to make legally required termination payments to employees. Badger argued that failure of a domestic company to make such payments due to insolvency would not be punishable under Belgian law. Belgium (and the Federation) pointed out that Badger was ultimately owned by Raytheon (US), which clearly possessed sufficient funds to make the required payments. The matter was eventually settled through OECD-sponsored negotiations, and some payments were made to the displaced workers. However, experience with this and similar incidents appears to have convinced most observers that organizations such as the OECD and the ILO do not have the capacity to establish binding policies or to pursue alleged violations on a case-by-case basis. (The authoritative account of the Badger case is Blanpain, 1977; see also Rowan and Campbell, 1983.)

The implication of the Badger case, along with other experiences such as the international infant formula controversy (discussed below), seems to be that multinational regime standards and penalties should probably be viewed as voluntary, not binding, among the participating parties. More recent developments, such as the UNCITRAL Model Law on International Commercial Arbitration, suggest the broad possibilities for international regime development based on voluntary and largely procedural, rather than binding and primarily substantive, norms and standards (Fleischhauer, 1986). It is indubitably the case that voluntary and recommendatory codes and standards are much easier to develop, and tend to gain acceptance much more readily, than mandatory regulations. In any event, the ultimate impact of these policy guidelines depends upon their acceptability among the parties involved and their integration into the operating practices and regulatory standards of enterprises and governments.

5.2.5. National Treatment

The Badger case also touches on the issue of *national treatment*, which has become a central substantive concern in the UN, OECD, ILO, and elsewhere. The national treatment principle requires that individual countries make no policy distinctions between domestically owned firms and the subsidiaries of foreign MNEs operating within their borders. As the Badger case clearly illustrates, the complex network of international ownership and control that has evolved during the post-World War II decades creates significant difficulties for determining the "nationality" of particular enterprises. When more and more operating units are owned through increasingly complex and frequently changing networks of international finance and investment, the task of distinguishing between domestic and foreign entities becomes insuperable, and national treatment becomes the only practical policy.

In spite of these realities, both nations and enterprises display mixed motivations with respect to the national treatment issue. Governments may well wish to offer selective incentives (loans or tax relief) either to domestic enterprises, to encourage their competitiveness, or to foreign subsidiaries, in order to attract them as stimulants for economic development. Host governments may also wish to place significant burdens (domestic content or export requirements) on foreign MNE subsidiaries in order to assure that specific development objectives are accomplished. And MNE subsidiaries may seek domestic status (i.e., national treatment) with respect to national subsidy or procurement programs, access to state-controlled resources, etc., and at the same time demand "guest" privileges with respect to disclosure of information or other responsibilities. At the present time, most governments and enterprises give lip service to the national treatment principle, but the exceptions in practice are very numerous.

5.3. UN Regime Initiatives Relating to Business

The broad scope of UN concerns and the diverse agencies through which it operates naturally lead to its involvement in numerous and varied international regimes, as reference to UN activities in the subsequent chapters will illustrate. In this section we examine a group of business-related UN initiatives that are significant examples of the UN's global and comprehensive orientation, but that are not related to other major functional regimes (see figure 5-1). One group of developments is centered around consumer protection issues, including specific concern with problems arising in the international marketing of infant food products. A second focus has involved business practices, particularly emphasizing restrictive arrangements, but including a variety of other matters as well. Consideration of these specific topics has also become intertwined with very general concerns about the impact of multinational enterprises, which are reflected in the draft Code of Conduct on Transnational Corporations, first proposed in 1974 and still pending before the General Assembly in 1991.

5.3.1. Consumer Protection

UN concerns about consumer protection arise from the perception of some member countries that collective arrangements for the regulation of MNEs may be more effective than (or may reinforce) independent national policies. This approach is illustrated by the WHO infant formula code, discussed in the first subsection below. That experience led UNECOSOC to prepare a more general set of guidelines for consumer protection, which is discussed in the second subsection.

5.3.1.1. Infant Formula. The story of the infant formula controversy is well documented and familiar (Dobbing, 1988; Greer, 1984; Sikkink, 1986; see also McComas, 1982, and the collection of documents in Nestle Coordination Center, 1983). It is usually, and accurately, presented as an extreme example of the clash between First World consumption patterns and marketing practices and Third World poverty and ignorance. It is also, however, a striking example of the evolution of an international policy regime: *first*, environmental, institutional, and behavioral factors combined to create a situation that appeared to require international policy attention; *then* these same forces led to an interactive response involving both governments and private enterprises.

A brief summary of the situation is as follows. Powdered food/chemical products that, when mixed with water, could be used as a breast milk substitute for infant feeding began to be produced and marketed in the US and Europe in the mid-nineteenth century. Over the years the product became a widely used supplement, and in many cases the food of choice, in infant nutrition throughout the world. In the post-World War II era, infant formula use expanded rapidly among the middle- and upper-income classes in many LDCs. Intensive marketing efforts by major international formula producers accompanied and increased this growth in demand. By the mid-1960s health workers in various countries came to believe that mothers unable to afford sufficient supplies of formula, and lacking the clean water,

| Description | I. Consumer Protection Initiatives | | II. Business Practices | | III. Code of Conduct on Transnational Corporations |
	A. General Guidelines	*B. Infant Formula Code*	*A. Restrictive Business Practices Code*	*B. Convention on International Sale of Goods*	*Broad statement of guidelines for both MNEs and governments*
Purpose and Scope	Identify broad goals for consumer protection throughout the world, including product quality and safety; promotion and distribution; redress of consumer grievances; specific attention to water, food, and pharmaceutical products.	Intended to reduce abuses in marketing infant food products in LDCs; specific attention to communications and advertising.	Identifies a list of specific business practices considered unacceptable in international competition; based on US antitrust tradition; applies to state-owned as well as private enterprises.	Intended to standardize terms used in international contracts and transactions, and to provide a basis for negotiation and settlement of disputes.	Intended to reduce ability of MNEs to take advantage of differences in national standards and practices, also to reduce discrepancies among national policies and protect MNEs from national discrimination; heavy emphasis on cooperation and disclosure of information.

Organizational Form	Stated as "principles" for implementation by individual governments.	Recommendatory guidelines for adoption and implementation by individual states.	Adopted as a *binding* agreement among participants; can be enforced through national courts or World Court.	Guidelines for adoption/implementation by individual states, and for reference in settlement of international disputes.	Addressed as guidelines to both MNEs and governments.
Status	Adopted by General Assembly in 1985.	Adopted by World Health Assembly in 1981; less than 50 countries have formally adopted or implemented.	Adopted by General Assembly in 1982.	Adopted by General Assembly in 1980.	Under development since 1974; still awaiting General Assembly action in 1991.

Figure 5-1. UN Regime Initiatives for International Business. UN-related functional regimes are listed and discussed in other chapters.

sterilization, and refrigeration facilities necessary for its proper use, were using formula products in ways that harmed, rather than helped, their children. Indeed, misuse of infant formula was thought to be responsible for some infant deaths. Aggressive marketing by international producers—and specifically by Nestle, the largest international producer and marketer—was believed to be an important contributing factor in this process.

Extensive publicity about this situation, and extensive controversy concerning its extent and causes, developed throughout the 1970s. The issue was addressed more than once by the World Health Assembly, and at length, in October 1979, WHO and UNICEF jointly sponsored an International Meeting on Infant and Young Child Feeding to address a broad set of issues relating to infant nutrition in the Third World, with infant formula marketing and use as the central concern. Participants in this gathering reached a limited consensus on a number of issues, including the idea that an international code of marketing practices supported by both importing and exporting countries should be developed. A WHO/UNICEF drafting group was constituted for this purpose; an industry coalition also prepared a draft code for consideration by this group.

Apart from the specific content of the draft code, a principal issue facing the drafting group was whether the code would be proposed as a WHO Regulation, directly binding upon all member states (unless a government gives formal notice to the contrary), or as a WHO Recommendation for modification and adoption by the member states in the light of their own specific circumstances. Eventually the latter alternative was chosen, and the WHO International Code of Marketing of Breast-Milk Substitutes was adopted by a vote of 118 countries in favor, three abstaining, and one (US) opposed, in May 1981 (WHO, 1981).

Implementation of the WHO Code clearly depended upon vigorous activity at the national level, particularly among importing countries, and also upon voluntary compliance by enterprises. Over the following decade, fewer than 50 countries have taken steps toward implementation, and not all of these have been completed. However, Nestle S.A. (Switzerland), the leading infant-formula marketing company in the world and the principal target of international criticism, formally adopted the Code as company policy and, in a significant innovation, appointed an independent Audit Committee of distinguished experts to monitor its own record of Code compliance. (The Audit Committee was disbanded in 1991.)

Experience with the infant formula controversy reflects many of the characteristics and problems associated with broad international policy initiatives. One is the difficulty of specifying exactly what is to be the scope and content of the desired regime. The WHO Code covers not only powdered formula mixtures but also other "milk products, foods and beverages" that might be marketed as breast milk substitutes, and related feeding equipment (bottles). It contains specific provisions governing advertising, consumer contact, sampling, and other marketing and communications practices. In spite of—and perhaps, in part, because of —these details, the precise implications of the Code remain subject to interpretation and controversy. A second problem is issue of adoption and enforcement, whether in various jurisdictions (as intended in this case) or through an international mechanism.

A third aspect of particular significance is the role of the WHO Code as a precedent for UN or other international regime development. Concern with consumer welfare was not part of the League of Nations tradition, and expansion of the UN into this area—primarily through the activities of WHO, FAO, and UNICEF—has been surrounded by controversy. A principal reason for criticism of many of the initial infant formula proposals, and ultimate opposition to the Code by some countries and enterprises, was the fear that this model (although perhaps appropriate on its own merits) might provide the basis for new initiatives in other areas: pharmaceuticals, pesticides, tobacco, alcohol, etc.

5.3.1.2. General Consumer Guidelines. In July 1981, almost simultaneously with the WHO adoption of the Infant Formula Code, UNECOSOC initiated consultations on the preparation of a general set of guidelines for consumer protection. This process eventually produced a draft document that was unanimously adopted by the General Assembly in April 1985. The guidelines deal with a number of topics: product safety and quality; promotion; distribution; education and information; and redress of grievances. They also deal with a few specific types of products: food, water, and pharmaceuticals. The food section endorses worldwide use of FAO standards and the WHO Codex Alimentarius, a comprehensive list of food terms and characteristics. The guidelines are presented as "principles" to be considered and implemented by individual governments within the context of their own economic and social circumstances; they also strongly recommend international exchange of information, consultation, and cooperation on consumer issues (Harland, 1987; Merciai, 1986).

During this same period, WHO explored the possibilities for developing a worldwide code for the marketing and use of drugs, particularly in LDCs. This activity, initiated in 1978, culminated in the Nairobi Conference on the Rational Use of Drugs in 1985, which involved representatives of governments, the pharmaceutical industry, and medical-consumer organizations. According to the summary report of this Conference, participants reached broad consensus on the responsibilities of both governments and the industry. It was also agreed that implementation would rest with individual governments, and with enterprises and user groups. Thus, these deliberations established a framework for a "voluntary" regime, with heavy reliance on adaptive behavior among participants (WHO, 1987 and 1988).

5.3.2. Business Practices

Unlike the League of Nations, the UN has at least since the mid-1960s maintained an active interest in the business practices of MNEs (Dell, 1990; Fisher and Turner, 1983; Keohane and Ooms, 1975; Sanders, 1982). As in the case of consumer protection, the UN member countries apparently believe that collective arrangements will be more effective than uncoordinated national action. Reflections of this belief include the UNCTAD Restrictive Business Practices Code and the Convention on Contracts for the International Sale of Goods, along with some other initiatives that are discussed briefly below.

5.3.2.1. Restrictive Business Practices. Both the WHO infant formula code and the broader UN Consumer Protection Guidelines reflect, among other things, a concern that aggressive competition among enterprises might lead to undesirable results. The possibility that the absence of competition due to monopolization, cartelization, and other forms of market control might also yield undesirable outcomes, not only for consumer welfare but also for the modernization and growth of less developed areas, has also been a concern of the UN from its beginnings. The special interest of LDCs in this issue was reflected in the initial establishment of UNCTAD (formed 1964), which eventually produced a set of principles dealing with restrictive business practices (referred to here as the "RBP Code") for General Assembly adoption in 1980.

The content of the RBP Code reflects primarily the US antitrust tradition and is aimed at situations involving "acquisition and abuse of a dominant position of market power" on the part of enterprises, whether domestic or multinational. Notably, the US is the only nation whose national procompetition policies are specifically applicable to foreign as well as domestic commerce. The "global" and "comprehensive" character of the RBP Code is specifically stated in the text: "[The Code] shall be universally applicable to all countries and enterprises regardless of the parties involved in the transactions, acts or behavior" (Section B, (i), 4). Inclusion of state-owned enterprises within the scope of the RBP Code was explicitly accepted by the USSR and its satellites during the late 1970s. Intergovernmental agreements, however, are excepted from the Code; and the status of subsidiary units within MNEs, although much discussed during Code negotiations, is not specifically addressed. LDC negotiators argued that intra-MNE arrangements should be specifically identified as possible sources of Code violations, while MNE representatives argued that they should be specifically exempt; in the end, the matter was left open for case-by-case consideration. The RBP Code is "voluntary;" it contains no provision for sanctions and lacks formal status as an element of "international law." It does, however, present a set of norms mutually agreed upon among many nations with diverse domestic economic systems. These Code provisions, therefore, constitute standards for internationally consistent domestic legislation, which may be particularly useful to the developing countries.[2]

5.3.2.2. International Sale of Goods. During the same time period that the RBP Code was under consideration, a separate UN initiative resulted in development of a comprehensive set of regulations and norms governing the international sale of goods (*UN Conference on Contracts*, 1981). The resulting *Convention*, eventually adopted by the General Assembly in 1982, includes a standard set of definitions of terms describing sales contract and conditions, with provisions for remedies and damages, applicable to both buyers and sellers engaged in international trade. The significant point about this *Convention* is not its contents, which are fairly standard among active trading countries, but the fact that it was adopted as a *binding* agreement among the participating parties, which included the USSR and its satellites, as well as most LDCs. This status means that its provisions can be enforced in national courts or, if necessary, through the World Court.

5.3.2.3. Other Concerns. Many other aspects of international business activity have attracted attention within UN debates and agencies. The most notable of these is probably the international transfer of technology. One of the most obvious advantages of advanced countries is their accumulated technological base; also, advanced countries are much more active in generating new technology, particularly through government sponsorship of research and development. LDCs are naturally eager to obtain access to both base technologies and new developments, but they are often unwilling to accept and enforce concepts of property rights in technology (e.g., patent protection). Even among advanced countries, there are wide variations in standards and provisions for the protection of intellectual property. Efforts to develop a UN code for technology transfer originated within UNCTAD during the 1970s and continued for some years, but no final resolution of the conflicting objectives and implementation techniques has been achieved. Transactions involving intellectual property rights have also been considered in recent GATT discussions.

The classic illustration of problems involved in technology transfer from advanced to developing countries is the December 1984 Bhopal chemical disaster in India (Shrivastava, 1987). In Bhopal, a leak of deadly methyl isocyanate gas from a pesticide plant owned by Union Carbide India, Ltd. killed more than 3300 people and injured perhaps 20,000 others. Bhopal was the world's worst industrial accident. In February 1989, India's Supreme Court ordered Union Carbide Corporation (USA) to pay the Indian government $470 million in compensation for all claims. Controversy about this matter revolves around two issues: 1) whether a properly safe technology for Indian operating conditions was used; and 2) whether local restrictions bore partial responsibility for the accident and its horrific consequences. One result of Bhopal was that the OECD began to study a set of guidelines (to be added to the existing "Guidelines for Multinational Enterprises") calling on MNEs to assess environmental consequences, to train personnel on safety matters, to use the best available technologies, to prepare contingency plans, and to provide timely information to governmental authorities (Gladwin, 1985).

Other UN concerns with business practices include accounting standards, reflected in the establishment of the Working Group of Experts on International Standards of Accounting and Reporting in 1982; illicit payments and other inappropriate interactions among businesses, government, and other political interests; and the responsibility of MNEs for disclosure of information, both to national governments and to international authorities. These concerns are reflected in various ways in the more general UNCTC Code of Conduct on Transnational Corporations, discussed below.

5.3.3.   The Code of Conduct on Transnational Corporations

Worldwide interest in the implications of the growth of MNEs for domestic economies—and particularly for developing economies—increased continuously throughout the postwar decades. Formal UN attention became focused on this issue as a direct result of the 1972 protest by the Chilean representative to the interference of ITT, a US-based MNE, in Chile's internal political affairs. The resulting UN resolution indicating general concern with MNE operations (UNESCO Resolution 1721) was therefore cast in a critical tone. The idea (apparently originating within the UN staff) that the UN's response to this concern would take the form of a "Code of Conduct" was adopted in 1974, but a much-revised draft document still awaits General Assembly action in 1992. Concern with these same issues, but without the controversial context, led the OECD to issue its 1976 *Declaration on International Investment and Multinational Enterprise*, which included a set of Guidelines jointly addressed by the member countries to MNEs operating within their borders. The ILO issued a corresponding document, *Tripartite Declaration of Principles Concerning Multinational Enterprises and Social Policy*, in 1977. (The entire code development experience is reviewed in Kline, 1985.)

The contrast between the rather rapid development of policy statements dealing with MNEs by both the ILO and OECD and the long and as yet inconclusive process underway in the UN is striking. The ILO statement is based largely on past Conventions and Recommendations, and devotes primary attention to employment and working conditions. The latter covers a wider range of topics, but reflects common interests among advanced countries. Both documents are phrased in very general terms and are expressed as voluntary guidelines for nations, enterprises and (in the ILO) trade unions.

By contrast, the UN Code was initially intended to harmonize the activities of MNEs—and, through them, those of advanced-country governments —with Third World demands for the New International Economic Order (NIEO), previously discussed. Over the intervening years, however, the environment in which the Code is evolving has changed considerably. Among these changes are the following:

1. Increasing two-way investment and trade among both advanced industrial countries and newly industrialized countries (NICs), so that home and host perspectives are equally relevant to nearly all major international economic participants.
2. Increasing numbers and diversity of active MNEs; the UN Centre on Transnational Corporations (UNCTC) "Billion Dollar Club" (enterprises with sales of $1 billion or more) now contains 600 members, with some large MNEs originating in NICs and LDCs.
3. Increasing ability of LDCs to strengthen desired impacts, and reduce undesired impacts, from foreign investment, along with increasing understanding of the benefits of foreign trade and investment, and hence of MNE activity, in the development process.

These changed circumstances, along with global experience with MNEs over the1980s decade, have led to a negotiated document that details responsibilities and standards for both governments and enterprises, and in terms that few appear to find offensive. Disclosure of information, an essential element of any enforcement activity as well as an end in itself, remains a central focus. Special topics include ownership and control, employment and industrial relations, balance of payments and financing, transfer pricing, taxation, competition, technology transfer, consumer protection, and environmental protection. A key objective of the Code, building on OECD and ILO experience, is "transparency" in the affairs of both governments and enterprises; that is, actual policies and practices should be made clear, and exceptions should be overtly identified and subject to challenge. The Code is now conceived as a purely recommendatory document, requiring implementation by national governments and intergovernmental agreements.[3]

5.4. Conclusion

The UN has played a critical role in the evolution of international policy regimes over the postwar decades, but not primarily by establishing new regulatory institutions under its own auspices. Instead, the UN has served as a multilateral forum for the identification of major international concerns, both substantive and procedural, and has provided a base for functionally specific agencies that have, in turn, become major elements of more narrowly focused regimes. The broad business-related regimes that have come from the UN itself, particularly the Restrictive Business Practices Code and the Code of Conduct on Transnational Enterprises, establish standards for implementation by individual governments and enterprises, but do not constitute elements of international law or formal regimes in their own right.

Notes

1. These issues have been widely discussed in the literature. A useful compendium of views is Horn, 1980; for a short and current review, see Behrman and Grosse, 1990, chapter 11.

2. Contemporary references to the RBP Code experience include Czako, 1981; and Davidow, 1980. For a more recent appraisal, following the 1985 UN review, see Dell, 1990, chapter 2.

3. Development of the UN Code has generated an extensive literature. Important early references are Feld, 1980, and Fikentscher 1982; see also Minta, 1988. More recent develop-

ments are reported in UNCTC, *The New Code Environment*, Series A, no. 16, April 1990; and *The UNCTC Reporter*, various issues, particularly No. 29, Spring 1990. A well-balanced current appraisal of the need for such a code is presented in Behrman and Grosse, 1990, pp. 315–333. The most recent draft of the UN Code is reproduced in the appendix. Some of the observations in this section are based in part on comments of participants in the "Symposium on the UN Code of Conduct on Transnational Corporations," Washington, DC, October 1990.

References

Behrman, Jack N., and Robert E. Grosse. 1990. *International Business and Governments*. Columbia, SC: University of South Carolina Press.

Blanpain, Roger. 1977. *The Badger Case and the OECD Guidelines for Multinational Enterprises*. Deventer, Netherlands: Kluwer.

Czako, Judith M. 1981. "Recent Development: The Set of Multilaterally Agreed Equitable Principles and Rules for the Control of Restrictive Business Practices," *Law and Policy in International Business*, vol. 13, pp. 313–337.

Davidow, Joel. 1980. "Multinationals, Host Governments and Regulation of Restrictive Business Practices," *Columbia Journal of World Business*, vol. 15, no. 2 (Summer), pp. 14–19.

Dell, Sidney. 1990. *The United Nations and International Business*. Durham, NC: Duke University Press.

de Rivero, Oswaldo. 1980. *New Economic Order and International Development Law*. New York: Pergamon.

Dobbing, John, ed. 1988. *Infant Feeding: Anatomy of a Controversy 1973–1984*. London: Springer-Verlag.

Feld, W.J. 1980. *Multinational Corporations and U.N. Politics*. New York: Pergamon.

Fikentscher, Wolfgang. 1982. "United Nations Codes of Conduct: New Paths to International Law," *The American Journal of Comparative Law*, vol. 30, no. 3, pp. 577–604.

Fisher, Bart S., and Jeff Turner. 1983. *Regulating the Multinational Enterprise: National and International Challenges*. New York: Praeger.

Fleischhauer, C.-A. 1986. "UNCITRAL Model Law on International Commercial Arbitration," *The Arbitration Journal*, vol. 41, no. 1, pp. 17–22.

Frederick, William C. 1991. "The Moral Authority of Transnational Corporate Codes," *Journal of Business Ethics*, vol. 10, no. 2 (February), pp. 165–177.

Ghosh, Pradip K., ed. 1984. *The New International Economic Order: A Third World Perspective*. Westport, CT: Greenwood.

Gladwin, Thomas N. 1985. "The Bhopal Tragedy: Lessons for Management," *NYU Business*, vol. 5, no. 2 (Spring/Summer), pp. 17–19.

Greer, Thomas V. 1984. "The Future of the International Code of Marketing of Breastmilk Substitutes: The Socio-Legal Context," *International Marketing Review*, vol. 1, no. 2 (Spring/Summer), pp. 33–41.

Gunter, Hans. 1982. "ILO Research on Multinational Enterprises and Social Policy: An Overview," Working Paper No. 15 (revised). Geneva: ILO.

Harland, David. 1987. "The United Nations Guidelines for Consumer Protection," *Journal of Consumer Policy*, vol. 10, no. 2, pp. 245–66. See also comments by Weidenbaum, pp. 425–432, and Peterson, pp. 433–439; and subsequent response by Harland, *Journal of Consumer Policy*, vol. 11, no. 1, 1988, pp. 111–115.

Horn, Norbert, ed. 1980. *Legal Problems of Codes of Conduct for Multinational Enterprises*. Deventer, Netherlands: Kluwer.

International Labour Organization (ILO). 1986. *Facts for Americans*. Washington, DC: ILO.

International Labour Organization (ILO). 1977. *Tripartite Declaration of Principles Concerning Multinational Enterprises and Social Policy*. Geneva: ILO.

Keohane, Robert O., and Van Doorn Ooms. 1975. "The Multinational Firm and International Regulation," *International Organization*, vol. 29, no. 2 (Winter), pp. 169–209.

Kline, John M. 1985. *International Codes and Multinational Business: Setting Guidelines for International Business Operations*. Westport, CT: Quorum Books.

Krasner, Stephen D. 1985. *Structural Conflict: The Third World against Global Liberalism*. Berkeley and Los Angeles, CA: University of California Press.

Kratochwil, Friedrich V. 1989. *Rules, Norms and Decisions: On the Condition of Practical and Legal Reasoning in International Relations and Domestic Affairs*. Cambridge, England: Cambridge University Press.

Luard, Evan. 1977. *International Agencies: The Emerging Framework of Interdependence*. Dobbs Ferry, NY: Oceana Publications.

McComas, Maggie, Geoffrey Fookes, and George Taucher. 1982. *The Dilemma of Third World Nutrition: Nestle and the Role of Infant Formula*. Vevey, Switzerland-Nestle: S.A.

Merciai, Patrizio. 1986. "Consumer Protection and the United Nations," *Journal of World Trade Law*, vol. 20, no. 2, pp. 206–231.

Minta, I.K. 1988. "The Code of Conduct on TNCs: In the Twilight Zone of International Law," *The CTC Reporter*, no. 25 (Spring), pp. 29–33, 37.

Nestle Coordination Center for Nutrition, Inc. 1983. *The Nestle Case*. Vevey, Switzerland-Nestle: S.A.

Robinson, Patrick. 1986. *The Question of a Reference to International Law in the United Nations Code of Conduct on Transnational Corporations*. UNCTC Current Studies, Series A, no. 1. New York: UNCTC.

Rowan, Richard L., and Duncan C. Campbell. 1983. "The Attempt to Regulate Industrial Relations through International Codes of Conduct," *Columbia Journal of World Business*, vol. 18, no. 2 (Summer), pp. 64–72.

Sanders, Pieter. 1982. "Implementing International Codes of Conduct for Multinational Enterprises," *The American Journal of Comparative Law*, vol. 30, no. 2, pp. 241–254.

Schneebaum, Steven M. 1983. "The Company Law Harmonization Program of the European Community," in Bart S. Fisher and Jeff Turner, eds., *Regulating the*

Multinational Enterprise: National and International Challenges. New York: Praeger, pp. 26–58.

Shrivastava, Paul. 1987. *Bhopal: Anatomy of a Crisis*. Cambridge, MA: Ballinger.

Sikkink, Kathryn. 1986. "Codes of Conduct for TNCs: The Case of the WHO/UNICEF Code," *International Organization*, vol. 40, no. 4 (Autumn), pp. 815–840.

Tharp, Paul A., Jr. 1976. "Transnational Enterprises and International Regulation: A Survey of Various Approaches to International Organizations," *International Organization*, vol. 30, no. 1 (Winter), pp. 47–73.

UN Centre on Transnational Corporations (UNCTC). 1990. *The New Code Environment*. Series A, no. 16 (April). New York: UNCTC.

United Nations Conference on Contracts for the International Sale of Goods. 1981. New York: UN Publications.

Vagts, Detlev. 1986. *The Question of a Reference to International Obligations in the United Nations Code of Conduct on Transnational Corporations: A Different View*. UNCTC Current Studies, Series A, no. 2. New York: UNCTC.

Weidenbaum, Murray L. 1985. "The UN as a Regulator of Private Enterprise," *Notre Dame Journal of Law, Ethics and Public Policy*, vol. 1, no. 3, pp. 349–365.

World Health Organization (WHO). 1987. *The Rational Use of Drugs*. Report of the Conference of Experts, Nairobi, 25–29 November 1985. Geneva: WHO.

World Health Organization (WHO). 1981. *International Code of Marketing of Breast-Milk Substitutes*. Geneva: WHO.

World Health Organization (WHO). 1988. *Ethical Criteria for Medicinal Drug Promotion*. Geneva: WHO.

6 REGIONAL AND ASSOCIATIVE REGIMES

The integration trend within the world economy involves regional and other associative arrangements, as well as global initiatives (Machlup, ed., 1976). Since the end of World War II, multinational economic agreements have proliferated, both reinforcing and counteracting the broad globalization trend itself. Not all of these arrangements constitute *regimes*; some, such as the Organization for Economic Cooperation and Development (OECD), are primarily consultative arrangements, and others are loose associations with limited structure and impact.

Most of these subglobal arrangements involve nations with strong similarities, including geographic location. The European Community (EC) is of this character. The European Free Trade Area (EFTA), which agreed in October 1991 to join with the EC into a European Economic Area, was by contrast comprised of small but otherwise dissimilar countries geographically removed from one another, that did not wish to join the EC. The OECD includes only advanced industrial countries, but spans the globe—Europe, North America, East Asia and the South Pacific. Many contemporary initiatives involve groups of less developed countries (LDCs)—at least three in Asia and the Arab Middle East, four in Latin America, and ten or so in Africa (depending on what is included), according to a recent analysis (Robson, 1987, pp. 8–10).

131

None of these developing-country schemes can be regarded as particularly successful compared to the EC or EFTA, although not all have dissolved. Another type of organization, the Council for Mutual Economic Assistance (CMEA), often referred to as the Communist Economies or COMECON, was basically a device for Soviet domination of its Eastern European satellites; it was formally dissolved in June 1991.

The General Agreement on Tariffs and Trade (GATT), which is discussed in detail in chapter 7 below, was intended to establish a global process for multilateral negotiations aimed at comprehensive trade liberalization. Successive rounds of GATT negotiations led to sharp reductions in tariff barriers, so that by 1989 tariff levels averaged less than 5% in the US, Japan, and the EC (European Documentation, 1989, p. 17). Tariff levels on individual products were nevertheless very uneven. The EC had only *one* product subject to tariff duties in excess of 20%; Japan had 35, and the US 185 (European Documentation, 1989, p. 17). (Japan tends to rely on nontariff trade barriers and domestic resistance to foreign products.) Schott observes that, since the Tokyo Round (1973–1979), "Many countries have sought to complement the multilateral GATT process with a variety of bilateral and regional trade initiatives. Concern about the efficacy of the GATT process has led some countries to focus more on such arrangements than on their participation in the multilateral negotiations" (1989, p. 1).

This redirection has been especially marked in both the EC and the US. The EC 12 have become increasingly focused on the 1992 elimination of all internal trade barriers in order to achieve a true European common market. The US, although the major organizer of the successive GATT negotiations, has turned increasingly to both unilateral pressure on trading partners and bilateral/multilateral negotiations in an effort to curb its continuing foreign trade deficit. These concerns and policy trends are clearly reflected in the US trade bills of the 1980s. Threats of unilateral retaliatory actions have been made against both Japan and the EC. Bilateral negotiation of free trade areas has been attempted with Israel (1985), Canada (1988), Australia and Japan (unsuccessfully), and most recently with Mexico.

Establishment of a North American Free Trade Area (NAFTA, comprising the US, Canada, and Mexico) is now in progress. The US has also proposed *multilateral* schemes in the Western Hemisphere: President Reagan's Caribbean Basin initiative and President Bush's recent "Enterprise for the Americas" initiative (echoing President Kennedy's earlier Alliance for Progress).

This chapter restricts attention to the most important multilateral arrangements and to recent US bilateral initiatives. The chapter makes no attempt to review the vast and varied literature on economic integration in general and on each of the specific current arrangements in particular. Instead, it offers an overview of the various forms of multinational economic integration and a survey of some of the major arrangements that are now in place. In the concluding section we examine the implications of these developments for the operation of multinational enterprises (MNEs) and for the evolution of global regime systems. The special importance of both 1) the evolving European Monetary System (EMS) for the International Monetary Fund (IMF) – based global monetary regime, and 2) EC and US trade policies for the global GATT process, are further discussed in chapter 7 below.

6.1. Multinational Arrangements: Types and Examples

Six general types of intercountry arrangements are included within our concept of regional or associative economic groupings. Listed in order of the degree of integration involved among their participants, the six types are as follows: association, free trade area, customs union, common market, economic integration, and political integration. By way of illustration, the major regional groupings created since World War II, not all of which may be formally termed *regimes*, are listed according to these categories in figure 6-1. Military and diplomatic arrangements such as the North Atlantic Treaty Organization (NATO), which may in fact have some significant economic aspects, are not included in this list. Some of these arrangements have significant political dimensions, while others do not. The EC aims at further political integration after formal economic union in 1992. By contrast, the Canada–US pact carries no such intention, nor do the EFTA countries intend to pursue political union with the EC.

Most of these intercountry groupings are literally "regional;" the countries involved are geographically proximate, and usually similar to each other in level and type of economic, social, and political development as well. However, there are clearly important exceptions. The three geographic clusters of the OECD countries (North America, Western Europe, and the Pacific Rim) are widely separated from each other, as are Israel and the US. And, indeed, a number of arrangements involving proximate and similar countries—such as the Andean Pact and the Central American Common Market—have proved unsuccessful. Some arrangements have been specifically designed to take advantage of intercountry

Type	Title and Membership	Founding and Ending Years
1. *Association*:	(1) Organization for Economic Cooperation and Development (OECD) 25 members: EFTA 7, EC 12, Australia, Canada, Japan, New Zealand, Turkey, US; plus Yugoslavia (special status)	1961
	(2) Council for Mutual Economic Assistance (CMEA) Bulgaria, Czechoslovakia, East Germany, Hungary, Poland, Romania, USSR; Cuba, Mongolia, Vietnam; Albania (1949–1951); plus Yugoslavia (special status)	1949–91
2. *Free Trade Area*:	no internal tariffs; independent national external tariffs	
a. *Bilateral*	(1) Australia–New Zealand Free Trade Agreement	1965
	Australia–New Zealand Closer Economic Relations Trade Agreement	1983
	(2) Ireland–UK Free Trade Agreement	1965
	(3) Israel–US Free Trade Agreement	1985
	(4) Canada–US Free Trade Agreement	1988
b. *Multilateral*	(1) European Free Trade Association (EFTA) Austria, Finland, Iceland, Liechtenstein, Norway, Sweden, Switzerland; Denmark, Ireland, UK (1960–73)	1960
	(2) Latin American Free Trade Area (LAFTA/ALALC) Argentina, Bolivia (1966 on), Brazil, Chile, Mexico, Paraguay, Uruguay, Venezuela (1967 on) Replaced 1980 by LAIA/ALADI (described below)	1960–80
	(3) Caribbean Free Trade Agreement (CARIFTA) Replaced 1973 by CARICOM (described below)	1967–73
	(4) Andean Group Bolivia, Chile (1969–76), Colombia, Ecuador, Peru, Venezuela (1973 on)	1969
	(5) Association of South East Asian Nations (ASEAN) Preferential Trading Arrangements Brunei (1986 on), Indonesia, Malaysia, Philippines, Singapore, Thailand	1977

Type			Title and Membership	Founding and Ending Years
		(6)	Latin American Integration Association (LAIA/ALADI) Argentina, Bolivia, Brazil, Chile, Colombia, Ecuador, Mexico, Paraguay, Peru, Uruguay, Venezuela	1980
		(7)	Southern Common Market Argentina, Brazil, Paraguay, Uruguay	1994
3.	Customs Union:		no internal tariffs; common external tariff (CET)	
	a. Bilateral		France-Italy Customs Union	1949
	b. Multilateral	(1)	BENELUX Customs Union Belgium, Luxembourg, Netherlands	1948
		(2)	European Economic Community (EEC 6) Belgium, France, Italy, Luxembourg, Netherlands, West Germany	1957
		(3)	Caribbean Community and Common Market (CARICOM) Antigua and Barbuda, Bahamas, Barbados, Belize, Dominica, Grenada, Guyana, Jamaica, Montserrat, St. Christopher and Nevis, St. Lucia, St. Vincent and the Grenadines, Trinidad and Tobago	1973
		(4)	Central American Common Market (CACM/MCCA) Costa Rica (1962 on), El Salvador, Guatemala, Honduras, Nicaragua	1960
4.	Common Market:		customs union plus free movement of capital, goods, people, services	
			European Community (EC 12) Belgium, France, Italy, Luxembourg, Netherlands, West Germany (1957 on); Denmark, Ireland, UK (1973 on); Greece (1981 on); Portugal, Spain (1986 on); plus Turkey (associate member)	1986
5.	Economic Union:		common market plus common or harmonized fiscal and monetary policies	
	a. Bilateral		Belgium-Luxembourg Economic Union (BLEU)	1921
	b. Multilateral	(1)	BENELUX Economic Union Belgium, Luxembourg, Netherlands	1958
		(2)	European Community (EC 92)	1992

Figure 6-1.   Important Contemporary Regional and Associative Groupings.

differences and complementarities rather than similarities; the CMEA is a striking example, but US initiatives in Latin America and scattered vestiges of older colonial empires also fit this description.

An *association* is a loose cooperation arrangement, through which member countries agree in principle to work together for mutual benefit on a limited or more general group of concerns. The OECD is the most important current example of such multilateral economic cooperation. Its membership includes virtually all the industrial market economies of the "Triad"—North America, Western Europe, and the Pacific Rim. The OECD is a loose grouping of industrial democracies for discussion of a fairly wide variety of economic and monetary topics including the activities of MNEs, economic relations with developing regions, and (until very recently) economic relations with the Soviet Union and its satellites. An important subset of OECD heads of government meets annually as the Group of Seven (G7) to coordinate fiscal and monetary policies: Canada, France, Germany, Italy, Japan, the UK, and the US. The CMEA was a very different kind of association and operated primarily as a means of economic subjugation and control over the countries of Eastern Europe by the USSR. Associations do not necessarily result in harmonization, much less integration, of policies and activities among their members. They are primarily consultative arrangements aimed at providing an organized forum for discussion of issues; the parties may agree on common practices in one instance and decide to follow different paths in another. The United Nations Conference on Trade and Development (UNCTAD) is a forum for discussion between advanced and developing countries.

Free trade areas and *customs unions* are limited functional arrangements aimed at narrowly defined goals: preferential trading among members in the first instance, and the establishment of a common external tariff in the second. A *free trade area* eliminates trade barriers at the borders of two or more countries, but permits each country to maintain its own restrictions against nonparticipants. Thus, a free trade area provides preferential access for member states at the expense of nonmembers, who may be treated quite differently by each of the members. Purely domestic activities of the members (such as taxation, regulation, and so on) need not be harmonized in any way. The 1988 Canada–US and 1985 Israel–US Free Trade Agreements are recent bilateral examples. The EFTA is a long-established multilateral free trade area. The Association of South East Asian Nations (ASEAN), whose six members are Brunei, Indonesia, Malaysia, the Philippines, Singapore, and Thailand, is often described as a free trade area, but this description is not fully accurate. ASEAN is better understood as a loose association of six geographically proximate countries with similar political objectives. Their economic objectives, circumstances, and trade and investment activities are significantly dissimilar. Indonesia, for example, is a member of the Organization of Petroleum Exporting Countries (OPEC). The ASEAN members do maintain preferential trading arrangements with each other; such arrangements are essential features of a conventional free trade agreement.

A *customs union* is, technically speaking, a free trade area whose members agree to maintain common trade restrictions against nonmembers, especially a common external tariff. The European Economic Community (EEC), as originally organized in 1957 with six members (Belgium, France, Italy, Luxembourg, the Netherlands, and West Germany), was a customs union, rather than a common market. Free trade areas and customs unions involve only trade in goods, while the concept of a common market connotes a fuller economic integration, as is explained below.

A *common market* provides for free movement among member countries of people, capital, and services, as well as goods. A common market necessarily includes a customs union, but involves many other features as well. The EC is scheduled to become a full common market, at least in principle, in 1992. A common market, however, need not involve complete economic integration. For example, although a common monetary and financial system like the European Monetary System (EMS) is undoubtedly desirable for the proper economic functioning of a common market, the existence of such a system is not a necessary feature. Since the EC is working toward the development of supranational institutions and processes for economic (and ultimately political) integration, it is evolving beyond the usual limits of a common market.

The leading example of a successful *economic union*, representing even further economic integration, is BENELUX, composed of Belgium, Luxembourg, and the Netherlands. This union evolved from an initial Belgium–Luxembourg Economic Union (BLEU), established in 1921, which joined in a customs union with Holland in 1948. BENELUX itself was created in 1950, and by 1970 all border controls among the countries were abolished. BENELUX was the first regional grouping to permit free movement of capital, labor, and services; it also provided for standardized postal and transport rates, and coordinated welfare policies.

A *political union* is an economic union with the addition of a central government structure, which may have broad or narrow functions. Political unions of previously independent jurisdictions often encounter difficult problems, as illustrated by the forces of dissolution currently at work within the former USSR. Bitter conflicts continue within the United Kingdom of Great Britain and Northern Ireland, originally formed in 1801 (the country of Ireland seceded in 1921). Imperial Germany (1871–1918) was a successful political union, but was clearly dominated by a single participating state (Prussia). Some EC member states apparently support full political integration with enthusiasm, although the resistance of some (specifically the UK) and the possible expansion of the EC to include EFTA and CMEA countries may delay this development.

The *degree of integration* involved in these various types of intercountry economic arrangements depends upon both the *scope* of activities included and the *goals* to be achieved. *Scope* may be either limited (and functional) or comprehensive; *goals* may include coordination, harmonization, or integration, and may vary among functional areas. *Coordination* simply involves mutual understanding and adaptation among the parties involved; their actual behavior need not be similar, nor even mutually supporting. *Harmonization* is generally associated with a functionally limited activity, such as taxation, which can be managed in such a way that it does not matter whether the activity occurs in one member's jurisdiction or another (see Andic, 1984; Shoup, 1967). Under a tax harmonization arrangement between two countries, an MNE with a specific level of net earnings would be subjected to the same level of taxation in either. The US harmonizes its taxation system for MNEs through bilateral tax treaties with other countries. *Integration* necessarily involves both more comprehensive scope and more ambitious goals; integrated regimes operate through a common set of institutions, norms, and behaviors involving multiple functional activities.

6.2. The European Community[1]

The world's largest and most important regional economic bloc is the 12-member European Community (EC). Under the Single European Act of February 1986 (effective July 1, 1987), the EC is scheduled to become a true common market after December 31, 1992, and is committed to pursue even fuller economic, and ultimately perhaps political, integration in the future (see Makridakis et al., 1991). The 1990 population of the EC 12 was almost one third greater than that of the US (see table 6-1). Their aggregate GNP (1988) was only slightly less, and is expected to increase by about 5% (in addition to normal growth) as a direct result of the final integration steps now underway (European Documentation, 1989, pp. 12–13). In addition to the 12 full members of the EC listed in table 6-1, Turkey is an associate member now applying for full membership; Turkey, Cyprus, and Malta are joined with the EC through customs unions. In October 1991, the

Table 6.1. Basic Statistical and Trade Data for the European Community with Selected Comparative Data for the US and Japan

	1988 Constant $ GNP		1990 Population		1988 GNP Per Capita (1988 $)	1988 World Trade Balance ($ Billions)	1988 Exports ($ Billions)	% Share of Exports To		% Share of Imports From	
	$ Millions (1988 $)	% Share	Millions (Estimated)	% Share				EC	US and Japan	EC	US and Japan
EC 12	4709	100.0	326.1	100.0		-11.6	1022.2				
EC 4	3768	80.0	232.0	71.1		3.4	759.0				
West Germany	1218	25.9	61.0	18.7	19,907	72.8	323.3	52.9	11.3	54.6	11.5
France	933	19.8	56.2	17.2	16,690	-15.1	161.7	60.6	8.7	65.7	8.6
Italy	810	17.2	57.7	17.7	14,095	-9.9	129.1	56.1	11.2	56.7	7.4
UK	808	17.2	57.1	17.5	14,152	-44.4	144.9	49.2	15.9	51.3	16.6
Other EC	941	20.0	94.1	28.9		-15	263.2				
Spain	338	7.2	39.6	12.1	8645	-20.1	40.2	59.1	8.2	54.9	12.3
Netherlands	226	4.8	14.9	4.6	15,312	3.8	103.1	75.7	14.7	61.5	11.1
Belgium	147	3.1	9.9	3.0	14,859	-0.1	92.0	74.0	6.0	72.4	7.9
Denmark	104	2.2	5.1	1.6	20,195	1.4	27.9	48.5	10.9	53.6	8.5
Greece	53	1.1	10.1	3.1	5223			67.1	7.6	61.2	6.7
Portugal	39	0.8	10.5	3.2	3750			71.3	7.3	63.5	8.8
Ireland	28	0.6	3.6	1.1	7795			73.5	9.5	71.3	17.8
Luxembourg	7	0.1	0.4	0.1	17,838	*	*	*	*	*	*
US	4881	100.0	250.4	100.0	19,813	-120.93	320.4				
Japan	2851	100.0	123.8	100.0	23,255	77.5	265.0				

Sources: Trade data from European Documentation, *Europe without Frontiers—Completing the Internal Market* (Luxembourg: 1989, 3rd edition); statistical data from *Statistical Abstract of the United States, 1990* (Washington, DC: US Department of Commerce, 1990).

Notes: *Luxembourg included in Belgium trade data. EC countries listed in order of 1988 GNP size. Some data not available. 1990 population for East Germany 16.6 million, 1987 current $ GNP 196.9 million.

% share of trade to/from other countries may be computed as difference 100% less EC, US, and Japan. 1988 imports may be computed from world trade balance and exports for each country.

EC and the EFTA reached an accord to create a European Economic Area by 1993. The arrangement will have a population of about 380 million and will account for more than 42% of the world's exports (see table 2-1). The EFTA will adopt most of the commercial, but not the agricultural, policies of the EC. Talks between the EC and the countries of Eastern Europe were underway in 1991. The outcome of these discussions will likely be some kind of "European Economic Space" embracing both Western and Eastern Europe. The EC has also established many bilateral and multilateral trading arrangements; in 1971 it adopted the Generalized System of Preferences (GSP) for trade with LDCs within the General Agreement on Tariffs and Trade (GATT) framework (see chapter 7 below for discussion of GATT and GSP).

Full common-market status will be achieved in principle when free movement of goods, services, people, and capital among the EC 12 is authorized in 1992. Some 300 internal barriers of various types are scheduled for elimination. The EC 12 have agreed to attempt harmonization of value-added taxes, unemployment insurance, social security, and agricultural subsidies. They have also agreed to seek exchange-rate stability by holding rates within agreed ranges. There will be increased harmonization of national legislation, national regulations, company law, taxation and so on (Price Waterhouse, 1987).

The degree of economic integration that will actually be achieved after 1992 is problematic, and political integration is even more uncertain. The EC 12 countries have much in common; but they are diverse in size and economic condition, as well as in culture and sociopolitical character. Per capita GNP of the richest countries (Denmark, Germany) is four or five times that of the poorest (Portugal, Greece), and even Ireland and Spain can be considered only "middle income" countries in a worldwide analysis (table 6-1). Inflation rates in 1987–1988 varied from 1.2% in Belgium to 11.5% in Portugal and 13.2% in Greece. Unemployment (total labor force measure) in 1988 varied between 1.6% in Luxembourg and 6.7% in Portugal at the low end, and 18.4% in Ireland and 19.5% in Spain at the high end. The average annual GNP growth rate during 1985–1988 varied from 0.7% in Denmark to 4.6% in Spain (European Documentation, 1989). Even before its integration with East Germany, West Germany was the largest unit within the EC, accounting for about one fourth of total EC GNP and one fifth of total EC population.

There are also significant differences in foreign trade patterns (table 6-1). Ireland, Portugal, and the Benelux countries export heavily to the rest of the EC; the UK and Denmark export heavily outside the EC. While West Germany enjoyed a strong positive overall trade balance in 1988, comparable to that of Japan, most other EC members had negative trade balances, some of them (e.g., the UK) very high. These disparities among the member countries may create substantial barriers to full integration after 1992.

The Maastricht agreement of December 1991, together with the October 1991 accord for a European Economic Association with the EFTA, strengthens the European integration movement. (As is discussed in section 6.2.2 below, the UK has not committed to the monetary policies of the Maastricht agreement.) In addition to monetary union and a single European currency by 1999, the EC formally designated the existing Western European Union (WEU), composed of nine EC members of NATO, to coordinate defense policies with NATO. The other three EC members will be invited to join WEU, together with Turkey (a member of NATO) as an associate member. The EC, except for the UK, agreed to a "social chapter" stipulating greater EC authority over labor policies. However, in foreign policy, the EC rejected France's proposal for majority voting in favor of the UK's insistence on unanimous polling (Smolowe, 1991).

6.2.1. EC Organizational Structure

The EC presently consists of three overlapping "communities" with the same membership: the European Coal and Steel Community (ECSC), established on April 18, 1951; the European Economic Community (EEC) and the European Atomic Energy Community (EURATOM), both established on March 25, 1957. A Convention also signed at Rome on the latter date joined the European Assembly (now the European Parliament), European Court of Justice, and Economic and Social Committee (ECOSOC)—entities created by the various treaties—into a common political structure; a subsequent treaty (April 18, 1965) created a single Council and Commission to govern the EC.

The 1957 EEC comprised six members: Belgium, France, Italy, Luxembourg, the Netherlands, and West Germany. It has evolved over time from a customs union (achieved in 1968) to its present state of economic integration; membership also expanded in stages, with new member countries given considerable time to adjust their tariffs and other regulations to common EC standards. (Spain and Portugal, which joined in 1986, were allowed seven years.) A European passport, introduced January 1, 1985, is being phased in as national passports are replaced.

The EC has a complex four-institution legislative structure. The *Council*, the ultimate elgislative body, currently consists of two elements:

1. The European Council, consisting of heads of governments of the member states, which meets only biannually and deals only with broad political and strategic issues; and
2. The Council of Ministers, which changes ministry composition depending upon the subject matter (e.g., taxation, transport, health) under consideration; foreign ministers are present for major policy decisions.

According to the EC treaties, the Council of Ministers is authorized to act solely on proposals put forward by the *Commission*, the secretariat of the EC. The Commission is specifically charged to ensure that all treaty objectives and provisions are carried out properly. The ethos of the Commission requires commissioners and staff to serve EC and not national interests. The Commission provides an annual report and a budget report to the Parliament, has a treaty right to speak before the Parliament, and can be dismissed only as a whole and only by a motion of censure in the Parliament.

The *European Parliament* (known before 1962 as the European Assembly) is a consultative body with no legislative role, but with certain specific powers, including power to dismiss (but not to appoint) the Commission, as noted above. In 1987, the Parliament consisted of 518 members, distributed roughly according to country size (France, Germany Italy, and the UK had 81 seats each; Spain, 60; the Netherlands, 25; Belgium, Greece, and Portugal, 24 each; Denmark, 16; Ireland, 15; Luxembourg, 6). Since 1979, members have been elected for five-year terms by direct universal suffrage in each country; they sit by pan-European party membership rather than in national groups. The European Parliament has the formal power to sue both the Council of Ministers and the Commission before the European Court of Justice for failure to take actions that are required under the treaty; its actual strength, however, comes from its right to "question" the Commission and its potential role in the budget conciliation process, including its right to reject the proposed EC budget as a whole.

The *Economic and Social Committee (ECOSOC)* consisted in 1987 of 189 members appointed by unanimous consent of the Council of Ministers. ECOSOC represents economic and social interest groups—employers, employees, and others. ECOSOC's role arises from the treaty requirement that it be "consulted" on certain specific issues, such as freedom of establishment and worker mobility, and in all cases where harmonization of national laws, regulations, or administrative actions requires amendment of national legislation. ECOSOC represents about 250 EC-wide sectoral interest groups, each of which functions largely as a confederation of national groups.

6.2.2. Critical Issues

The essence of the Single European Act is that it modifies all of the EC treaties to establish qualified majority voting on customs duties, freedom of commercial establishment, professional qualifications, movement of capital and people, common transport policy, and harmonization of national standards.[2] No single country can veto a majority decision on any of these important steps toward a common market. A unanimous vote is still required, however, on some issues, such as harmonization of indirect and direct taxation among the member states.

Although the EC has been highly successful in reducing trade barriers against nonmembers, there are still strong pressures for trade protectionism, investment controls, and continuation of agricultural subsidies within the member states. At least half the foreign trade of EC countries takes place within the bloc, but in 1988 the EC 12 had a collective negative trade balance with the rest of the world. Among the member countries, the UK, Spain, and France had substantial external deficits, whereas Germany (West) had a very strong positive trade balance at the same time (US Department of Commerce, 1990).

Harmonization of domestic policies and practices is a major issue within the EC. This problem can be readily illustrated by a comparison of the various tax structures (see table 6-2). Considering just the five largest EC countries, the proportion of gross domestic product collected as tax revenues ranged from 36% to 45% in 1987. There is also substantial variation in the mode of tax collection. The UK collects a relatively low proportion of revenue from social security taxes and is heavily dependent on excises and other sources, such as the local property tax. Corporate tax revenues are relatively low in France and Germany; individual income tax revenues are relatively low in France and the UK.

Full economic integration will require integration of money and capital movements, and probably freedom of establishment and operation of financial services such as banks, insurance companies, and brokerage and securities firms (see European Documentation, 1982b). Separate stock markets can be operated in various locations, as in the US. The European Monetary System (EMS) was established in 1979, but Greece, Portugal, Spain, and the UK did not join. The EMS is operated through the European Monetary Cooperation Fund (EMCF) founded in 1973. The

Table 6-2. Tax Harmonization in Selected OECD Countries, 1987

	1987 Tax Revenue as % of Gross Domestic Product (GDP)	1987 Percentage Distribution of Tax Receipts by Type of Tax						
		Individual Income	Corporate Profits	Employee Social Security	Employer Social Security	General Consumption	Specific Consumption (Excises)	Other
France	44.8	12.7	5.2	12.3	27.2	19.5	8.9	14.2
Italy	36.2	26.3	10.5	6.7	24.1	14.6	10.3	7.5
Netherlands	48.0	19.7	7.7	18.8	17.0	16.4	7.4	13.0
UK	37.5	13.6	10.6	8.3	9.4	16.1	13.6	28.4
US	30.0	36.2	8.1	11.1	16.6	7.4	7.2	13.4
West Germany	37.6	29.0	5.0	16.1	19.1	15.7	8.6	6.5
Japan	30.2	24.0	22.9	10.2	14.8	0.0	11.1	17.0

Source: Statistical Abstract of the United States, 1990 (Washington, DC: US Department of Commerce, 1990).

Notes: 1987 Tax Revenue as % of GDP: Belgium 46.1, Denmark 52, Greece 37.4, Ireland 39.9, Luxembourg 43.8, Portugal 31.4, Spain 33.
"Other Taxes": Property taxes, employer payroll taxes other than social security contributions, capital gains taxes, contributions of self-employed, taxes on production, sales, transfer, leasing, and delivery of goods and services and rendering of services, and miscellaneous taxes.

member countries transferred 20% of their gold and dollar reserves to the EMCF in return for a common reserve currency called the ECU (European Currency Unit). The ECU is valued in terms of weighted amounts of all member currencies. The ECU is presently a reserve unit and instrument for settling central-bank balances resulting from joint market-intervention activities. (The ECU is thus analogous to the SDR created by the International Monetary Fund, as discussed in chapter 7 below.) Money, credit, and capital are extremely sensitive to national economic policies, and capital movements among the EC countries have been much smaller than movements of goods. The EC has also established a nonprofit European Investment Bank (EIB), which uses loans and loan guarantees to facilitate both balanced and common development within the EC. Funds for the EIB consist of both member state contributions and capital market borrowings. The Maastricht agreement of December 1991 stipulated creation of a "cohesion fund" with the objective of promoting balanced development through investment in the poorer countries of the EC (Greece, Ireland, Portugal, and Spain).

The Maastricht agreement will change present monetary arrangements in stages that create a monetary union by 1991. (The UK did not commit to these arrangements, that presently embrace just the other 11 EC members. The UK's Parliament will vote on adoption of the ECU at some future date.) On January 1, 1994, a European Monetary Institute will begin coordinating EC monetary policy. The ECU will become a European currency when at least seven EC members meet certain economic criteria (e.g., total government debt must be decreased to below 60% of gross national product and the government budget deficit must be held to no more than 5% of gross domestic product). Only three countries currently meet these criteria (Smolowe, 1991, p. 29). The European currency will become automatically invoked on January 1, 1999, in any case for qualifying countries. The European Monetary Institute will eventually become a European central bank.

Strategic business alliances are common in Europe, and since passage of the Single European Act there has been a merger and acquisition boom within the EC. This boom followed on the heels of a similar merger wave in the US. Between 1985 and 1989, the US experienced more than 6000 such transactions, with a total value of more than $1 trillion. While there had been earlier restructuring movements in the US and the UK in the 1960s, neither Europe nor Japan had experienced such activity. In 1990, however, US merger transactions were expected to be less than half of the total value of global merger transactions, due to increasing European activity. During 1985–1989, about 60% of non-US transactions were intra-European (with a total value of $196 billion); an additional $156 billion represented Europe/non-Europe transactions, mainly in the US (Smith and Walter, 1991).

The growth of intra-European business organizations, anticipated to increase rapidly after 1992, has led to the development of a new "European company statute," which offers MNEs the option of registration under a single body of law applicable throughout the EC, rather than under individual national codes. (The most recent developments with respect to this initiative are discussed in Schelpe, 1991.)

6.2.3.   The European Free Trade Association (EFTA)[3]

The EC will form a free trade association with the EFTA by 1993. The EFTA is like the CMEA an arrangement now of only historical interest. A brief comment on that history is therefore sufficient. The EFTA, organized in 1960, was originally viewed as a rival or alternative to the EC as a means to economic integration in Western Europe. The EFTA currently has seven members: Austria, Finland, Iceland, Liechtenstein, Norway, Sweden, and Switzerland. Denmark and the UK were formerly members, but shifted to the EC. Norway applied for EC membership in the early 1970s, but withdrew its application after a national referendum disapproved membership. All these countries are small and, except for Norway and Sweden, have little in common with each other except high levels of per capita income, and (at least initially) lack of desire to become fully integrated into the EC. The EFTA was, in fact, not so much a regional economic group as an organization of non-EC members, with little independent role or purpose.

6.3.   US Agreements: Bilaterals and NAFTA[4]

In addition to its leadership role in the GATT process and other globally focused economic initiatives, the US has pursued its international objectives through both bilateral and multilateral initiatives. Successful agreements have been reached with both Israel and Canada, and negotiations toward an agreement with Mexico and an ultimate North American Free Trade Area (NAFTA) are in progress in 1991. On the other hand, Australia and Japan have declined US free trade proposals. The US had also launched multilateral initiatives involving other parts of the Western Hemisphere —the Caribbean Basin initiative and "The Americas" initiative.

The US made its initial foray into bilat
framework with the Israel–US free trade a$
at the elimination of all tariffs between the \
(Greenaway, Hyclak, and Thornton, eds., 1
more symbolic than practical, since US tarif
were already set at zero under the General.
(GSP) for developing countries. The basic effec
1) guarantee continuation of preferential statu
eliminate the EC preference created by the 1
agreement; and 3) schedule new tariff reduction.
zero levels on both sides by 1995. The agreem   ....eu "best
efforts" to negotiate rules on services trade. The gr ...est importance of the
Israel–US pact may be its role as a model for the Canada–US Free Trade
Agreement of 1988. Both of these agreements established special administrative bodies for the resolution of disputes among the parties. These resolution procedures are highly important, because tariff reductions have
led to increasing emphasis on countervailing-duty and antidumping laws
in the US.

6.3.1. NAFTA: US, Canada, Mexico[5]

Canada and the US are the world's largest bilateral traders. Their bilateral
merchandise trade (exports and imports) was $125 billion in 1985,
compared to $108 billion for EC 10–US trade (the EC 10 does not include
Portugal and Spain) and $88 billion for Japan–US trade in the same year.
Ontario Province alone is the largest buyer of US exports; the four next
largest buyers are Japan, the rest of Canada, Mexico, and the UK
(Wonnacott, 1987a, p. 2). In 1987, Canada received 23.6% of total US
exports and provided 17.9% of total US imports (Schott, 1988, in Schott
and Smith, eds., p. 9).[6] Trade with the US is even more important for
Canada; more than 70% of Canadian exports go to the US, and the US
share of Canadian imports is almost as great, at 67% in 1987 (Schott, 1988,
in Schott and Smith, eds., p. 10).[7] In 1986, Canada invested $18.5 billion
(annual flow) in the US (up from $11.7 billion in 1982), and the US
invested $50.2 billion in Canada (up from $43.5 billion in 1982) (Schott,
1988, in Schott and Smith, eds., p. 146).[8]

Canada and the US functioned as a free trade area during 1854–1866,
but that arrangement was terminated by the US because of difficulties
connected with the Civil War. By 1987, when the most recent negotiations
began in earnest, 65% of US exports to Canada and 80% of US imports

already were duty free, with more cuts scheduled under ᴊATT agreements (Wonnacott, 1987a, p. 3). However, major ᴍs remained because of high tariffs in certain sensitive industries ᴎ as textiles, apparel, footwear, and furniture, and because of nontariff barriers (NTBs). The 1988 agreement commits both parties to reduce all tariffs to zero over a ten-year period, beginning in 1989, and to eliminate nontariff restraints on trade in energy and automotive products. This agreement also opens more government procurement contracts to competitive bidding and bars most border restraints on bilateral investment. As noted above, the Canada–US agreement provides formal procedures for dispute resolution as well. Implications of the 1988 agreement for automotive trade are particularly important. Automotive products constitute one third of US–Canada merchandise trade, and the 1965 Auto Pact provided for duty-free passage of original equipment parts and new vehicles between the two countries. The 1988 free trade agreement removes tariffs on replacement parts, and commits Canada to ending its embargo on used car imports within five years.

Estimates of the likely effects of the Canada–US agreement vary widely. Overall GNP effects in either country are likely to be relatively small (although even small effects in these large economies can be substantial in absolute amount). Specific sectoral effects may be substantial. Elimination of most restrictions on oil and gas imports should reduce costs and improve competitive efficiency in the US. Gradual reduction in Canadian restrictions on foreign investment should provide a boost for its own economy. The pact will undoubtedly increase trade between the two countries and cause some trade diversion away from Japan and Western Europe; however, expected aggregate growth effects will probably generate new trade opportunities for those external partners as well (Schott, 1989, p. 5).

The Canada–US pact is much broader than typical bilateral trade agreements. The US succeeded in establishing precedent-setting rules for service trade and investment between the two countries. Particular problems affecting the auto and energy sectors, where relations had been strained for several years, were addressed. Canada sought and obtained secure access to US markets, a significant objective in the light of concerns raised by US trade legislation in the 1980s. As in the case of EC–US discussions, domestic subsidies remain the principal unresolved problem between the two countries.

The Mexico–US Framework Agreement of 1987 established consultation procedures for liberalizing trade and investment. The subsequent Trade and Investment Facilitation Talks, concluded in October 1989, extended the earlier agreement and added formal procedures for sectoral negotiations. Pursuant to GATT and IMF/World Bank programs, Mexico cut its average tariff rate from 28.5% in December 1985 to 11.8% in December 1987 (Schott, 1989, p. 45). Mexican interest in a free trade agreement with the US has been propelled by two concerns: 1) a fear that EC 1992 and East European investment opportunities will limit future European investment in Mexico; and 2) the failure of Mexico's liberalized investment rules (May 1989) and the Brady Plan for foreign debt relief to stimulate desired levels of foreign investment. Mexico is the third largest trading partner of the US, after Canada and Japan; about 65% of Mexico's total exports (and 85% of its manufactured exports) go to the US.

Negotiation of a formal free trade agreement with the US was proposed by Mexico in 1990. The Salinas Government also announced that it would reprivatize the banking industry (nationalized in 1982) by selling its share in the country's 18 largest commercial banks. The Mexico–US trade negotiations are intertwined with two sensitive political issues: 1) labor immigration from Mexico into the US; and 2) foreign ownership and development of natural resources (especially energy) in Mexico. The energy resources of Mexico are regarded as a national patrimony; in 1938 these resources were nationalized, and a state monopoly, Petroleos Mexicanos (PEMEX), was created to control and exploit them.

Negotiations between Mexico and the US are in progress at the time of this writing, and it is now generally anticipated that a North American Free Trade Area (NAFTA) comprising Canada, Mexico, and the US will eventually emerge. There are, however, profound economic differences between the US and Canada, both of which are advanced industrial countries with closely integrated economies, and Mexico, classifiable as a newly industrialized country (NIC). In 1990, Mexico's GNP per capita was only a tenth of that in the US and Canada, and its real GNP growth rate was only 0.5% compared to 3.3% in both Canada and the US. Mexico's inflation rate of 20% was four to five times higher than the rates of its North American neighbors. Mexico can offer a large labor force (its 1990 population was estimated at 84.3 million compared to 26.2 million in Canada and 249.4 million in the US) and low average wages ($2.30 per hour compared to $14.30 in the US and $14.70 in Canada).[9]

6.3.2. Conclusion on US Agreements

Completion of some kind of agreement with Mexico, which seems likely at present, will probably terminate this type of activity for the US for the fore-seeable future. Continued expansion of such agreements to include, for example, Australia, the ASEAN countries, Japan, South Korea, and Taiwan has been suggested from time to time, but these developments do not seem likely (Schott, 1989). Mexico and Canada are geographically linked with the US (resulting in low transport and other costs), and heavily dependent on it for imports, exports sales, and investment. The link with Israel is political and strategic, but very strong. No other trading partner matches these qualifications. The key issue with Japan, perhaps the most likely candidate for consideration, is the large bilateral US trade deficit. The US and Japan are making both unilateral and bilateral moves to improve their trade relations, but the development of a general agreement between them does not seem likely at this time, given Japan's 1988 rejection of a US free trade proposal.

6.4. Other Regional Arrangements

Regional economic arrangements other than those of the EC and Canada–US have not been very successful, primarily because trade and investment issues elsewhere are dominated by economic development problems and conflicts. The regional arrangements in the developing world are not really free trade areas, much less customs unions, in the conventional senses of those terms. Their focus is primarily on import substitution, export promotion, and the control of economic development (see Robson, 1987, for a detailed discussion).

In point of fact, economic progress in the LDCs may be far more dependent on developments taking place within the GATT and UNCTAD frameworks than on regional initiatives. Establishment of the Generalized System of Preferences (GSP), which sets low tariff levels for imports from LDCs, is among the most important of these developments. In addition, the US, EC, Japan, and other countries have taken a variety of bilateral and multilateral initiatives aimed at improving the economic development prospects of the LDCs. In 1987, the Development Assistance Committee (DAC) provided $66 billion in LDC aid; OPEC provided an additional $4.1 billion in aid (1985), and CMEA's European members provided $5 billion (1987) (US Department of Commerce, 1990, based on OECD data).[10]

6.4.1.   Council for Mutual Economic Assistance (CMEA)[11]

The Council for Mutual Economic Assistance (CMEA), often called COMECON (for Communist Economies), officially dissolved in June 1991;

it nevertheless merits mention here as a type of regional economic organization quite different from those discussed above. CMEA was basically little more than a Soviet device for economic domination of the six East European members: Bulgaria, Czechoslovakia, East Germany (GDR), Hungary, Poland, and Romania. (Albania was a member only during 1949–1951.) Cuba, Mongolia, and Vietnam were non-Euopean members of CMEA, but with little apparent involvement in its activities. By contrast, Yugoslavia was never a member, but was accorded equal economic status. The USSR has also long maintained a special trading relationship with Finland, which was never a CMEA member. The GDR became unified with West Germany in 1990. The traditional Communist regimes have been overturned throughout Eastern Europe and the USSR itself has disintegrated into a Commonwealth of Independent States. Hungary, Poland, Romania, and Yugoslavia are members of the World Bank—a status requiring prior membership in the International Monetary Fund (IMF); Czechoslovakia and Bulgaria applied for IMF/World Bank membership in 1990, and the USSR applied in 1991. Fourteen Commonwealth of Independent States members were approved for membership in April 1992.

The European CMEA members were intimately linked by trade as well as by geographic proximity and political–strategic considerations. Most production in these economies originated in state-owned enterprises (SOEs), and export–import activities were handled by government-controlled trading companies. Such organizations find it difficult to deal with market-oriented enterprises and were also noncompetitive. There is now a strong movement toward privatization, decentralized market pricing and trading, and dismantling of state administrative apparatus in all these countries. However, immediate integration into the global economy or even Western Europe is not a realistic economic or political likelihood. Soviet domination isolated these economies from worldwide developments; they are structurally interdependent and noncompetitive, and they can gain little from cooperation or integration with each other. The CMEA experience reveals some of the potential dangers of regional economic arrangements, especially in developing regions, that isolate their members from global economic trends.

6.4.2. Latin America and the Caribbean[12]

During the postwar decades, five regional economic arrangements have been attempted in Latin America and the Caribbean:

The Latin American Free Trade Association (LAFTA, or ALALC in Spanish), founded in 1960 and succeeded in 1980 by the less ambitious *Latin American Integration Association* (LAIA/ALADI);

The Central American Common Market (CACM/MCCA), also founded in 1960;

The Caribbean Free Trade Association (CARIFTA), founded in 1965 and followed by the 1973 *Caribbean Community* (CARICOM), consisting of English-speaking island-nations that were members of the British Commonwealth;

The Andean Group, formed in 1969 by a subset of LAFTA members; and

a newly formed *Southern Common Market*, scheduled to be in effect by the end of 1994.

None of the terms (*free trade, common market,* etc.) in the titles of these organizations are properly descriptive of their actual characteristics. LAIA, CARICOM, and the Andean Group are tariff preference zones, with the latter two aiming at establishment of a common external tariff among their members. CACM is a free trade area also aiming to establish a common external tarift. The basic purpose behind all these schemes has been to increase intraregional trade in order to alleviate perennial foreign exchange crises. The common strategy has been to enlarge internal markets and restrict imports from hard currency countries.

Latin America and the Caribbean are characterized by tremendous cultural, political, and socioeconomic variety. The area itself is vast, geographically diverse, and populated by large and dissimilar groups— European (Spanish, German, Italian), Indian, Negro, and mestizo. Spanish, Portuguese, English, French, and Dutch languages are spoken in various parts of the region. There are also tremendous differences in income and degree of urbanization. Mexico City and Sao Paulo are expected to have populations of approximately 24 million by the year 2000, placing them among the largest cities in the world (US Department of Commerce, 1990). Argentina, Brazil, Chile, and Mexico are usually considered "newly industrialized countries" (NICs), and many other states in the region qualify as "middle-income countries" according to most classifications. Others, however, such as Nicaragua, El Salvador, Honduras, and Bolivia, are very poor. Ecuador and Venezuela are OPEC members; Mexico (a major petroleum and natural gas producer) is not. Most Latin American and Caribbean economies are heavily dependent on imports from outside the region and are not integrated with each other; only landlocked Bolivia obtains even half of its imports from within the region (see table 6-3).

Prior to the Great Depression of the 1930s, there was a general approximation of free trade throughout Latin America; formal trade barriers among countries did not exist. The Depression, however, led to widespread implementation of import substitution and protectionist measures. In the 1950s and 1960s, the UN Economic Commission for Latin America (ECLA/CEPAL) promoted industrialization through import substitution strategies associated with what was intended to be temporary protection against external competition. In any event, protectionism became permanent, and the program tended to establish and preserve inefficient industrial sectors characterized by high capital intensity and low productivity (Edwards and Savastano, 1989, in Greenaway, Hyclak, and Thornton, eds., p. 190).

The movement toward various forms of regional economic integration during recent decades has been driven by a desire to obtain larger-scale markets for these industrial sectors while continuing to practice external protectionism. During the late 1960s and 1970s, the importance of export promotion beyond Latin America and the Caribbean also received significant emphasis.

6.4.2.1. LAFTA and LAIA.

LAFTA was formed by the Treaty of Montevideo (effective June 1, 1961) as a free trade association among six countries: Argentina, Brazil, Chile, Mexico, Paraguay, and Uruguay. Bolivia joined in 1966 and Venezuela in 1967. LAFTA evolved into the looser form of LAIA in 1980 because the multilateral-negotiations strategy originally adopted did not work as expected. The 1960 treaty envisioned continuous multilateral negotiations leading to a gradually liberalized free trade area. However, none of the negotiation mechanisms worked very well, and intraregional trade never rose to 14% of total group exports (Edwards and Savastano, 1989, in Greenaway, Hyclak, and Thornton, eds., p. 194).

The generally poor performance of LAFTA led first to the formation of the Andean Group (Cartagena Agreement or Andean Pact of May 1969) and then to LAIA (Treaty of Montevideo, 1980). The Andean Group, also known as the Andean Common Market (ANCOM), was formed by Bolivia, Chile, Colombia, Ecuador, and Peru. Venezuela participated in the negotiations but did not join until February 1973. Adoption of the Andean Code for Foreign Investment led to Chile's withdrawal in 1976. The basic rationale for the Andean Pact was that most foreign direct investment (FDI) from advanced countries was going to Argentina, Brazil,

Table 6-3. Import and External Public Debt Data for Selected Latin American Countries

	1990 Population (Millions)	1986 Country Share of Imports by Origin (% of Total)			1987 External Public Debt ($ Billions)
		Industrial Market Economies	Latin America and Caribbean	Other	
NICs					
Argentina	32.3	63.1	31.5	5.4	47.5
Brazil	153.7	61.3	9.7	29.0	91.7
Chile	13.0	56.3	24.9	18.8	15.5
Mexico	109.4	93.0	3.1	3.9	82.8
Andean Group					
Bolivia	6.7	38.5	57.0	4.5	4.6
Colombia	32.6	77.5	19.2	3.3	13.8
Ecuador	10.5	77.1	17.0	5.9	9.0
Peru	21.9	69.3	26.5	4.2	12.5
Venezuela	19.6	85.3	11.2	3.5	25.2
Other					
Costa Rica	3.0	71.3	23.5	5.2	3.6
Dominican Republic	7.3	48.1	43.3	8.6	2.9
Guatemala	9.3	61.3	34.9	3.8	2.3
Panama	2.4	54.5	12.3	33.2	3.7
Uruguay	3.0	39.9	43.2	16.9	3.0

Sources: Population and external public debt data from *Statistical Abstract of the United States, 1990* (Washington, DC: US Department of Commerce, 1990), based on World Bank data.

Import data from Sebastian Edwards and Miguel Savastano, "Latin America's Intra-Regional Trade: Evolution and Future Prospects," in David Greenaway, Thomas Hyclak, and Robert J. Thornton (eds.), *Economic Aspects of Regional Trading Arrangements* (New York: New York University Press, 1989), table 9-4, pp. 202–203.

Notes: External Public Debt excludes military equipment purchases and any private debt not guaranteed by a governmental entity. Missing Latin American and Caribbean countries not reported.

and Mexico. The Andean Group members were poorer and more economically homogeneous; they intended to pursue economic development through comprehensive industrial planning. The Andean Group agreed to a complex schedule of automatic annual internal tariff reductions and planned to adopt a common external tariff. They also agreed to reallocate industries so as to foster balanced regional development and focus investment on a few "strategic" industrial sectors; four such programs (for the metalworking, petroleum, automotive, and telecommunications industries) were negotiated. The Andean Group adopted the 1971–1987 Andean Code for Foreign Investment (Declaration 24), which severely limited the permissible share of foreign capital in domestic ventures. None of these plans proved to be particularly successful. Intraregional trade never reached 5% of total group exports; the common external tariff was never fully developed (and exceptions were routinely granted in any event); and the industrial programs were not implemented.

The transformation of LAFTA into LAIA in 1980 reflected a shift of emphasis toward export promotion and a decision to rely on bilateral commercial agreements as the basis for subsequent regional cooperation. Each country was left to determine its own tariff preferences, both regional and external. This bilateral approach, similar to and consistent with that adopted by the US during the 1980s, has proved to be somewhat more efficient. However, the major problem faced by Latin American countries during the 1980s was foreign debt repayment, made more difficult by a 40% decline in external financing between 1981 and 1983 (Edwards and Savastano, 1989, in Greenaway, Hyclak, and Thornton, eds., p. 191).

The NAFTA discussions and President Bush's "The Americas" initiative have stimulated discussion of the possibility of an "Inter-American Free Trade Zone" embracing the Western Hemisphere. In March 1991, Argentina, Brazil, Paraguay, and Uruguay signed the Treaty of Asunción setting up a Southern Common Market (MERCOSUR) by December 31, 1994 (this arrangement would not include Chile). Other countries are invited to join in the future. The four member countries have a combined gross national product (GNP) of about $400 billion (51% of the total GNP of Latin America and the Caribbean) and a combined population of 195 million (46% of the total population). The arrangement will have a common external tariff and may include sectoral complementation agreements. Paraguay and Uruguay are granted more extensive exceptions and given an additional year to implement the common market process.[13]

6.4.2.2. Central America and the Caribbean.

Central America has a history of efforts at regional integration going back into the mid-nineteenth century. An Organization of Central American States was formed in 1951. The Central American Common Market (CACM/MCCA) was established in 1960 by El Salvador, Guatemala, Honduras, and Nicaragua; Costa Rica joined in 1962. (Panama has never been a member of any regional grouping.) A Central American Bank for Economic Integration was created in 1961. Inspired by the European Payments Union Agreement, the central banks of the five countries gradually formed a Central American Clearing House (1961–1963) to provide multilateral payments clearing; a Central Monetary Stabilization Fund (January 2, 1970), Monetary Union (February 25, 1974), and Monetary Agreement (August 24, 1974) followed.

CACM was virtually abandoned in the 1980s due to the political and military disturbances within the region. A major stumbling block was inability to agree on free movement of labor within the region. There was a brief border war in 1969 between El Salvador and Honduras over alleged mistreatment of Salvadoran migrant labor. CACM tried unsuccessfully to allocate an industrial sector to each country, but there was not enough foreign investment to sustain this effort. In 1970, Hondoras imposed tariffs on regional imports. These developments, aggravated by subsequent military conflicts, marked the end of economic integration efforts.

The efforts of the English-speaking Caribbean states to form a political federation was also short lived.[14] The basic problem is that no political consensus exists among these countries on how to constitute and operate common procedures. The Caribbean Common Market (CARICOM), formed in 1973 as a successor to the Caribbean Free Trade Agreement (CARIFTA), contained a special Eastern Caribbean Common Market (ECCM) for the less developed members of the community. The CARICOM region contains only 5 million people and a combined GNP of only $7 billion. The membership is geographically dispersed and their economies are competing rather than complementary. The US Caribbean Basin initiative was intended to provide special financing, investment, and trade preference programs for the benefit of these countries from the US, Canada, Mexico, Venezuela, and international financial organizations.

6.4.3. Africa and the Middle East[15]

Probably the least successful efforts at economic integration have taken place in Africa and the Middle East, due to wide cultural differences, lack of economic complementarities, and political–diplomatic turmoil. A Regional Co-operation for Development scheme organized among Iran, Pakistan, and Turkey to achieve limited sectoral industrial integration dissolved with no better success than that of the Andean Group. After some 50 years of operation in various forms, the East African Community (EAC)—finally comprising Burundi, Kenya, Rwanda, Somalia, Tanzania, and Uganda (originally organized among Kenya, Tanzania, and Uganda and operating as the East African Common Services Organization, EACSO, during 1961–1967)—failed in 1978.

A wide variety of schemes have been attempted in Africa. The EAC aimed at a common market with common currency. In 1969, a Southern African Customs Union was established among South Africa (which in 1948 had formed a customs union with Southern Rhodesia), Botswana, Lesotho, and Swaziland. The Southern African Development Coordination Conference organized in 1980 aimed only at economic coordination rather than creation of a formal trade bloc. The 1981 Preferential Trade Area for Eastern Africa included 15 countries.

West African countries, which are culturally very diverse and relatively small in size, have attempted a number of arrangements: the Communauté Economique de l'Afrique de l'Ouest (CEAO), established in 1974 (Ivory Coast, Mali, Mauritania, Niger, Senegal, Upper Volta—now Burkana Faso—with Benin joining in 1985), was linked in a monetary union (except Mauritania, which maintains economic relations with the Arab Middle East) with Benin and Togo. The 1973 Mano River Union (MRU) created a Liberia–Sierra Leone customs union joined by Guinea in 1980. The 1975 Economic Community of West African States (ECOWASI) attempted to unite some 16 countries inlcuding CEAO and MRU members. In Central Africa, the 1964 Union Douanière et Economique de l'Afrique Centrale (UDEAC) united the People's Republic of the Congo, Gabon, Cameroon, the Central African Republic, and Chad (to 1968 only), and subsequently Equatorial Guinea in a monetary union. The 1976 Communauté Economique des Pays des Grands Lacs (CEPGL) included Burundi, Rwanda, and Zaire. In 1983, the Communauté Economique des Etats de l'Afrique Centrale (CEEAC) associated ten countries: the UDEAC and CEPGL member together with Chad, Equatorial Guinea, and São Thomé et Principé. The problems in West and Central Africa closely resemble those of the Caribbean.

Economic cooperation efforts in the Arab Middle East have been strongly affected by the political–diplomatic turmoil within the region, and the divisions among the Arab members of the Organization of Petroleum Exporting Countries (OPEC). A Council of Arab Economic Unity was organized in June 1957 (Iraq, Jordan, Kuwait, Libya, Mauritania, the PLO, Somalia, Sudan, Syria, United Arab Emirates, and both Yemens) but did not meet until 1964. In 1964, an Arab Common Market contained Iraq,

Jordan, Libya, Mauritania, and Syria. The Arab Fund for Economic and Social Development organized in May 1968 involved the 21 members of the Arab League (founded 1945) plus the PLO. The Arab Monetary Fund (April 1976) contained the same membership except for the PLO. None of these efforts has been much more successful than the short-lived political union between Egypt and Syria (the "United Arab Republic").

6.4.4.   ASEAN [16]

The Association of South East Asia Nations (ASEAN) was created by the Bangkok Declaration of August 1967. Its membership consists of six countries: Brunei (which joined in 1986), Indonesia, Malaysia, the Philippines, Singapore, and Thailand. (Basic economic data on the five largest members of ASEAN are provided in table 6-4.) There are enormous political, economic, and social differences among these countries. Singapore and Brunei are extremely small in size and population. Indonesia is extremely large in both, with Thailand and the Philippines being intermediate. The Philippines is the only Christian country in Asia (with a large Muslim minority in the southern islands); Indonesia is the world's largest Muslim country, while Malaysia is also Muslim. Singapore is predominantly Chinese. Thailand is a Buddhist country. Singapore and Malaysia are relatively high-income NICs, with substantial FDI and export activities. Brunei and Indonesia are members of OPEC, but by comparison receive relatively little FDI on a proportional basis.

It is not fully accurate to term ASEAN a free trade area. ASEAN is a loose association of geographically proximate states with mutual political and economic interests. Trade and investment relations are handled largely by administrative regulation. There is very little likelihood of a true customs union developing. Balasubramanyam concludes:

> The ASEAN has had little success in promoting its stated objectives. . . . [T]he main stumbling block in the way of progress appears to be the marked differences in the development strategy and economic philosophy of the principal member countries. . . . The ASEAN has had little impact on either the magnitude or the pattern of FDI in the region (1989, pp. 185–186).

6.5.   Regional Regimes and MNEs

Regulation of MNE activities in general, and of FDI in particular, has been a major concern in most of the regional regimes. Conspicuous examples in

Table 6-4. Basic Economic Data for ASEAN Members, Selected Years

	Indonesia	Malaysia	Philippines	Singapore	Thailand
1990 Population (Millions)	191.3	17.1	66.6	2.7	56.5
1985 $ GDP Per Capita	530	2000	580	7420	800
1983 FDI Stock ($ Billions)	6.8	6.2	2.7	7.9	1.4
% Share of Exports to:	100.0	100.0	100.0	100.0	100.0
ASEAN Members, 1985	10.9	26.6	11.7	24.7	14.8
Industrial Market Economies	77.8	56.7	75.7	48.0	58.5
Other Economies	11.3	16.7	12.6	27.3	26.6
% Share of Imports from:	100.0	100.0	100.0	100.0	100.0
ASEAN Members, 1985	9.1	23.1	14.8	24.1	15.3
Industrial Market Economies	72.9	63.4	55.9	50.8	61.4
Other Economies	18.1	13.5	29.3	25.1	23.3
1985% of GDP from:	100.0	100.0	100.0	100.0	100.0
Agriculture	24.9	19.5	25.3	0.8	17.4
Construction	5.7	5.2	5.7	11.4	5.1
Manufacturing	12.0	20.5	25	24.0	19.9
Mining	17.7	9.8	1.8	0.3	2.8
Services	38.9	43.4	40.9	61.3	52.7
Utilities	0.8	1.6	1.3	2.2	2.1
1985 Foreign Trade as % of GDP	33.5	88.4	31.8	254.4	39.5
1983 FDI as % of GDP	8.7	21.1	7.8	47.5	3.5

Sources: V.N. Balasubramanyam, "ASEAN and Regional Trade Cooperation in Southeast Asia," in David Greenaway, Thomas Hyclak, and Robert J. Thornton (eds.), *Economic Aspects of Regional Trading Arrangements* (New York: New York University Press, 1989), pp. 167–188, based on various official sources.

Population data from *Statistical Abstract of the United States, 1990* (Washington, DC: US Department of Commerce, 1990).

Notes: Brunei not reported. GDP = gross domestic product. FDI = foreign direct investment.

the industrial market economies are the OECD guidelines for MNEs and the Canada–US auto pact. Canada has limited FDI by US firms through the screening procedures of FIRA, and the investment part of the Canada–US free trade agreement may be unstable (Wonnacott, 1987, p. 9). The EC has generally been open to both intragroup and external FDI, except for France, which attempted unsuccessfully to restrict US investment. The CMEA was largely closed to FDI; former CMEA countries are now trying to encourage FDI, particularly joint ventures, but hard-currency payment requirements and other restrictions have limited the interest of foreign investors.

Latin American countries have attempted to regulate MNE activities in a variety of ways. The "sectoral programming strategy" of the Andean Group, although never implemented as planned, restricted internal free trade to firms with at least 51% Andean Group ownership, which discouraged FDI. LAIA used company complementation agreements, which tended to reduce tariff duties for the companies involved. Although some 25 such agreements were concluded in a variety of industries, including chemicals, pharmaceuticals, electrical appliances, and telecommunications, they did not prove successful in attracting FDI.

The Andean Foreign Investment Code (1971–1987) illustrates the widespread desire in the developing countries to stimulate local ownership participation. The Andean Code subjected FDI and the entry and operation of foreign-owned enterprises to common rules enforced by separate (and nonharmonized) national laws in the member states. Foreign ownership in enterprises was to be reduced to 49% within 15 years (20 in Bolivia and Ecuador); enterprises not meeting this criterion lost tariff preferences. Profit remittance, reinvestment, and use of patents and trademarks to protect industrial technology were all limited, and reporting requirements were increased. New FDI was forbidden in certain nonmanufacturing sectors (e.g., public services, insurance, banking, electricity, telecommunications, and news media). In addition, each country was allowed to restrict foreign ownership in other sectors to 20% of company value. Grosse analyzed the impact of the Andean Code through management interviews and other relevant data, and concluded that the Code had a substantial negative impact on MNE entry decisions and operating flexibility. FDI slowed during the first few years of the code, and there was a significant shift in new entry ownership toward host-country joint ventures (Grosse, 1983). Chile withdrew from the Andean Group in 1976 in order to enact legislation more attractive to FDI; and the Code itself was replaced in 1987 by a new set of rules aimed at stimulating foreign investment. This change was driven by the foreign debt crisis of the 1980s.

The ASEAN approach has been much more accommodating to FDI and MNEs, although not much more successful in practice. While the regional pact provided for industrial complementation agreements along Andean Group lines, MNEs were admitted to the process on both company (as in LAIA) and industrywide levels. The agreement process never functioned successfully, however, because it was largely left to enterprises without government participation, and conflicts among enterprises prevented agreements.

The general experience with regional codes or guidelines for regulating FDI and other MNE activity is that they have tended to work poorly even in the industrial market economies and to fail in other settings. The various "guidelines" developed within the OECD carry no sanctions and have apparently had little influence either on member states or on MNEs. However, if—as seems likely—regional regimes become stronger and expand their activities in the future, their ability to influence MNE operations will probably increase. Such increased influence will probably be used to stimulate some forms of MNE activity and FDI, while restricting others in order to achieve regime objectives.

Notes

1. This section is based principally on material contained in European Documentation, 1982a; European Documentation, 1989; and Price Waterhouse, 1987. See also Emerson, 1989; Sapir and Jacquemin, eds., 1990.

2. Qualified majority voting means that voting rights are weighted. In the Council of Ministers, unanimous, simple majority, and qualified majority voting are specified for different types of decisions. In the commission, with 17 commissioners appointed by the national governments (two each from France, Italy, Spain, the UK, and West Germany, and one each from the other member countries), decisions are reached on the basis of simple majority voting.

3. This section is based on Schott, 1989.

4. This section is based on Schott, 1989.

5. This section is based on material contained in Greenaway, Hyclak, and Thornton, eds., 1989; PBEC, 1990; Schott, 1989; Schott and Smith, eds., 1988; Smith and Stone, eds., 1987; Wonnacott, 1987a, 1987b.

6. Based on US Department of Commerce, Bureau of the Census, *Advance Report of U.S. Merchandise Trade: December 1987*, FT 900 ADV, 12 February 1988.

7. Based on International Monetary Fund (IMF), *International Financial Statistics* (Washington, DC: February 1988), and *Direction of Trade Statistics Yearbook* (Washington, DC: 1987).

8. Based on US Department of Commerce, *Survey of Current Business* (Washington, DC), August issues, 1985–1987.

9. Data reported in "Future Growth in North American Trade," *Deloitte & Touche Review* (May 20, 1991), p. 5.

10. The Development Assistance Committee (DAC) is an association of a subset of OECD governments formed for the purpose of coordinating development aid to LDCs. Its member countries are Australia, Austria, Belgium, Canada, Denmark, Finland, France, Germany, Iceland, Italy, Japan, the Netherlands, New Zealand, Norway, Sweden, Switzerland, the UK, and the US.

11. This section is based on material contained in Drabek, 1989, in Greenaway, Hyclak, and Thornton, eds.; and Schrenk, 1990.

12. This section is based on material contained in Nunez del Arco, Margain, and Cherol, eds., 1984; Edwards and Savastano, 1989, in Greenaway, Hyclak, and Thornton, eds.

13. Information is taken from a document announcing the Southern Common Market issued by the Argentine Embassy (Washington, DC).

14. This paragraph is based on Lewis, 1984, in Nunez del Arco, Margain, and Cherol, eds.

15. This section is based on Robson, 1987; see also Boyd, 1991, for general information.

16. This section is based on Balasubramanyam, 1989, in Greenaway, Hyclak, and Thornton, eds.

References

Andic, Fuat. 1984. "Tax Harmonization and Economic Integration," in Jose Nunez del Arco, Eduardo Margain, and Rachelle Cherol, eds., *The Economic Integration Process of Latin America in the 1980s*. Washington, DC: Inter-American Development Bank, Institute for Latin American Integration, pp. 205–228.

Balasubramanyam, V.N. 1989. "ASEAN and Regional Trade Cooperation in Southeast Asia," in Greenaway, Hyclak, and Thornton, eds., *Economic Aspects of Regional Trading Arrangements*. New York: New York University Press, pp. 167–188.

Behrman, Jack N. 1972. *The Role of International Companies in Latin American Integration*. Lexington, MA: Lexington Books.

Boyd, Gavin. 1991. *Structuring International Economic Cooperation*. London: Pinter Printers.

Drabek, Zdenek. 1989. "CMEA: The Primitive Socialist Integration and Its Prospects," in Greenaway, Hyclak, and Thornton, eds., *Economic Aspects of Regional Trading Arrangements*. New York: New York University Press, pp. 235–254.

Edwards, Sebastian, and Miguel Savastano. 1989. "Latin America's Intra-Regional Trade: Evolution and Future Prospects," in Greenaway, Hyclak, and Thornton, eds., *Economic Aspects of Regional Trading Arrangements*. New York: New York University Press, pp. 189–234.

Emerson, Michael. 1989. *The Economics of 1992: The E.C. Commission's Assessment of the Eocnomic Effects of Completing the Internal Market*. New York: Oxford University Press.

European Documentation. 1982a. *The European Community's Industrial Strategy*. Luxembourg: Office for Official Publications of the Communities.

European Documentation. 1982b. *The European Financial Common Market*. Luxembourg: Office for Official Publications of the Communities.

European Documentation. 1989. *Europe Without Frontiers—Completing the Internal Market*, 3rd edition. Luxembourg: Office for Official Publications of the Communities.

Greenaway, David, Thomas Hyclak, and Robert J. Thornton, eds. 1989. *Economic Aspects of Regional Trading Arrangements*. New York: New York University Press.

Grosse, Robert E. 1983. "The Andean Foreign Investment Code's Impact on Multinational Enterprises," *Journal of International Business Studies*, vol. 14, no. 1 (Winter), pp. 121–133.

Lewis, Vaughan A. 1984. "Regional Integration and Theories of Regionalism in the Commonwealth Caribbean," in Nunez del Arco, Margain, and Cherol, eds., *The Economic Integration Process of Latin America in the 1980s*. Washington, DC: Inter-American Development Bank, Institute for Latin American Integration, pp. 27–42.

Machlup, Fritz, ed. 1976. *Economic Integration: Worldwide, Regional, Sectoral— Proceedings of the Fourth Congress of the International Economic Association (1974)*. New York: Halsted.

Makridakis, Spyros G., et al. 1991. *Single Market Europe: Opportunities and Challenges for Business*. San Francisco, CA: Jossey-Bass.

Nunez del Arco, Jose, Eduardo Margain, and Rachelle Cherol, eds. 1984. *The Economic Integration Process of Latin America in the 1980s*. Washington, DC: Inter-American Development Bank, Institute for Latin American Integration (January).

Pacific Basin Economic Council (PBEC). 1990. "Mexico-US Free Trade Agreement," *International Bulletin* (May 31).

Price Waterhouse. 1987. *European Communities*. New York: Price Waterhouse.

Robson, Peter. 1987. *The Economics of International Integration*. 3rd revised edition London: Allen & Unwin,

Sapir, Andre, and Alexis Jacquemin, eds. 1990. *The European Internal Market: Trade and Competition*. New York: Oxford University Press.

Schelpe, Dirk. 1991. "A Statute for a European Company," *The CTC Reporter*, no. 31 (Spring), pp. 17–19.

Schott, Jeffrey J. 1988. "The Free Trade Agreement: A US Assessment," in Schott and Smith, eds., *The Canada–United States Free Trade Agreement: The Global Impact*. Washington, DC: Institute for International Economics, pp. 1–35.

Schott, Jeffrey J. 1989. *More Free Trade Areas?* Washington, DC: Institute for International Economics (May).

Schott, Jeffrey J., and Murray G. Smith, eds. 1988. *The Canada–United States Free Trade Agreement: The Global Impact*. Washington, DC: Institute for International Economics.

Schrenk, Martin. 1990. "Future of the CMEA," *Socialist Economies in Transition*, vol. 1, no. 1 (April), pp. 3–5 (World Bank, Country Economics Department, Socialist Economies Unit).

Shoup, Carl S., ed. 1967. *Fiscal Harmonization in Common Markets*, 2 vols. New York: Columbia University Press.

Smith, Murray G., and Frank Stone, eds. 1987. *Assessing the Canada–U.S. Free Trade Agreement.* Halifax, Canada: Institute for Research on Public Policy.

Smith, Roy C., and Ingo Walter. 1991. *The First European Merger Boom Has Begun.* Formal Publication No. 103, Washington University, Center for the Study of American Business, St. Louis, MO (January).

Smolowe, Jill. 1991. "European Community—Blueprint for the Dream," *Time*, vol. 138, no. 25 (December 23), pp. 29–30.

Wonnacott, Paul. 1987a. *The United States and Canada: The Quest for Free Trade—An Examination of Selected Issues.* Policy Analyses in International Economics 16, Institute for International Economics, Washington, DC (May).

Wonnacott, Paul. 1987b. *The US–Canadian Free Trade Agreement; A View from South of the Border.* PEAP Policy Study No. 87–2, University of Toronto, Institute for Policy Analysis, Policy and Economic Analysis Program, Toronto, Canada (December).

7 TRADE, EXCHANGE, AND INVESTMENT REGIMES

The most extensive and complex international economic regimes that have evolved during the postwar period are those governing trade, currency exchange, and financial relationships among and between the economically active countries of the world. For most of the period, the USSR and its former satellites were not formal participants in these regimes; however, most of them are now or will soon become regular participants. In any events, the great bulk of world commerce and financial activity has been governed by these regimes, and they should therefore be considered *global* in character. Although their functional scope is limited, their effects on the entire system of international business and economic activity are complex and pervasive.

Even before the beginning of World War II, there was widespread international agreement, particularly in the United States and Great Britain, that a totally new system of monetary and trade relationships was needed. It was generally believed that international trade conflicts and exchange disequilibria were principal causes of worldwide economic instability during the interwar period and thus, ultimately, of the war itself. Establishment of a trade regime based on multilateral competition, with the elimination of all country preferences and exchange controls, became a particular objective of US policy. A second, although transient, concern was the need to facilitate reconstruction in the war-damaged economies. And a third concern, continuing down to the present, was the promotion of long-term economic and social development in the less developed countries (LDCs) of the world.

A series of international conferences, begun while the war itself was still in progress, explored these issues and examined possible alternatives for dealing with them. Ultimately, the first concern—trade and currency exchange arrangements among countries at various levels of development and with various resource endowments and productive capacities—came to be embodied in two institutions: the International Monetary Fund (IMF) and the General Agreement on Tariffs and Trade (GATT). These two institutions, although very different in character, were aimed at a common objective: *mutually beneficial multilateral trade should be encouraged to the greatest extent possible.* Unrestricted International competition, facilitated by reliable currency exchange arrangements, was the means adopted to achieve this goal.

Reliance on competition and freedom of contract was not, however, adopted as the guiding principle with respect to international investment and capital flows. One reason for this difference was a fear that some countries—primarily LDCs, but initially including the war-damaged economies as well—would not be able to obtain sufficient support for long-term reconstruction and development projects from existing sources. The International Bank for Reconstruction and Development (IBRD, or World Bank) was created to provide a pool of funds, supplied by cooperating governments, for loans to countries needing this type of assistance. The second reason for rejecting open competition as the paramount principle for capital flows was a general recognition that various states—and not, as it turned out, only the poorer ones—might wish to control either inward or outward capital flows in order to pursue their own economic development objectives.

The worldwide boom in foreign investment and the related growth of multinational enterprises (MNEs) was not anticipated during the immediate postwar period. Only now, nearly a half century later, are some elements of a comprehensive international investment regime beginning to emerge (see chapter 2 discussion above). Over the intervening decades, however, the growth of investment has impacted the trade and exchange regimes in varied and important ways. Foreign investment is both a substitute and a stimulus for trade; hence, the growth of investment may "solve" some trade problems, while giving rise to others (see chapter 2 discussion above). In addition, both investment and trade operate through the currency exchange system, but often with opposite effects. Thus, a trade imbalance may induce an equilibrating movement in exchange rates, but contemporaneous capital flows may offset or reverse the process. Hence, as a practical matter, it is not possible to analyze the operation of trade and payments systems without attention to investment activity as well.

In this chapter, we examine the evolution of the closely related regimes for trade and monetary exchange during the past half century, and then look more briefly at developments associated with the possible evolution of a regime for international investment.

7.1. The Trade Regime: GATT[1]

The principle of international economic relations agreed upon by the victorious Allied nations of World War II was unrestricted freedom for, and indeed maximum encouragement of, mutually beneficial multilateral trade. However, development of a set of institutional arrangements and behavioral norms to implement this principle was not a simple matter. The fundamental problem was (and still is) that individual countries have traditionally protected various domestic industries and interests from foreign competition, and/or promoted their development through subsidies and other devices, for a variety of reasons: long-term development goals, concern for politically important interests or disadvantaged groups, and national defense considerations. The phasing out of these protection/ promotion policies typically creates costly economic and political disloca- tions in domestic economies. In fact, the trade regime has repeatedly confronted various forms of "new protectionism," which work directly against the long-term goal of liberalization.

The concept of unrestricted multinational free trade had been embodied in US bilateral trade agreements during the 1930s and was reflected in the Atlantic Charter (1941) and the Lend-Lease Agreement (1942). A US proposal for establishment of an International Trade Organization (ITO) under UN auspices was circulated for international discussion in 1945. As with the related (and logically secondary) process of establishing an international monetary regime, a series of international conferences and negotiations took place at various levels, and in 1947 a codification of trading relations among an important group of trading nations was signed in Geneva. This document, the General Agreement on Tariffs and Trade (GATT), was viewed as a transitional step toward the ITO. The ITO proposal reached its final form in the Havana Charter, which was signed by more than 50 countries in 1948. However, by that time differences among

Scope	Worldwide trade, with primary emphasis on manufactured goods.
Purpose	Promote unrestricted, multilateral trade, primarily through the reduction of tariff barriers.
Organizational Form	The General Agreement on Trade and Tariffs (GATT): A consultative and negotiating mechanism established under UN auspices; many related agreements among selected participants, some inconsistent with GATT principles.
Decision and Allocation Modes	Decisions based on consensus among participating parties; costs and benefits allocated through the trading process itself.
Strength and Change	1948–present: Successive negotiation "rounds" reduced tariff barriers worldwide; increasing numbers of nations participating.
	1986–1991: Most recent "round" not yet successful in expanding agreements on agriculture and services, or in resolving other controversial issues (e.g., intellectual property).

Figure 7-1.   The GATT Trade Regime.

the wartime allies—reflected in the creation of both the Council for Mutual Economic Assistance (CMEA) and the Organization for European Economic Cooperation (OEEC) (see chapter 6 above)—and concerns about special trade relationships on the part of both advanced countries and LDCs had undermined the immediate postwar consensus. Even in the US, the original sponsor, the ITO proposal provoked great opposition, and President Truman eventually withdrew the proposal from Congressional consideration in 1950.

The result was that GATT, which was never intended to be anything other than a transitional agreement, became the primary formal expression of international commitment to a liberal trade regime (figure 7-1). GATT is not an established agency in the same sense as the IMF or ILO; its staff has gradually increased but remains well under 500. GATT signatories are referred to as "contracting parties," and their deliberations are carried out in periodic rounds of major negotiations that take place over an extended time period. The eighth and most recent of these negotiations, the Uruguay Round, began in 1986. The GATT document provides for majority rule, with one vote per country, but decisions are actually arrived at by consensus. Although GATT has been the vehicle for multilateral trade negotiations for more than 40 years, it has never been given formal treaty status by any major trading country. Its strength rests in its mechanisms for dispute settlement and the threat of collective retaliation against violators.

GATT represents an international commitment to the principles and processes of trade liberalization; its strength as an effective forum may lie in its relative weakness as an organization. Finlayson and Zacher describe GATT as a "peculiar and entirely accidental institution," the central element in a regime "concerned with one international trade issue area, namely, trade barriers" (in Krasner, ed., 1983, p. 274). This is something of an overstatement, since dumping, subsidization, and some other important matters are also included in GATT negotiations. However, it remains true that GATT is not the core of a comprehensive international trade regime. (Repatriation of earnings, for example, is not included within the GATT framework.) Some of the trade issues not included in GATT are, of course, addressed in other UN-based initiatives.

7.1.1. Key Concepts and Issues

The postwar commitment to trade liberalization embodied in GATT involves two key concepts. One is the reduction of trade barriers, and the other is the elimination of discrimination and preferences among trading partners. These two ideas are quite distinct, since it is possible (indeed, historically typical) to reduce barriers or grant preferences for some trading partners while maintaining or even increasing them for others (thus maintaining or increasing discrimination). The principle of nondiscrimination is therefore the fundamental idea, a fact reflected in its priority position in Article 1 of the basic GATT agreement. The principle of nondiscrimination is formally expressed as "most favored nation" treatment (MFN), meaning that the most favorable treatment accorded any trading partner will be extended to others. Reciprocal MFN agreements were initially developed by the US during the interwar period. When reductions in trade barriers are negotiated in a multilateral, reciprocal MFN setting, the efficiency-increasing and welfare-enhancing effects of liberalization are extended to all participating parties.

Three major types of obstacles have delayed and complicated the establishment of a fully liberalized international trade regime centered on GATT:

1. Traditional industry protections and trade-partner preferences, the types of restrictive arrangements to which the postwar trade negotiations were initially addressed; some of these arrangements are actually multiplying and taking new forms (e.g., protection of service industries);
2. Concern that LDCs cannot overcome historic disadvantages without preferential treatment (i.e., discrimination in their favor) in their dealings with more advanced countries; and
3. Establishment of regional and other "customs union" and "free trade" agreements, which, although permitted by GATT, by their nature violate MFN principles, since participants in such agreements favor each other over outsiders.

The last of these obstacles has proved the least troublesome, since the new regional group agreements evolving over the postwar period have usually provided for greater liberalization among their own members, rather than increased restrictions on others (see chapter 6 above). In 1989, GATT contained 98 member countries. More than half of the current GATT membership (accounting for a much larger portion of world trade) belong to regional groupings.

Concern that LDCs would not be able to compete successfully in a completely nondiscriminatory trading system was a major factor undermining worldwide support for the initial ITO proposal. After a number of years of discussion and negotiation, a set of criteria for preferential trade treatment of these countries, known as the "Generalized System of Preferences" (GSP), was developed. The idea is that all countries meeting certain criteria (i.e., LDCs) would be accorded the same preferential treatment by all other countries (i.e., advanced countries) participating in the agreement. The GSP system, although it involves discrimination, is considered to be consistent with the liberal trade regime's fundamental goal of worldwide economic development and growth. The principal problems encountered have been connected with the reluctance of GSP countries to "graduate" (i.e., lose GSP status) as their levels of economic development and trade competitiveness increase.

Paradoxically, traditional industrial protection and discriminatory practices have accounted both for GATT's greatest achievements and for its most troublesome continuing problems. The MFN principle has become generally recognized, and tariff levels have been repeatedly reduced. Indeed, GATT has been criticized for an overemphasis on numerical tariff reductions, without regard to their significance or scope, and for neglecting nontariff barriers. More important, however, has been the persistence of protection for historical political interests in advanced countries (e.g., agriculture in Western Europe, Japan, and the US), and the appearance of "new protectionism" for some important manufacturing industries, particularly in the US. Since the "new protectionism" tends to rely on nontariff barriers, quotas, "voluntary" restraints, etc., these developments conflict both with the basic principles of trade liberalization and with GATT's specific emphasis on tariffs as the principal form of trade restriction.[2] The weakness of GATT's legal structure and its inability to impose sanctions or resolve disputes arising from either "old" or "new" forms of protectionism have been the major points of criticism (see, for example, Lipson, in Krasner, ed., 1983, and Schott, ed., 1990).

GATT ceased to function very effectively during the 1980s for a number of reasons. First, a great many trade disputes have arisen due to the economic changes of the 1970s and 1980s, and unilateral adoption of industrial policies and protectionist practices has become widespread. Protectionism has turned increasingly to domestic regulatory controls as well as to nontariff barriers. Second, as discussed in chapter 6 above, regional economic integration has become more important in both Western Europe and North America, regions which account for a dominant portion of global trade.

Other problems of the GATT system are inherent in its design. Multilateral negotiation is necessarily a slow and complex process; the successful Tokyo Round of negotiations lasted six years (1973–1979), and the current Uruguay Round involves 15 different negotiating groups. The de facto consensus rule permits a single country to halt the entire process until its interests are satisfied. There are numerous exceptions and other loopholes in the GATT, so that only about 60% of world trade is covered, and the GATT rules themselves are "inadequate and inadequately enforced" according to some analysts (Schott, 1989, pp. 7–9). Finally, the GATT consultative process cannot respond well to the rapid pace of change in international capital markets, information technology, service industry competition, and other areas.

7.1.2. Product and Commodity Agreements Within the Trade Regime

Within the broad international commitment to free trade embodied in GATT, there is also a set of subsidiary regimes involving explicit and significant commitment to an opposite notion, the principle of restricted competition or "managed trade" (Waldmann, 1986). Volatility in demand, supply, and price of agricultural commodities and other raw materials had led to the development of many different types of international stabilization arrangements, some of which date back to the prewar era. Agricultural products and raw materials were granted broad exemptions from the basic GATT principles from the beginning, and attempts to bring these areas of trade into the GATT framework have thus far proved unsuccessful. In addition, in recent years, bilateral and multilateral agreements have been used to limit competition, imports, and/or exports in a number of important manufacturing sectors and product lines. Since manufactured goods are the main focus of GATT negotiations, these departures from free trade principles require some kind of explicit justification. GATT's "safeguards" provisions create a basis for these exceptions.

Whether "managed trade" arrangements are made within or outside the context of GATT, they constitute departures from basic free trade principles for the purpose of limiting the effects of international competition and preserving spheres of economic activity, investment, and employment in particular nations and regions. The desire of various countries to "manage" their trade relationships and to insulate their economies from international competition is the central problem of the current Uruguay Round of GATT negotiations. It is widely believed that various schemes for trade management, as opposed to open competition, will be put forward in the near future. Hence, the character and impact of these "managed trade" regimes, and their connection with the larger free trade system, merit brief examination. We focus on two main examples: the Multifiber Agreement (MFA) involving trade in textiles and apparel; and the attempt to develop a comprehensive system of international commodity agreements during the 1970s.

7.1.2.1. The Multifiber Agreement (MFA).[3] Textiles, apparel, fibers, and related products accounted for 9% of total world trade in manufactures in 1982 (Cline, 1990, p. 51). Textile production typically appears early in the industrialization process, and one of the consequences of worldwide economic development during the postwar decades has been the successive creation of new sources of textile production in emerging economies. There new industries first provide import substitutes for domestic markets, and then become international competitors. The appearance of these new sources of supply and competition inevitably leads to pressures for protection in the established production and trading countries.

Ad hoc policy responses to increasing world textile competition during the 1950s evolved into international agreements with respect to cotton goods during the 1960s and eventually into the MFA in 1974. Unlike some other postwar trade arrangements, the textile regime has proved surprisingly durable and relatively stable; its purpose and character have been much the same over time, although its coverage has expanded continuously and its detailed provisions have changed in response to changing circumstances.

An important consideration accounting for initial attention to cotton goods was the fact that US producers had to buy raw cotton at the protected US domestic price, while their competitors purchased US cotton at the lower world price. In 1960, under US pressure, GATT enlarged the scope of exceptions from the basic free trade policy to recognize "Avoidance of Market Disruption" (i.e., rapid change in existing production and trading patterns), and international agreements to limit competition in cotton textiles soon followed. Within these agreements, bilateral consultations established limits on the growth of exports of cotton products from various LDCs and Japan into the US and European countries. Pressures for additional protection in the US persisted during the following decade, and the fact that restrictions on US imports often diverted textile products into European markets increased support for a more comprehensive international agreement. By the early 1970s, negotiations were initiated to pursue the following goals: expand coverage to all natural and manmade fibers; distribute export and import effects among all involved parties; avoid more restrictive unilateral actions, particularly by the US; and integrate the arrangement within the GATT framework. Although the eventual demise of MFA has been contemplated from its very beginnings, its basic structure has been expanded and strengthened during renewals in 1977, 1982, and 1986.

The MFA is generally recognized as an embarrassing breach of GATT principles, particularly because it overtly discriminates against LDC textile exporters (Zheng, 1988). MFA's reliance on physical quota limits, rather than tariffs, is also counter to the entire thrust of GATT. In fact, the MFA contains specific provisions insulating the GATT responsibilities and rights of participants from their contradictory MFA commitments. In spite of these apparent contradictions, however, textile exports from LDCs to advanced countries have grown continuously under the MFA. The MFA has certainly been "stabilizing," in the sense of providing for gradual rather than sudden change in trading patterns; and it may even have been "liberalizing," at least in comparison with various realistic alternatives. Textile industry representatives in the US insist that MFA restrictions are insufficiently protective, while critics from the opposite camp contend that they are nevertheless very costly to consumers. Ultimately, the MFA—like less elaborate arrangements in other industries—seems to have been less of a departure from the basic free trade regime than its formal structure and occasional short-term impact might suggest.

7.1.2.2. Commodity Agreements.[4]   The idea of using government policy to mitigate the effects of fluctuations in the supply and demand for basic commodities is very old and a variety of schemes to stabilize international commodity markets have been put forward over the past century. Many of these schemes have centered on supplier cartels; establishment and operation of the Organization of Petroleum Exporting Countries (OPEC) during the 1970s is the most recent and successful example. However, OPEC, like many similar arrangements, collapsed because of the diversity of interests among its participants, and also because of objections and counteractions by impacted customers.

The OPEC experience—both its initial success and its evident weaknesses and problems—stimulated interest in a comprehensive approach to international commodity markets, including foodstuffs (grains, coffee, sugar, cocoa), other agricultural products (cotton, rubber), minerals (bauxite), and metals (tin, copper). Since many LDC economies depend heavily on exports of these products, the concept of a comprehensive trade stabilization system for commodities became a major item on the agenda of the UN Conference on Trade and Development (UNCTAD). (Similar schemes, however, had been proposed by various interests and experts during the interwar period and by Keynes and others in the immediate postwar negotiations.)

The central theme of the new approach, which came to be referred to as the Integrated Program for Commodities (IPC), was that most internationally traded raw materials encountered similar instability problems, particularly on the demand side, and that piecemeal approaches involving only individual countries and commodities on an ad hoc basis were inevitably irrational and discriminatory. The IPC proposal of 1980 contained two main elements: 1) provision for international purchase and ownership of buffer stocks of commodities that are in temporary worldwide oversupply; and 2) compensatory financing mechanisms to cover short-term declines in export earnings due to commodity demand and price fluctuations. The central institutional innovation was a "Common Fund for Commodities," from which resources needed for these purposes would be drawn. Individual international commodity agreements (ICAs), representing both suppliers and customers for various commodities, would have access to the Common Fund as need arose. Individual countries, both advanced (particularly the US) and less developed, would be suppliers in some ICAs and customers in others. This broad mutuality of interests was a major consideration in the development of the entire proposal.

Only four ICAs involving both producer and consumer interests—coffee, cocoa, sugar, and tin—were in force at the time of the IPC discussions; charges levied on transactions governed by these agreements were available for financing the Common Fund. However, no such financing base existed for the 14 other commodities—many traded in much larger volumes and under much more volatile conditions—that were also involved in the negotiations. Ultimately, the lack of an adequate financial base, as well as the diversity and complexity of production/consumption conditions for the various products and the difficulty of obtaining agreement among all major parties, led to the abandonment of the comprehensive IPC initiative and the concept of the Common Fund for Commodities. Individual commodity agreements of varying scope and effectiveness are proposed, adopted, and abandoned from time to time.

7.1.2.3. Evaluation. The conclusion to be drawn from all this experience is that efforts to establish new international regimes that would operate very differently from the basic free trade regime of GATT have not been highly successful. On the other hand, in both raw materials (particularly agricultural products) and finished goods, individual country policies and bilateral agreements involving both simple protectionism and "managed trade" constitute major departures from free trade principles. Although these latter arrangements are persisting, and possibly even expanding, in numerous countries at various development levels, the fact that these arrangements are *not* supported by comprehensive international agreements may indicate their long-term weakness. In any event, the single most important *international* arrangement based on non-GATT principles, the CMEA, has collapsed within the last decade, and most of its members are attempting to adapt their economies for participation within the GATT framework (see discussion in chapter 6 above).

7.2. The Monetary Exchange Regime: IMF[5]

Commitment to a system of worldwide multilateral free trade, even if such an objective is only partially achieved, necessarily involves a parallel commitment to an international monetary system that contributes to, or at least does not impede, this objective. Establishment of such a monetary system, however, inevitably involves a loss of national autonomy with respect to foreign exchange arrangements and monetary policies. A country can participate in the open international trading system only to the extent that it can offer currency (or, equivalently, goods and services) acceptable to its various trading partners and, ultimately, to the international community as a whole. Hence, establishment of an open trading system requires parallel creation of a supportive system of currency exchange, including a mechanism for stabilizing and/or adjusting rates in response to changing developments over time.

A fundamental question about any international arrangement established for this purpose is the extent to which such rate settings and adjustments will be "automatic" or "discretionary," that is, whether they will occur without case-by-case policy intervention or, on the other hand, will require specific and detailed negotiations and agreements. Although little serious consideration was given in the postwar discussions to a return to the international gold standard, the theoretically "automatic" adjustment mechanism of the gold standard is generally regarded as a point of reference for the evaluation of other international monetary regimes. A brief description of the gold standard therefore provides an appropriate starting point for our analysis.

7.2.1. The Gold Standard [6]

Gold, along with other precious metals and commodities, has been used as a store of value and means of payment since ancient times, but its only lengthy period of use as the central element in the international monetary system was 1870–1914. After serving as a de facto standard for about a century, gold was formally established as the basis for the value of the British pound sterling in 1821. As Britain became the leading world economic and military power during the nineteenth century, other countries voluntarily adopted similar arrangements (sometimes, as in the US, over considerable domestic opposition), and a worldwide system of currency valuation and exchange in terms of gold evolved. The absence of centralized discussions and formal agreements in the establishment of the nineteenth-century gold-standard regime is one of its most curious features; as Cooper remarks, the nineteenth-century gold standard "was in a sense an accident of history" (1987, p. 44).[7]

The essential idea of the gold standard is that the value of each country's currency is established in terms of a specific quantity of gold. According to the oversimplified textbook explanation, the system operates as follows: foreigners coming into possession of a particular currency in amounts in excess of their immediate needs (as a result of export sales greater than corresponding imports, for example) may convert the currency to gold and return it to their own country, reconverting it there into their own currency. This operation will draw down gold stocks in one country and increase gold stocks in the other. If gold flows of this sort are substantial and persistent, the money supply and prices will decline in the gold-exporting country, and increase in the gold-importing country, and these relative price movements will continue until the basic disequilibrium in import–export relationships is corrected. Thus, in theory, the gold standard tended to stabilize international economic relationships in two important ways:

1. Establishment of currency values in terms of gold provided security for international transactions and facilitated easy conversion of one currency into another, reducing the need for actual gold movements and stimulating multilateral trade; and
2. In the event of persistent disequilibrium and substantial gold flows, the money supply and price effects resulting from the gold standard would induce reequilibrating developments in the countries involved.

Although these theoretical features of the gold standard are clearly demonstrable in the abstract case of a two-country, two-currency world, actual experience with the gold standard was substantially different. For a variety of reasons, not all due to the operation of the gold standard itself, prices, trade volumes, production, and employment in the major trading countries were quite unstable throughout the gold-standard era. The time periods required for supposedly reequilibrating adjustments proved to be long, and the domestic economic adjustments involved would, according to Cooper, be considered "intolerable" in the contemporary world (1987, p. xiii). He notes that the late nineteenth-century reign of the gold standard ended in something that was then called the "Great Depression," until the worldwide economic collapse of the 1930s took over that title. In a more technical analysis, Cooper shows that the gold standard did not produce price stability either in the short or long term, in either the US or Great Britain, and that the unemployment rate in both countries was higher during the gold-standard decades than during a comparable time period following World War II (1987, chapter 2). Meltzer reaches similar conclusions, but points out that there is "a higher probability that the long-term price level would remain constant under the gold standard" than under postwar arrangements (in Campbell and Dougan, eds., 1986, p. 150). The fear that the gold standard would have a permanently depressing effect on both prices and the level of economic activity throughout the world was, in fact, one of the reasons for its rejection in the postwar discussions.

7.2.2. The Bretton Woods Institutions

Dissatisfaction with international trade and monetary arrangements during the interwar period and the desire to create a framework for unrestricted international trade in the postwar era led to the development of a variety of proposals for new exchange arrangements to be put in place at the close of World War II. After considerable consultation among the wartime allies (which at that time included the USSR), the UN Monetary and Financial Conference convened at Bretton Woods, New Hampshire, in July 1944, to address two interrelated problems: 1) creating an orderly basis for international currency exchange, including both stabilization and adjustment mechanisms; and 2) providing loans to support reconstruction in war-damaged countries and economic growth and development in poorer countries. These two different purposes led to the creation of two different institutions—the International Monetary Fund (IMF) and the International Bank for Reconstruction and Development (IBRD, or World Bank). As was noted at the time, the names of these institutions are somewhat confusing, since the IMF was established to carry out exchange, reserve, and short-term loan functions normally associated with a bank, while the IBRD is essentially a fund for providing long-term loans. The term *World Bank* is particularly unfortunate, since the IBRD provides financial assistance only to a selected group of countries and for very limited purposes. It performs none of the functions, such as currency issue and monetary policy control, that would be associated with a worldwide central bank. From the time of their creation, the two Bretton Woods institutions have evolved in very different ways, and the IBRD, although playing a highly significant role in some countries and with respect to some important facets of worldwide economic development, is a peripheral element of the worldwide trade and monetary exchange systems. (See further discussion of the IBRD in connection with international investment, below.)

7.2.3. From Fixed to Floating Rates

The basic idea reflected in initial plans for the IMF was to create a system of international currency exchange that would have the desirable properties of the theoretical gold standard, while avoiding its destabilizing and deflationary effects. In a modification of the "gold exchange" standard that operated briefly during the interwar period, gold convertibility of key currencies (ultimately only the dollar) was to be maintained, and exchange rates among currencies would be established from this reference point. The result was a set of exchange rates pegged to the dollar, which became the key reserve currency and the source of international liquidity. The exchange rates for all other currencies were to be stabilized during periods of short-run disequilibrium by loans from a reserve fund established at the outset by contributions from all member countries. In the event of substantial and persistent disequilibrium in a particular currency, revaluations would be negotiated among the member contributors. In principle, the IMF system with pegged exchange rates would create the same fungibility between domestic and foreign currencies that had characterized the gold standard; and, since currency revaluations were expected to be rare, the stability of contracts provided by the gold standard was anticipated as well.

Initial establishment of both specific exchange rates and the reserve fund was facilitated by the fact that the dollar had already become the de facto international currency standard, and the US was the largest contributor to the reserve fund itself. Subsequently, economic recovery in other major trading nations and inadequacy of the total gold/currency reserve in the light of expanding world trade led to the creation of a new form of reserve credit, *Special Drawing Rights (SDRs)*, defined as a "basket" of major currencies in 1969. SDRs are the internal accounting units used by the IMF to describe the contribution quotas and indebtedness of its members and to settle accounts among them.

Creation of SDRs both reflected and facilitated the declining role of both gold and the dollar in the international monetary system. In August 1971, in response to continuing high rates of inflation and balance of payments deficits, the US made a dramatic break with the worldwide monetary regime by terminating the gold convertibility of the dollar and imposing a 10% surcharge (in effect, a temporary tariff) on all dutiable imports. This shift marked the end of the de facto "dollar standard" of the postwar era. By 1973 a worldwide system of flexible exchange rates, supervised by the IMF and hence referred to as "managed float," had evolved.

There is some debate in the literature as to whether or not the developments of the 1970s marked the end of the initial postwar monetary regime. Not only did the managed float arrangement reduce the need for conventional IMF stabilization loans, but also 1) the increase in oil prices greatly increased the need for short-term payments financing, and 2) the private credit market, partially funded with oil revenues, became much more available for this purpose. These developments brought about substantial changes in the role and activities of the IMF, referred to by some analysts as the "dissipation" of the regime (Cohen, in Krasner, ed., 1983, p. 327). However, there was in fact no change in the basic purposes and functions of the regime during the period, and the IMF secretariat continues to play a major role in the administration of the system, including extensive consultation with individual countries concerning their exchange rate problems. Since the IMF now involves more than 150 members, with post-Communist and other countries still in the process of joining, it remains the major multinational forum for consideration of worldwide monetary and exchange issues (see figure 7-2). The IMF thus continues to provide focus and support for the regime's fundamental objectives—providing an supportive exchange framework for expanding multinational trade—although the specific activities carried out, both by the IMF and by other entities, both governmental and private, have by the IMF and by other entities, both governmental and private, have changed in response to changing circumstances. The norms and behaviors associated with the post-war monetary regime are essentially unchanged. The fact that ultimate objectives can be pursued without reference to the fixed exchange rates and stabilization loans that were the IMF's principal initial features is a sign of the regime's long-term success.

7.3. International Investment: The Search for a Regime

The role that foreign direct investment (FDI) would play in the postwar international economic order was not anticipated when the foundations of the trade and payments regimes were put in place. Earlier foreign financing of economic development—British financing of North American development, for example—was primarily in the form of portfolio investment; foreign investors bought shares or provided loans to domestic enterprises, taking little if any control over actual operations. Prior to World War II, FDI was confined almost entirely to natural resource exploitation (oil, metals) and specialized agriculture (e.g., bananas). Nestle, Singer, and Unilever stood out as the rare large MNEs in manufactured products.

Postwar interest in international investment was primarily focused on the reconstruction of war-damaged economies and, secondarily, on the creation of favorable development conditions in postcolonial states. As its name implies, the International Bank for Reconstruction and Development (IBRD, or World Bank) was created in response to these concerns. Like the IMF, the World Bank initially dealt directly only with

Scope	Exchange rates and mechanisms among nations engaged in world trade and finance.
Purpose	Establish orderly process for monetary exchange—including setting, stabilizing, and modifying exchange rates—to promote growth of world trade and investment.
Organizational Form	International Monetary Fund (IMF): A formal organization controlled by a Board of Governors representing the membership and operated by a professional secretariat. The actual "fund" consists of the contributions of member nations, established by quota.
Decision and Allocation Modes	Weighted voting on policy issues, based on relative contribution. Loans from stabilization fund largely controlled by professional staff within policy guidelines. Currency revaluations negotiated between major involved parties and IMF staff.
Strength and Change	Initial scheme aimed at maintenance of pegged exchange rates ended in early 1970s, when current "floating rate" system was introduced. Result has been a changed *role* for IMF, but not a decline in importance.

Figure 7-2. The IMF Monetary Exchange Regime. Alongside the IMF, periodic conferences among the major trading nations, referred to as the Group of Five (G5) or the Group of Seven (G7) depending on the number of participants, have attempted to stabilize or revise exchange rates among major international currencies, with varying degrees of success.

governments. It provided financing for types of projects—namely, large-scale and long-term—for which private financing is difficult if not impossible to obtain; and, again like the IMF, World Bank assistance was often tied to substantial resource and policy commitments by the receiving country. The initial focus of World Bank activity was on the replacement of war-damaged infrastructure, and infrastructure projects such as port facilities, power systems, and so forth continued to receive primary emphasis when attention shifted to development of poorer nations and regions. Agricultural and rural development projects have been emphasized more recently (van Meerhaeghe, 1987, pp. 67–100).

The IBRD has been augmented by the creation of two related institutions: the International Finance Corporation (IFC, 1956), which aims at expanding funds available for private enterprise; and the International Development Association (IDA, 1960), which aims at improving loan terms on projects in LDCs. The provision of technical assistance for the design and execution of investment projects has become an increasingly important World Bank function over time. The impact of the World Bank on worldwide economic development and integration during its half century of existence is literally incalculable, since the roughly $200 billion made available through its operations has been multiplied many times through the activities of domestic governments and private investors (van Meerhaeghe, 1987, pp. 67–100).

The IBRD was not conceived as the core element of an international investment regime, and in spite of the creation of the IFC, it has not evolved in that direction. The difference between IBRD-related activities and a comprehensive international investment regime was emphasized in the widely cited article "Toward a GATT for Investment" by Goldberg and Kindleberger (1970). Their list of investment-related concerns meriting international policy attention is quite broad, and includes some issues, such as taxation and competition, subsequently covered in Organization for Economic Cooperation and Development (OECD) and UN discussions and elsewhere (see chapter 5 above). They also identified a number of investment-related issues, such as the impact of exchange controls, export controls, and varied national standards of securities regulation on MNE activities, that have not yet received systematic international attention. Goldberg and Kindleberger, however, did not emphasize the international investment issue that has received the greatest attention over the subsequent decades—insurance against political risks.

The US developed an investment guarantee program to encourage private investment in the reconstruction of Europe after World War II. This program gradually expanded to include other countries, and in 1959 it was modified to focus exclusively on investment in developing countries. The current agency, the Overseas Private Investment Corporation (OPIC), was established in 1971, with various revisions thereafter. Several other major investor countries, led by Germany and Japan, have also developed nationally based investment insurance schemes, and there are some private providers as well (Shelp, in Goodwin and Mayall, eds., 1980). The provision of some sort of protection against political risk is widely believed to be essential to continuing and increased advanced country investment in the LDCs.

Proposals for some kind of *multilateral* insurance arrangements have circulated for several decades. Such arrangements appeared to be needed because of conflicts and gaps in national and bilateral schemes; also, multilateral arrangements would be appropriate for investor and/or recipient groups that were themselves multinational. A major sticking point, however, was LDC resistance to the use of international mechanisms for dispute resolution. Such mechanisms are obviously critical, since the principal risk to be insured is expropriation, and the point of an insurance scheme is to provide some recourse for the foreign investor other than decisions of domestic governments and courts (Holthus, Kebschull, and Menck, 1987).

After many years of debate and discussion under World Bank auspices, the Multilateral Investment Guarantee Agency (MIGA) became operational in April 1988. Both advanced and developing countries join MIGA voluntarily, accepting their roles and responsibilities when they do so. (Advanced countries supply capital to the insurance fund in accordance with an established formula.) MIGA guarantees eligible investments against non-commercial risks of several types, including:

1. transfer risks arising from currency restrictions (the first concern raised by Goldberg and Kindleberger, 1970);
2. loss from legislative or administrative actions, whether or not such actions constitute formal expropriation;
3. government repudiation of contracts; and
4. armed conflict and civil unrest.

MIGA is intended to supplement, but not supplant, national and private investment insurance programs. It is also intended to take an active role in research, technical assistance, and other functions that would contribute to increased foreign investment in LDCs ("The Legal Framework: MIGA Launched," 1988).

Experience with MIGA has been too brief for any conclusions to be drawn as to its effectiveness and impact. If it meets the needs of advanced-country investors and developing-country recipients, then one would expect membership to increase and MIGA's functions to expand accordingly. As an additional agency within the complex of the World Bank and the IMF, MIGA might over time become the nucleus for a regime that would address securities regulation, corporate governance, and other investment-related issues on a multinational basis. (See figure 7-3 for elements of an international investment regime.) On the other hand, MIGA's resources may prove inadequate or its settlement procedures may fail to satisfy the various parties involved; if so, the need for "a GATT for investment" will remain unfilled.

Scope	Worldwide international investment, including rights/responsibilities of both governments and investors.
Purpose	Establish ground rules for relations between and among nations and enterprises in order to promote world development and trade through international investment; reduce unilateral controls on capital flows; protect foreign investment against default and expropriation.
Organizational Form	(1) World Bank: Provides long-term loans and technical assistance for major projects in less developed countries. (Only IMF members may join.) Supplemented by IDA and IFC. (2) MIGA: Provides insurance against political risks for investments among signatory countries. (Only World Bank members may join.) (3) UN Code of Conduct on Transnational Corporations: Draft statement of concerns and responsibilities for both governments and enterprises involved in international investment; not yet formally adopted. (4) OECD Declaration on International Investment and Multinational Enterprise: Guidelines on MNE investment for home and host countries.
Decision and Allocation Modes	(1) World Bank: Policy controlled by governing board; detailed decisions made by secretariat. (2) MIGA: Policy set in basic agreement; administered by staff. (3) UN Code of Conduct on Transnational Corporations: Developed within UNECOSOC; awaiting General Assembly action.
Strength and Change	No comprehensive investment regime is yet in place; critical missing elements are common international understandings about accounting standards, corporate governance, repatriation of funds, etc.

Figure 7-3.   Elements of an International Investment Regime.

Julius proposes two general principles as the basis for an international "policy environment" providing "neutrality or non-discrimination" in foreign direct investment: 1) national treatment (i.e., "equal treatment of foreign and domestic firms in the home market"); and 2) neutrality between trade and investment (1990, p. 97). In her view, this neutral policy environment would maximize the efficiency gains from FDI. This view is based on four arguments about FDI (Julius, 1990, p. 96). First, FDI provides direct economic benefits, just as cross-border trade does. Second, the balance of indirect benefits and costs associated with FDI is impossible to quantify. Third, foreign-owned and domestic enterprises behave in much the same way. Fourth, most advanced countries both invest in and receive investment from each (see chapter 2 above), and enterprises have multiple investment choices (excluding Japan); policy flexibility is therefore necessary.

7.4. The Trade and Exchange Regimes: Evaluation

In the context of this analysis, the international exchange and trade regimes described above require evaluation from at least three perspectives. First: are these regimes substantive, or merely institutional— that is, do they have genuine effects on the international business and economic relationships within their intended scope? Second: how are these regimes related to the growth and success of MNEs during the postwar decades? In particular, is there a cause–effect relationship in either direction? Third: what does experience with these regimes tell us about the general nature of regimes, their origins and evolution?

7.4.1. Substantive Impact

With respect to the substantive impact of the regimes—that is, in what way is the world different because of their existence?—a definitive conclusion is not possible, since we lack a second environment in which to conduct parallel experiments. However, it is indisputable that, by any measure or comparison, world trade has grown more rapidly, and the benefits of trade have been more widely distributed among regions, nations, and industries, during the postwar decades than at any other time in world history. Hence, it is hard to believe that the postwar money and trade regimes have failed in their primary purpose, which was and is to expand the volume and extend the benefits of worldwide multilateral trade.

With respect to more specific evidence of impact, empirical studies by Cooper (1987), Meltzer (in Campbell and Dougan, eds., 1986), and Schwartz (in Campbell and Dougan, eds., 1986), previously cited, confirm that the postwar monetary regime has led to greater stability (or at least no greater instability) in several indicators of economic performance as compared to a similiar time period under the nineteenth-century gold standard. If there is a long-term trade-off between inflation and unemployment, as many people believe and as the gold standard/IMF comparisons suggest, then the postwar experience (more inflation and less unemployment) is probably in the direction that would be chosen by most contemporary regime participants. With respect to the trade regime, it is indisputable that average tariff levels have been reduced, and duties in many specific areas eliminated altogether. Many protectionist policies and discriminatory barriers remain, but the commitment to the principles of liberalized trade has unquestionably influenced both domestic policies and international agreements throughout the world.

Strange argues that "the 'golden years' of growth in the 1950s and 1960s are better explained by the steady expansion of credit . . . than by the reduction in the barriers to trade or the observance of rules regarding exchange rates" (1988, p. 105). However, there is some circularity in this viewpoint. Establishment of the trade and exchange regimes preceded the credit expansion, and there is no reason to believe that the expansion itself would have occurred in their absence.

It may be argued that both regimes have "weakened" in the more recent decades—the monetary regime by its acceptance of floating rates and the trade regime by its tolerance of continued (or even increased) discrimination and restrictions. The counterarguments, of course, are that 1) the "managed float" system is more supportive of trade expansion in a rapidly changing world than a fixed rate system would be; 2) the regional and GSP exceptions to MFN are understood to involve objectives that will contribute to growth and liberalization over the long term; and 3) the "new protectionism," although objectionable, falls within the permissible safeguards provided in the initial GATT agreement, and does not involve abandonment of the regime's initial and continuing norms. (This is essentially the position taken by Lipson and by Ruggie, both in Krasner, ed., 1983; it is also consistent with numerous proposals for technical modifications within the regime, cf. Williamson and Miller, 1987.) According to this perspective, the regimes have adapted to changing circumstances, a sign of strength and persistence rather than of weakening. At a minimum, both regimes may be said to have promoted constraint in the management of international economic relations, both by individual countries and by multinational groups, and to have reduced uncertainty, which "may well be the single most important" barrier to the growth and development of the international economy (Finlayson and Zacher, in Krasner, ed., 1983, p. 314).

7.4.2. Regimes and MNEs

The evolution of the postwar trade and exchange regimes is peculiarly associated with the growth of MNEs in both numbers and scale. On the one hand, trade liberalization and ease of currency exchange created a favorable setting for the expansion of international business activity in all forms, and for the growth of multinational firms. The theory of the MNE involves the optimization of investment; therefore, facilities, production and marketing among various locations, ease of movement for both capital and output, and reductions in exchange controls and tariffs, all contribute to MNE expansion. On the other hand, the growth of MNEs takes a large amount of international economic activity out of the "market" arena and into the internal control of individual firms. Once MNE structures are established, local revenues become available for expenditure in various jurisdictions, and local capital sources become accessible as well; the need for international financial transfers is correspondingly reduced. Similarly, MNEs may choose to transfer products and services among jurisdictions in ways that avoid or minimize the impact of tariffs and other trade restrictions; or, conversely, they may accept restrictions (such as "voluntary" trade restraints) that fall outside the scope of multilateral negotiations. In a sense, the growth of the MNEs, nurtured within the framework of convertible currencies and liberalizing trade, has created a situation that makes the framework itself less important. The apparent weakening of the regimes may be in fact a reflection of the strengthening of the forces that have grown up within them.

7.4.3. Regime Theory

With respect to the theoretical analysis of the creation and evolution of regimes, formation of the trade and exchange regimes unquestionably owes much to the economic and political dominance of the US at the end of World War II. Both GATT and the IMF may be said to have been born, or at least conceived, in Washington, DC. However, the norms and behaviors of both regimes, along with their institutional forms, have remained intact even as the US abandoned its primary supporting role and, indeed, took actions—such as the 1971 break with gold and the "new protectionism" for textiles, autos, and steel—that conflicted with fundamental regime commitments. The conclusion seems to be that the ongoing strength and character of the trade and exchange regimes owes more to mutuality of interest and fundamental commitment to principles among the membership than to the power and goals of any hegemon. In a sense, what appears to be a weakening of both regimes in recent years may be a sign of their fundamental success, in that the basic norms and standards have become so widely accepted in the international community that 1) they can be pursued through multiple means, private as well as governmental and intergovernmental, and 2) great variations in short-term behavior can be tolerated without serious threat to the underlying principles and norms of the regimes themselves.

Notes

1. The structure and evolution of GATT are described in innumerable publications; Kelly et al., 1990, Schott, ed., 1990, and van Meerhaeghe, 1987, are recent and authoritative. Major analyses of the world trading system from an "international regimes" perspective include Kihl and Lutz, 1985, and papers by Finlayson and Zacher, Lipson, and Ruggie, all in Krasner, ed., 1983.

2. The argument for focusing primarily on tariffs is that they are 1) "transparent"—i.e., the amount of restriction can be readily observed—and 2) easily revised through across-the-board reductions, rather than requiring case-by-case negotiations. However, tariff reductions are often offset by the development of nontariff barriers (Grieco, 1990).

3. This section is based primarily on Cline, 1990; The Multifiber Agreement, 1987; Tussie, 1987; and Zheng, 1988.

4. This section is based primarily on Goodwin and Mayall, eds., 1980; and Tait and Sfeir, 1982; see also Hathaway, 1987.

5. Principal references for this section include Campbell and Dougan, eds., 1986; Classen, ed., 1990; Cooper, 1986, 1987; Cooper et al., 1989; Hamouda et al., eds., 1989; Maddison, 1989; Weil, 1983; and Williamson and Miller, 1987. The papers by Cohen and Ruggie, both published in Krasner, ed., 1983, specifically deal with the international monetary system from an "international regimes" perspective.

6. Principal sources for this section include Cooper, 1987, chapter 2; papers by Meltzer and Schwartz, both in Campbell and Dougan, eds., 1986; and Eichengreen, in Cooper et al., 1989.

7. Actual operation of the gold standard depended heavily on the supportive policies of the British government and the use of the pound sterling as a key currency.

References

Campbell, Colin D., and William R. Dougan, eds. 1986. *Alternative Monetary Regimes*. Baltimore, MD: Johns Hopkins University Press.

Classen, Emil-Maria, ed. 1990. *International and European Monetary Systems*. New York: Praeger.

Cline, William R. 1990. *The Future of World Trade in Textiles and Apparel*, revised edition. Washington, DC: Institute for International Economics.

Cohen, B.J. 1983. "Balance-of-Payments Financing: Evolution of a Regime," in Krasner, ed., *International Regimes*. Ithaca, NY: Cornell University Press, pp. 315–336.

Cooper, Richard N. 1986. *Economic Policy in an Interdependent World*. Cambridge, MA: MIT Press.

Cooper, Richard N. 1987. *The International Monetary System*. Cambridge, MA: MIT Press.

Cooper, Richard N., Barry Eichengreen, C. Randall Henning, Gerald Holtham, and Robert D. Putnam. 1989. *Can Nations Agree?: Issues in International Economic Cooperation*. Washington, DC: Brookings Institution.

Eichengreen, Barry. 1989. "Hegemonic Stability Theories of the International Monetary System," in Cooper et al., *Can Nations Agree?* Washington, DC: Brooking Institution, pp. 255–298.

Finlayson, J.A., and Mark Zacher, 1983. "The GATT Regime and the Regulation of Trade," in Krasner, ed., *International Regimes*. Ithaca, NY: Cornell University Press, pp. 273–314.

Goldberg, P.M., and C.P. Kindleberger. 1970. "Toward a GATT for Investment: A Proposal for Supervision of the International Corporation," *Law and Policy in International Business*, vol. 2, no. 2 (Summer), pp. 295–325.

Goodwin, Geoffrey, and James Mayall, eds. 1980. *A New International Commodity Regime*. New York: St. Martin's.

Grieco, Joseph M. 1990. *Cooperation among Nations: Europe, America, and Non-Tariff Barriers to Trade*. Ithaca, NY: Cornell University Press.

Hamouda, Omar F., et al., eds., 1989. *The Future of the International Monetary System*. Armonk, NY: M.E. Sharpe.

Hathaway, Dale E. 1987. *Agriculture and the GATT: Rewriting the Rules*. Washington, DC: Institute for International Economics.

Holthus, Manfred, Dietrich Kebschull, and Karl Wolfgang Menck. 1987. *Multilateral Investment Insurance and Private Investment in the Third World*. New Brunswick, NJ: Transaction Books.

Kelly, Margaret, et al. 1988. *Issues and Developments in International Trade Policy*. Occasional Paper 63, IMF, Washington, DC.

Kihl, Y.W., and James M. Lutz, 1985. *World Trade Issues: Regime, Structure, and Policy*. New York: Praeger.

Krasner, Stephen D., ed. 1983. *International Regimes*. Ithaca, NY: Cornell University Press.

"The Legal Framework: MIGA Launched." 1988. *The CTC Reporter*, no. 25 (Spring), pp. 19–21.

Lipson, Charles. 1983. "The Transformation of Trade: The Sources and Effects of Regime Change," in Krasner, ed., *International Regimes*. Ithaca, NY: Cornell University Press, pp. 233–272.

Maddison, Angus. 1989. *The World Economy in the 20th Century*. Paris: OECD.

Meltzer, A.H. 1986. "Some Evidence on the Comparative Uncertainty Experienced Under Different Monetary Regimes," in Campbell and Dougan, eds., *Alternative Monetary Regimes*. Baltimore, MD: Johns Hopkins University Press, pp. 122–153.

The Multifiber Agreement. 1987. *Law and Policy in International Business*, vol. 19, no. 1 (Special Issue).

Ruggie, J.G. 1983. "International Regimes, Transactions and Change: Embedded Liberalism in the Postwar Economic Order," in Krasner, ed., *International Regimes*. Ithaca, NY: Cornell University Press, pp. 195–232.

Schott, J.J. 1989. *More Free Trade Areas?* Washington, DC: Institute for International Economics.

Schott, J.J., ed. 1990. *Completing the Uruguay Round*. Washington, DC: Institute for International Economics.

Schwartz, Anna J. 1986. "Alternative Monetary Regimes: The Gold Standard," in Campbell and Dougan, eds., *Alternative Monetary Regimes*. Baltimore, MD: Johns Hopkins University Press, pp. 44–72.

Shelp, Ronald K. 1980. "Private Sector Investment and Political Risk: A Comparative Study of OPIC and Other Schemes," in Goodwin and Mayall, eds., *A New International Commodity Regime*. New York: St. Martin's, pp. 186–228.

Strange, Susan. 1988. *States and Markets*. New York: Basil Blackwell.

Tait, R.T., and G.N. Sfeir. 1982. "The Common Fund for Commodities," *The George Washington Journal of International Law and Economics*, vol. 16, no. 3, pp. 483–538.

Tussie, Diana. 1987. *The Less Developed Countries and the World Trading System*. New York: St. Martin's.

van Meerhaeghe, M.A.G. 1987. *International Economic Institutions*, fifth revised edition. Dortrecht, Netherlands: Kluwer.

Waldmann, Raymond J. 1986. *Managed Trade: The New Competition Between Nations*. Cambridge, MA: Ballinger.

Weil, Gordon. 1983. *Exchange-Rate Regime Selection in Theory and Practice*. New York: Graduate School of Business Administration, New York University.

Williamson, John, and Marcus H. Miller. 1987. *Targets and Indicators: A Blueprint for the International Coordination of Economic Policy*. Washington, DC: Institute for International Economics.

Zheng, Henry R. 1988. "Defining Relationships and Resolving Conflicts Between Interrelated Multinational Trade Agreements: The Experience of the MFA and the GATT," *Stanford Journal of International Law*, vol. 25, no. 1, pp. 45–101.

8 SEA AND AIR TRANSPORT REGIMES

Among the institutional and behavioral arrangements governing various aspects of international business, those dealing with sea and air transport are among the most interesting to examine from an "international regimes" perspective. Strange (1988) notes that, although it is easy to view "the political economy of transport systems" as a matter of only marginal significance, the truth is that the governance and operation of international transport has become increasingly salient. Both the volume of world trade and the amount of world transport activity have been growing much faster than world production for several decades, and transport services are spanning ever greater distances at ever greater speeds (Strange, 1988, p. 137). As the world becomes smaller and more interdependent, the forces of shrinkage and linkage become more, not less, important.

In spite of their obvious differences in technology and purpose—air transport primarily involves the movement of people, and sea transport the movement of goods—these two industries have many common features. Their economics is dominated by the pressures of high fixed/low variable costs and highly unstable demand; the equipment involved is costly and has few alternative uses; and the cost of trips is much the same, whether the equipment is full or empty. In addition, both activities have very significant network and systemic attributes; they serve multiple geographic points from central and interlinked nodes. Each industry also involves technological aspects requiring fairly high levels of expertise; and both safety/performance aspects and intercarrier standardization are important features.

Although both sea and air transport services are operated by business enterprises (whether private or state owned) rather than by political management, both industries are subject to substantial policy attention by national governments. Krasner (1985, chapter 8) emphasizes that international sea transport has evolved over several hundred years on the basis of market-oriented principles and norms, whereas the air transport regime has been "authoritarian" (i.e., primarily under government control) from its very beginnings. This distinction is broadly accurate, but may give insufficient weight to the important role of domestic government policies in developing and supporting commercial shipping activities in the major sea-transport countries. These mutually tolerated and interwoven domestic transport policies created an international regime that was at least partially governed by nonmarket forces even before the new and more authoritarian intergovernmental agreements of the late 1960s. On the other side, the international air transport regime is becoming increasingly market oriented. Hence, the sea and air regimes, although having very different histories, are somewhat more alike today than they have ever been in the past. Our research also suggests that these two regimes have followed a common evolutionary pattern over the post-World War II era that has not been clearly observed in prior studies.

8.1. The Ocean Shipping Regime[1]

Ocean shipping is one of the very few international business activities that has no substantial domestic counterpart. Air transport, telecommunications, banking, and, of course, commercial trade and investment all take place primarily within sovereign states, and only secondarily between them. By contrast, even for the US, where domestic ocean shipping is a significant mode of transport, international shipments account for roughly two thirds of total ocean tonnage and much higher shares of total ton-miles and value of shipments. (Domestic ocean shipments are primarily bulk commodities of low unit value.)

Surprisingly, however, the overwhelmingly international character of ocean shipping has not led to the development of a strong international network of intergovernmental and interenterprise understandings and agreements. On the contrary, and in contrast to the ubiquitous state interest in both air transport and telecommunications, the international shipping industry has evolved in an atmosphere of almost complete private ownership and control. National policies toward ocean shipping have a history going back to Vasco da Gama, Columbus, and Sir Francis Drake. However, both historically and at present, these policies have tended to support, promote, and protect, rather than restrict, the operations of home-country entrepreneurs and carriers.

Shipping was the subject of one of the first international conferences concerned with the conduct of routine business activity (the International Maritime Conference, convened by the US in 1889). But the agreement coming out of that conference dealt only with navigational issues, and the US proposal for creation of an international maritime commission received little attention. Subsequent international conventions and agreements have addressed safety issues, working conditions, and skill qualifications, as well as other operating concerns, but fundamental economic issues—particularly entry into the industry, the critical issue upon which all others depend—were not addressed multilaterally until 1958. The current international policy regime for ocean transport involves a combination of essentially private interenterprise aggreements, national policies, and international conventions, the latter dealing with both economic and noneconomic issues affecting the industry. (Principal elements of the regime are summarized in figure 8-1.)

8.1.1. Background and Regime Characteristics

Many factors explain the absence of a strong regulatory tradition, both domestic and international, in ocean shipping. One is certainly the long historical evolution of the industry and the prominence of both entrepreneurial initiative and colonialist ambitions in its development. A second factor is the diversity of the industry, particularly the segmentation of markets in both geographic and product-service dimensions. These functional differences give rise to differences in cost and demand conditions among carriers and shippers, which in turn inhibit uniform approaches to policy issues and even handicap the carriers' own efforts to reach and maintain agreements among themselves. A third factor is that the ocean shipping industry lacks the prominent natural monopoly features that characterize many transport and communications activities and that typically give rise to some form of state intervention.

As a result of the natural openness of ocean shipping to competitive forces, the national policies of most states involved in the industry have,

Description	Liner Conferences	IMO/UNCTAD
Institutional identification	Conference agreements (1880s–present)	IMO (1958) UNCTAD Code (1974/1983–present)
Purpose and Scope		
Purpose	Restrict competition	IMO: Noneconomic aspects UNCTAD: Permit/control entry
Scope	Entry, capacity, schedules, rates	IMO: Technology, safety, data entry UNCTAD: Participation
Organizational Form		
Structure	Enterprise-level, decentralized (some government recognition)	Multilateral (governments)
Power/concentration	Decentralized/concentrated within trade routes	Increasingly diffused among both carriers and governments
Decision and Allocation Modes	Negotiated (within multiple cartels)	Market/administrative
Strength and Change		
Peak strength	Up to early 1970s	1980s
Current (1980–1990)	Medium, and declining	Medium
Why change?	Economic, technological and political change; new sources of competition; new industry participants	

Figure 8-1.   The Ocean Shipping Regime.

both historically and more recently, emphasized the promotion of domestic carriers and the suppression of foreign competition. According to the traditional home-country perspective, the shipping industry deserves promotion as a contributor to national wealth and power; any cost burdens involved can be shifted to trading partners or third-country shippers. Even the US, in spite of its traditional commitment to market competition, has long provided its domestic shipping industry with subsidies (for ship construction and labor training, as well as for operations) and with protection from foreign competition, as well as some exemption from domestic anti-trust requirements. Other major shipping countries have typically been more restrictive of foreign competitors, and have tolerated strong anticompetitive agreements among carriers.

The historic means of suppressing competition in ocean shipping is the *liner conference*, a nongovernmental organization of scheduled (nonbulk) carriers serving a specific trading route. The conference system developed in the late nineteenth century with the advent of steamships, which made it possible to offer regularly scheduled service along established routes. *Closed* conferences are classic cartels that limit membership, allocate business, and pool revenues and costs; *open* conferences set rates but do not formally restrict membership (although they may discourage entry in other ways). US law requires that all conferences serving American ports—which means conferences carrying about 20% of the value of total world trade —be open; most others are closed. There have been 300 to 400 active conferences operating in the worldwide shipping trade in recent decades.

The purpose of liner conferences was and is to control entry and to discourage the intense price competition that often arises in industries with high fixed/low variable cost ratios and highly variable demand. Although liner conferences are, in principle, highly restrictive business arrangements, their effectiveness has varied constantly as a result of changes in demand, technology, and capacity, and in response to political developments.

8.1.2. Strength and Change

The immediate post-World War II decades were high points of conference effectiveness. The world shipping industry recovered rapidly from the war, but total carrying capacity maintained a rough balance with demand. As a result, the conference system was able to preserve a minimum rate structure and take advantage of periods of high demand to achieve substantial profits. However, by the early 1970s the conference system gradually began to weaken as a result of changes in economic, technological, and political conditions. On the economic side, rate agreements lacking full cartel status are difficult to monitor, and the sanctions and remedies available to control violations are relatively weak. The US open-conference requirement thus had significant impact on the worldwide cartel environment; and the cartel compliance of US carriers, with more than 90% of their international tonnage operating under foreign "flags of convenience" to escape domestic labor and safety requirements, has tended to be erratic.

Moreover, even the strongest conference rate agreements involve only conference members. Independent liner operators may solicit business among the same routes and shippers, and the tendency to violate or by-pass conference agreements increased steadily as the switch to larger container-carrying vessels resulted in worldwide overcapacity in the industry. In addition, a substantial and increasing amount of tonnage is carried in bulk, in which case an entire vessel filled with a single commodity makes a point-to-point voyage at a negotiated price. Bulk cargo, both freight and tanker, now accounts for about three fourths of all ocean shipping tonnage and perhaps a quarter of all shipments by value.

Additional economic and technological trends weakening the power of the conferences include 1) vertical integration by large MNEs into the carriage of their own merchandise in their own vessels (Kindleberger, 1985); 2) development of land routes that provide alternatives to traditional ocean shipments; and 3) increasingly aggressive organizations of shippers who use combined bargaining power to negotiate favorable freight rates or develop alternatives to conference rate shipments. As a result of all these developments, although the traditional conference structure appears to constitute a classic cartel, its actual effects have been uneven with respect to nations and carriers as well as to types of shipments and trade routes, and have also been highly variable over time, declining (except for peaks associated with the oil crises) since the early 1970s. The international political environment also changed in ways that eventually produced new multinational policy initiatives concerning ocean shipping. Three features of the postwar environment were of critical importance in this process: 1) US political and economic leadership in the non-Communist world, which gave traditional US resistance to restrictive business practices in international trade an increased importance; 2) European economic recovery, along with traditional European government support of the liner conference system; and 3) appearance of numerous postcolonial states—the less developed countries (LDCs)—on the world scene, and their strong drive toward economic independence and evelopment.

The first important international policy developments arising out of this context were the 1958 International Maritime Organization (IMO) and the 1958 Geneva Convention on the High Seas. The IMO was established under UN auspices to serve as custodian for a number of existing international conventions and subsequently as the source of new agreements concerning noneconomic aspects of the maritime industries (i.e., safety, pollution, data collection). These concerns were greatly increased in the postwar years because of the increase in ocean traffic and in the size of vessels. The High Seas Convention, an output of the first UN Conference on the Law of the Sea, addressed issues of national registration and attempted to reduce the use of "flags of convenience" as a means of avoiding operating costs required to meet advanced-country (and international) safety and labor standards. Reducing use of "flags of convenience" did not have US support and was not attained. Both of these developments reflect the power of the US with respect to international shipping policy, in spite of the fact that US carriers (both national flag and "flag of convenience") account for less than 10% of total world shipping tonnage.

The most important international policy development involving ocean shipping, however, arose from the third feature of the postwar environment, the desire for economic independence and development among the LDCs. This desire became focused in the demand for a New International Economic Order (NIEO, eventually formalized in UN resolutions in 1974). A major vehicle for the creation of NIEO was the UN Conference on Trade and Development (UNCTAD), first convened in 1964 and ultimately established as a permanent UN agency. Ocean shipping—its cost, service, and national control—had been of concern to many of the LDCs during their years of colonial status, and UNCTAD became the focus of these concerns from its inception. The ultimate goal of the LDCs can be described as *participation* in the operation and management of the world shipping industry, particularly insofar as their own imports and exports were affected. The practical dimensions of such participation would include both 1) reservation of some portion of LDC shipments to national carriers, many of which might be state owned; and 2) generally increased LDC government involvement in the heretofore private (and largely First World dominated) world of international shipping.

After a decade of debate, the UNCTAD Code of Conduct for Liner Conferences was adopted in 1974 and came into force in 1983 when it was ratified by nations accounting for more than 25% of the relevant tonnage. Since 58 nations were required to reach this level of coverage, the abstention of several major shipping states, as well as the principal states offering "flags of convenience" (Liberia and Panama), is apparent. European Community (EC) member countries ratified the Code only after it was agreed that intra-EC shipments would be excluded from coverage and that the entire EC would be considered one "national state" for purposes of cargo allocations. The USSR and other East European countries also retained substantial flexibility even after becoming signatories to the Code.[2]

The UNCTAD Code responds directly to LDC concerns about their historically unfavorable position vis-a-vis ocean shipping. Recognizing that the existing liner conference system could not be easily displaced, the Code requires that "national shipping lines" of any nation served by a

conference be automatically allowed to join the conference as a full participant; moreover, the consent of such "national lines" to all major conference decisions affecting the relevant country is required. Conferences are
also required to consult with shippers about rates and related matters.
Since many of the LDC enterprises involved in these relationships,
whether as carriers or as shippers, are state-owned enterprises or closely
related to national governments in other ways, these provisions effectively
include LDC governments within the information and decision-making
systems of the relevant conferences. Moreover, designated carriers of the
LDCs are guaranteed actual participation in the provision of shipping
services through the most widely discussed aspect of the Code, the "40–
40–20" formula for allocating shipments. Unless mutually agreed otherwise, the Code requires that all conference shipment revenues between two
nations shall be equally divided between their national line carriers, except
that third-country carriers have the right to carry "a significant part, such as
20%" of the total. Although the language of the Code applies to "conference" shipments only, the intent of most LDCs seems to be that the
40–40–20 formula would apply to all liner shipments, whether conference or independent; bulk shipments, however, are not involved in the
arrangement.

The US, Canada, and Japan, along with some LDCs having divergent
interests, have abstained from the UNCTAD Code up to the present time.
However, the US has long been involved in bilateral agreements with a
few important trading partners (Brazil, Argentina, and China, at present).
These agreements have essentially the same structure—reserving the
relevant two-way trade for equal division between the national carriers of
the two countries involved.

8.1.3. Impact of the Current Regime

The combination of cartel rate setting through the liner conferences and
government allocation of cargo under the UNCTAD Code might be
expected to yield a rigidly controlled international shipping regime.
However, basic economic and technological trends tending to widen the
scope for competitive forces in the industry remain at work. Continuing
increases in economies of scale, at both the vessel and the enterprise level,
make small-scale operations increasingly uneconomic; some LDCs have
found that their only viable strategy is to lease their 40% cargo rights back
to some international carrier. In addition, the US responded to the changed

environment of the 1970s with the Shipping Act of 1984. This legislation strengthened the participation of American carriers in the liner conferences in certain respects, but weakened their power in others. In brief, the Shipping Act increased somewhat the immunity of conference agreements from US antitrust requirements and authorized the use of "service contracts," which tend to foreclose entry, between conferences and individual shippers or shipper associations. At the same time, however, the Shipping Act strengthened the rights of conference members to take "independent action" (i.e., individual rate setting) and more flexible approaches to price and service decisions. Required registration of all US trade conference agreements with the US Federal Maritime Administration (FMA) appears to convert that agency into an enforcement arm of the cartels; however, the FMA also has a watchdog role in that it can disapprove such agreements. The overall effect of the 1984 Act has been a subject of continuing debate up to the present (Grifman, ed., 1988).

In short, although the UNCTAD Code adds another non-competitive dimension to the liner conference portion of worldwide ocean shipping, and although this dimension involves both some increase in the number of market participants and some protection of their interests, neither the Code nor the conferences to which it is linked can completely alter the effect of basic economic forces—economies of scale, overcapacity, demand instability, ease of entry, etc.—which account for the fundamentally competitive structure of the ocean shipping industry.

8.2.   The Air Transport Regime[3]

International commercial air transportation presents a perfect example of the complex network of contacts and activities, involving both enterprises and governments, that characterizes the contemporary multinational business environment. As Kasper notes, "An airline hub diagram could just as easily illustrate a telecommunications network, a marine cargo transport system, or even a financial clearing house operation" (1988, p. 8). During the postwar period, international air transport has been affected by extreme forms of nationalistic protection and international cartelization; at the same time, economic and technological trends, as well as domestic political developments in a number of countries, have stimulated competitive forces and liberalized international air transport policies.[4]

The international air transport regime consists of three main elements (see figure 8-2):

Description	Bermuda	IATA/ICAO
Institutional identification	Bilateral agreements (1946–present)	IATA (1945–present) ICAO (1947–present)
Purpose and Scope		
Purpose	Establish and allocate	IATA: Cartel system to set fares ICAO: Standardize technology/procedures
Scope	Routes, entry, capacity	IATA: Rates, commercial practices ICAO: Technical issues
Organizational Form		
Structure	Governmental/bilateral/ decentralized	IATA: Interenterprise ICAO: Intergovernment Both: multipartite/ centralized
Power/concentration	Origin: US/UK dominance Later: Bilateral power	IATA: Dispersed among participants ICAO: Originally US (FAA) dominated; now dispersed
Decision and Allocation Modes	Bilateral negotiations	IATA: Cartel agreements ICAO: Technical negotiations
Strength and Change		
Peak strength	1946–1977 (declining)	IATA: 1946–1977 ICAO: Continuously strong to present
Current (1980–1990)	Low	Medium
Why change?	Change essentially due to changes in number/power/ interests of actors, particularly: (1) Entry and increasing capacity—especially on US–Europe routes (2) Domestic deregulation and pressure for international liberalization (3) Mergers and joint agreements	

Figure 8-2.   The Air Transport Regime.

1. Bilateral agreements among governments allocate international air routes to their respective *national* control. These are generally referred to as "Bermuda-type" agreements, although their characteristics vary widely.
2. The International Air Transport Association (IATA) is a price-setting cartel of airlines and related enterprises; it is recognized by, but does not directly involve, governments.
3. The International Civil Aviation Organization (ICAO) is an intergovernmental organization that deals with technical and safety issues and has important informational functions.

8.2.1. Background

From the beginning of international air travel, it has been assumed that government approval is required before a foreign plane can land on its territory. At the outset, individual carriers simply negotiated the relevant permissions on their own, but during World War II, national government interest in airline operations and the increase in international flights caused the US government to assume responsibility for these negotiations on behalf of US firms. (Prior to World War II, Pan Am was the only US airline significantly involved in international flights, and only a few other carriers were operating anywhere in the world.)

In 1944, representatives of the Allied Powers met in Chicago to consider alternative postwar policy regimes for international air transport. Conflict between a US commitment to "open skies" (i.e., essentially the idea that carriers should be free to offer service, with a minimum of government intervention) and a desire on the part of most other nations to protect and promote the development of their own national carriers prevented the development of global policies with respect to the allocation of routes and other commercial aspects of air transport. As a result, the "Convention on International Civil Aviation" (usually referred to as the "Chicago Convention") reflected agreement on technical and safety issues alone, and did not address commercial traffic issues.

The Chicago Convention came into force in 1947 when it was ratified by the required 26 national governments; ICAO was formed to carry out the purposes of the Convention on a continuing basis. Although ICAO is not directly involved in economic issues, its activities are commercially important for two reasons: 1) technical standards and arrangements affect costs and often provide foundation or ancillary elements of commercial agreements; and 2) the absence of any other official international body has led ICAO to assume very significant informational and administrative functions. ICAO apparently was and is seen as a vehicle to prevent complete US dominance of the international air transport regime; at the same time, the US Federal Aviation Administration (FAA) has been a dominant technical force within ICAO during most of its history. Since neither the Chicago Convention nor ICAO embodied any understanding about route allocations, regularization of international commercial air transport service was left in the hands of the various governments and carriers involved. The primary national participants in international commercial air transport at the end of World War II were the US and the UK, the former having the major fleet of planes and the latter controlling landing rights at important locations around the globe. Representatives of these two nations met in Bermuda in 1946 and worked out an agreement involving bilateral exchange of landing rights along specific routes. In effect, the two nations agreed to permit flights by each other's national carriers between specific destinations (e.g., New York–London). The national governments involved then allocated these flights among their own airlines as they saw fit.

The Bermuda Agreement, which became the model for the eventual worldwide network of bilateral arrangements, did not address the issue of fares, but essentially assumed the existence of a separate international fare-setting mechanism, which was, in fact, already in operation. The International Air Transport Association (IATA) took on its present form in 1945. When the 1944 Chicago Convention failed to come to agreement on the commercial issues of entry, capacity, and pricing, the international airlines themselves reorganized their existing trade association and converted it into a vehicle for rate setting, standardization of commercial practices, and exercise of political influence. IATA membership, including both airlines and affiliated enterprises, and influence increased continuously over the following years, along with the growth in international air travel. However, challenges to IATA's authority have also been continuous, and the volume of non-IATA travel (both charter and scheduled) has been substantial for a couple of decades.

8.2.2. Regime Characteristics

Although bilateral intergovernmental route agreements and the international airline fare-setting cartel are formally distinct institutions, they are in fact complementary elements of a single international policy regime for commercial air transport. ICAO is this regime's supporting technical branch. (See figure 8-2 for a summary of regime characteristics.) Bermuda-type agreements define international airline routes in terms of departure points, intermediate points, destinations, and "beyond points" (i.e., extensions). A single "route" may include numerous permutations of these features, and may thus involve service to various third countries as well as to the two nations directly participating. Most agreements not involving the US also specify the service capacity (size of planes, number of flights) to be provided by the contracting parties; US agreements provide only for ex post government review of capacity developments. IATA and ICAO recognize a number of air transport regions (e.g., North America–Europe), and "rate conferences" composed of the carriers serving each such region or subunit thereof determine among themselves the fares to be charged for service along specific routes. The power of this classic cartel arrangement is constrained, however, by several considerations. Not all IATA members providing service in a particular area necessarily participate in the relevant rate conferences, and, as noted above, the volume of non-IATA traffic can also be substantial. IATA rate agreements must also be submitted to the various governments involved for approval. Although such agreements are generally approved, if one is not approved or if no agreement is reached among the carriers, then the conference is declared "open" and individual carriers submit their own rate filings to relevant national authorities. For all of these reasons, and because of underlying changes in the volume, economics and technology of air travel, the actual cartel power of IATA has varied considerably both among regions and over time.

8.2.3. Strength and Change

The 1946 Bermuda Agreement between the US and the UK became the model for a worldwide intergovernmental system of air route allocations through a very natural process. At the end of World War II, the US had a large and comparatively well-developed domestic airline industry, and a single US carrier (Pan Am) accounted for almost all international commercial travel. The UK was the only other significant participant in the industry, with the advantage of control of important landing sites in the Middle and Far East and in the Caribbean, as well as the position of London as the gateway for North American flights to Europe. Commercial air transport was an infant industry in most other countries.

Once the US and UK had reached agreement about conditions of mutual access, similar agreements were made with other nations desiring landing rights on their respective territories. And as the air traffic of these third countries developed, the Bermuda model, with various modifications, was extended throughout the world. The power of IATA developed in a parallel manner, since US and UK airlines were initially the dominant members. In fact, Pan Am alone accounted for over half of all international commercial travel until the late 1950s.

The Bermuda–IATA regime remained essentially stable for more than three decades and continues in place up to the present time. However, the strength of the regime has varied among regions and routes, and was gradually being eroded by economic and technological change before it was substantially modified in 1978. The basic change-inducing factors include

1. A vast expansion in the volume of international air travel during the 1960s and 1970s, with a corresponding increase in total carrying capacity;
2. Increases in the size of planes and changes in the technology of related support activities (e.g., computerized reservation systems) that resulted in significant economies of scale; and
3. Increases in the number of airlines providing international commercial air transport, many of which are government owned or subsidized and enjoy monopoly status within their home jurisdictions.

The total number of international passenger-kilometers increased from an infinitesimal level when the Bermuda–IATA regime was put in place to about 100 billion in 1965, to almost 300 billion in 1975, and then to 600 billion by 1985. More than 200 million passengers now travel internationally each year, accounting for almost one fourth of all scheduled airline service (domestic and international together) throughout the world. At the same time, the number of airlines providing scheduled international service increased from 44 in 1950 to more than 170 by the 1980s. Only about two thirds of these airlines are IATA members, and they account for a comparable share of total scheduled air traffic. In addition, under the umbrella provided by the IATA fare structure, nonscheduled (charter) international services expanded rapidly during the 1960s and accounted for almost 40% of total international service in the early 1970s (Dresner, 1989).

These changes brought a number of different pressures to bear on the Bermuda–IATA regime. Growth in demand increased the opportunity for competition and weakened the power of the cartel. The success of independent charters on densely traveled and vacation routes caused some IATA carriers to expand their own charter activity, while others responded with deep fare discounts. Increasing economies of scale reinforced pressures for high-capacity operations and stimulated fare reductions for this purpose as well. At the same time, the availability of scale economies strengthened the positions of the largest carriers (including large, primarily domestic carriers) vis-a-vis smaller firms. Moreover, many of the new international airlines were small, were unable to take advantage of scale economies, and required monopoly-cartel protection (as well as government subsidies) in order to operate at all. By the mid-1960s a majority of IATA member airlines were based in developing countries, and most of these enterprises were small, state-sponsored monopolies established for reasons of national prestige. This change in membership greatly increased the role of governments in the cartel and strengthened support for its activities. (However, some important new national airlines—particularly those of Singapore, Malaysia, Thailand, and Hong Kong—remained outside the cartel and competed vigorously and successfully for international traffic.) The net result of all these developments was a strengthening of competitive forces on the one hand and a strengthening of support for anticompetitive restrictions on the other.

These conflicting developments fragmented IATA's structure and strained its cohesiveness. Although fare reductions succeeded in stemming the growth of charters, which now account for only about 10% of total traffic, the price-setting power of the cartel was clearly being eroded. At the same time, concerns of governments—European as well as Third World—for the welfare of their national carriers increased the restrictiveness of bilateral access agreements, including limitations on flight capacity and frequency, as well as provisions for revenue pooling. By the mid-1970s even the US became sufficiently concerned with carrier protection to accept British proposals for capacity and entry controls in a second Bermuda Agreement (Bermuda II, 1977).

However, the expansion of national protectionism embodied in Bermuda II proved to be short-lived. The same underlying forces that had been increasing competitive pressures in international markets—appearance of new competitors, scale economies, etc.—had also been at work in the large US domestic market. And US domestic policy was moving in the direction of deregulation across the board, with the airline industry a major focus of activity. Hence, by 1978 Bermuda II became essentially a dead letter, and the US negotiated new bilateral agreements forbidding government restrictions on airline pricing, capacity, and entry (including charters). The inducement of asymmetric access—greater foreign access to

US destinations—was used to induce acceptance of these liberalizations by foreign negotiators.

The net result of all these developments has been a considerable and continuing liberalization of the international air transport regime over the past decade, although the combination of bilateral government agreements and an enterprise-level cartel remains in place. In some markets, particularly the heavily traveled North Atlantic region, competition has increased to the point that IATA fare setting is irrelevant; in other regions IATA has designated "fare zones," leaving room for flexibility on specific fares. Some current US agreements contain a "double disapproval" feature that allows airlines to set whatever fares they choose unless *both* governments deny permission. Joint service agreements among international carriers have opened up each other's domestic markets to indirect competition from foreign sources, and foreign investment combinations (SAS–Continental, KLM–Northwest, Swissair–Delta, and Hawaiian Air–JAL) have begun to emerge. These developments, along with use of common computerized reservation systems and other linkages, are creating multinational entities that partially escape home-country control and that may be harmed, rather than helped, by restrictive national policies.

In addition, liberalization of international airline competition is an important aspect of Europe 1992. The European Civil Aviation Conference (ECAC) is the focus of this activity. The ECAC does not yet have the authority to assign routes, and hence cannot engage in bilateral agreements on behalf of the entire European Community (EC); it may, however, become the basis for a future phase of multilateral regime development.

8.3. Conclusion

This analysis of the international regimes for air transport and ocean shipping leads us to two substantive conclusions:

1. These regimes "matter," in the sense that they influence the actions of enterprises and governments, and hence the content and outcome of international business activity.
2. These regimes display a common evolutionary pattern over the postwar decades that has not been clearly observed in previous analyses.

This concluding section summarizes our findings on these two substantive issues.

8.3.1. The Impact of Regimes

The question of whether or not regimes "matter" requires some expli-
cation: Do regimes "matter" as compared to *what*? It is impossible to
imagine exactly what the international business environment would be like
if none of the institutional developments of the postwar decades had taken
place; and, in any event, some forms of government involvement and
international cooperation/conflict would inevitably exist in these and many
other industries. Hence, the relevant question is this: do the regimes
examined here have discernable direct consequences? We address this
issue in terms of the four specific questions derived from the Haggard and
Simmons (1987) analysis (see our earlier discussion in chapter 4).

1. Has the regime altered the situation so that cooperation (or conflict)
among enterprises and states becomes more (or less) likely? Our answer to
this question is "yes" in both cases, although it is difficult to draw a net
balance between the forces of cooperation and conflict involved. On one
hand, both regimes are based on principles of cooperation, usually with
cartel aspects. At the same time, these sophisticated and complex
arrangements also increase the possibilities for conflict, both between
regime participants and outside parties and, even more conspicuously,
among the participating governments and enterprises. Hence, the general
conclusion seems to be that more, and certainly very different, possibilities
for both cooperation and conflict arise in each industry because of the
existence of the regimes. In particular, although market forces are now of
great importance in both cases, the basic regime structure in air transport,
and the postwar developments in shipping, have tended to shift the focus
from market forces to the political arena.

2. Has the regime altered actors' goals and behavior options? Again,
our answer is affirmative in both cases; the reasoning is presented in section
8.3.2 below.

3. Has the regime tended to weaken national boundaries? Our answer is
negative in both cases. The UNCTAD Code clearly strengthened national
interests, and the contemporary weakening of national identity among the
airlines is occurring at the expense of, not because of, the international
policy regime. However, it should be noted that, although the weakening of
national boundaries is assumed to be desirable by some regime enthusiasts,
this view is neither unambigous nor universal. Indeed, Krasner (1985)
appears to believe that more "authoritarian" regimes are probably more
desirable from the viewpoint of LDCs, and such regimes necessarily
involve the strengthening, rather than the weakening, of national authority
in some respects.

4. Did the regime strengthen coalitions? The answer is affirmative in both cases, although the coalitions stimulated were typically less than universal and not necessarily benign. Both the Bermuda–IATA regime and the liner conferences were established as coalitions, and they in turn stimulated countervailing coalitions aimed at getting a share of the pie.

Our overall conclusion is that both the air and sea regimes do "matter," in the sense that their respective industries involve different constituents and operate in different ways than they would if no similar institutional and behavioral arrangements were in place. However, this conclusion is neither as obviously benign as some regime analysts may have anticipated, nor as clearly malign as some critics may have feared. Our positive conclusion is that these regimes have had very significant effects; the normative analysis of these effects—whether they are on balance desirable or undesirable, and from whose perspective—is a question we leave to others.

8.3.2. The Evolutionary Pattern

The first phase of regime evolution common to both of these cases is an increase in government participation within the system of market relationships and agreements previously worked out among enterprises. The initial enterprise-level arrangements are, of course, IATA and the ocean liner conferences. Increased government participation involves both 1) increases in the *number* of governments participating, and 2) more extensive government *involvement*, particularly more government initiative in stimulating and directing enterprise-level activities. Illustrative examples are the international air transport agreements leading up to Bermuda II and the UNCTAD Code.

Increased government involvement and nationalistic protectionism leads directly to an increase in the number of enterprise participants in the industry. Some of these are new competitors (whether state owned or private) attracted by cartel price umbrellas; others are created by governments to achieve national representation in international markets. Examples are charter flights and new national airlines, and bulk ocean carriers and UNCTAD national freight allocations. These increases in the number of actors, both government-sponsored and private, in each industry place fundamental strains on the system of government controls and protections. On the one hand, there are more potential sources of competitive behavior within the industry; on the other hand, many of the new participants can exist only within a protected environment, and increases in their numbers lead to demands for increased protection. The result in the case of airlines, where the cycle is essentially complete, has been the outbreak of competition from both new and old sources, partial abandonment of the protective regime, and a wave of failures, mergers, and new international investments that is still (1991) in progress. In ocean shipping, the growth of bulk carriage, which escapes coverage by both the conferences and the UNCTAD Code, and the leasing of small UNCTAD-guaranteed shipment rights to larger established carriers are comparable developments.

A cursory survey of international economic relationships in a wide variety of industries and areas suggests that this three-phase pattern of evolution has been fairly typical of the post-World War II era. Certainly there has been an increase in government involvement in all aspects of international business and economic activity. And, because of the increase in the number of economically active governments in the world, as well as for other reasons, there have been substantial increases in the number of enterprises and actors in most industries, as well as increases in interindustry competition. Hence, tension inevitably increases between protective-controlling regimes, on one hand, and ever more numerous and diverse enterprises and governments—each of which is a potential source of competition, and some of actual rivalry—on the other. The likely outcome, most clearly observed here in the case of international air transport, is a weakening of regime controls and a period of shake-out and consolidation among the potential competitors, both states and enterprises.

Notes

1. This section is primarily based on Garvey, 1984; Stopford, 1988; and White, 1988; see also Waldmann, 1980, chapter 5. Comments and suggestions from Professor George A. Garvey, School of Law, Catholic University, are gratefully acknowledged.

2. Important references on the UNCTAD Code include Juda, 1983; Kyle and Phillips, 1983; and Larsen and Vetterick, 1981; see also Stopford, 1988, chapter 4.

3. This section is based primarily on Dresner, 1989; Jonsson, 1987; Kasper, 1988; and Taneja, 1988; we have also made use of various official documents. We are particularly grateful to Assistant Professor Martin Dresner, College of Business and Management, University of Maryland, University Park, for suggestions and materials.

4. The theory that international regimes are created by a powerful hegemon or coalition, and decline when hegemonic power wanes, has been tested in three case studies of international airlines. Jonsson (1987) found the theory inadequate and developed an alternative "process model" of regime transformation. Busza (1987) found the theory helpful, but introduced a shift in the importance of goals (from national security interests to carrier interests) on the part of the hegemon (US) as a major explanatory factor. In the most rigorous study, Dresner (1989) found the hegemonic stability theory to be supported by three instances of regime change and not supported in one.

References

Busza, Eva. 1987. *The Civil Aviation Cartel.* Unpublished master's thesis, University of British Columbia.

Dresner, Martin. 1989. *The International Regulation of Air Transport: Changing Regimes and Price Effects.* Unpublished doctoral dissertation, University of British Columbia.

Garvey, George E. 1984. "Regulatory Reform in the Ocean Shipping Industry," *George Washington Journal of International Law and Economics*, vol. 18, no. 1, pp. 1–54.

Grifman, Phyllis, ed. 1988. *The Shipping Act of 1984: A Debate of the Issues.* Los Angeles, CA: Sea Grant Program, University of Southern California.

Haggard, Stephan, and Beth A. Simmons. 1987. "Theories of International Regimes," *International Organization*, vol. 41, no. 3 (Summer), pp. 491–517.

Jonsson, Christer. 1987. *International Aviation and the Politics of Regime Change.* New York: St. Martin's.

Juda, Lawrence. 1983. *The UNCTAD Liner Code.* Boulder, CO: Westview.

Kasper, Daniel M. 1988. *Deregulation and Globalization: Liberalizing International Trade in Air Services.* Cambridge, MA: Ballinger.

Kindleberger, Charles P. 1985. "Multinational Ownership of Shipping Activities," *The World Economy*, vol. 8, no. 3 (September), pp. 249–265.

Krasner, Stephen D. 1985. *Structural Conflict: The Third World Against Global Liberalism.* Berkeley and Los Angeles, CA: University of California Press.

Kyle, Reuben, and Laurence T. Phillips. 1983. "Cargo Reservation for Bulk Commodity Shipments: An Economic Analysis," *Columbia Journal of World Business*, vol. 18, no. 3 (Fall), pp. 42–49.

Larsen, P.G., and V. Vetterick. 1981. "The UNCTAD Code of Conduct for Liner Conferences," *Law and Policy in International Business*, vol. 13, no. 1, pp. 223–280.

Stopford, Martin. 1988. *Maritime Economics.* London: Unwin Hyman.

Strange, Susan. 1988. *States and Markets.* New York: Basil Blackwell.

Taneja, Nawal K. 1988. *The International Airline Industry.* Lexington, MA: D.C. Heath.

Waldmann, Raymond J. 1980. *Regulating International Business through Codes of Conduct.* Washington, DC: American Enterprise Institute.

White, Lawrence J. 1988. *International Trade in Ocean Shipping Services.* Cambridge, MA: Ballinger.

9 ENVIRONMENTAL REGIMES

International efforts to control and protect the water, air, and land resources of the globe are numerous, diverse, incomplete, and in many cases highly controversial. In spite of their varied subjects and purposes, most of these efforts are based on the idea that the natural environment of the earth constitutes, in some sense, a "commons," a collection of resources to be shared among all the earth's inhabitants, present and future. The familiar "tragedy of the commons" is that excessive use of "free" common resources by some may ultimately lead to reduced welfare for all (Hardin, 1968). This result, one of the classic examples of "market failure," arises because each user rationally seeks to maximize individual benefit from use of the common resources. The individual user confronts no "price" or "cost" for such common resources and ignores or does not perceive collective costs. Policy regimes, whether local, national, or international, that are designed to deal with this type of problem attempt to alter the behavior of individual users in order to increase the aggregate benefits available to all over the long term. Whether such corrective regimes can, in fact, be designed and implemented, and whether other "tragedies" or "failures" will occur as a consequence, are matters of considerable controversy. In addition, in many areas of environmental concern there is substantial uncertainty about the actual impact of specific resource uses on the flow of potential benefits, both present and future, and these uncertainties add significantly to the complexity of the policy debate.[1]

Although the idea is widely accepted that some features of the planet should be viewed as a "commons," there is no general agreement as to which specific domains are encompassed by this concept and what kinds of understandings should govern their appropriate use. The high seas, for example, have been historically viewed as a "commons" beyond control or expropriation by private persons and individual states. On the other hand, territorial jurisdiction is a fundamental characteristic of the nation state, and the extension of national sovereignty to cover adjacent natural domains—airspaces and coastal waters—is also conventionally accepted. And when "commons" uses and nation-based activities overlap—as, for example, in the disposal of wastes—national authority is typically called upon to protect common-access resources. After extensive discussion and debate, the Stockholm Conference on the Human Environment (1972) eventually incorporated both "commons" and national perspectives into the following statement:

> Nations . . . have the sovereign right to exploit their own resources . . . , and the responsibility to insure that activities within their jurisdiction or control do not cause damage to the environment of other States, or of areas beyond the limits of national jurisdiction (Declaration of the United Nations on the Human Environment, Principle 21, Stockholm, 1972).

The evolution of international environmental regimes during recent decades has affirmed and extended both national and common domains. The existence of a "global commons" has been formally recognized, and its scope specifically enlarged in some respects, by international agreement. At the same time, nation-state jurisdiction over some portions of the heretofore "common" natural environment has also been regularized and extended. In spite of these developments, numerous and pressing environmental issues remained to be resolved by other means. The fact is that relatively few environmental problems are truly "global" in character, and a "commons" is a difficult entity to manage under the best of circumstances. On the other hand, it is clear that "the entire ecology of the planet is not arranged in national compartments" (Kennan, 1970, pp. 401– 402). Hence, it is universally agreed that some kinds of international understandings and agreements are required in this area, although their precise scope, purpose, and mode of operation are subjects of controversy. The United Nations Environmental Program (UNEP), which was created at the 1972 Stockholm Conference, was not intended to be, and has not become, the basis for a comprehensive international environmental regime. However, it has served as a catalyst for a number of specific initiatives and "proved indispensable to the process of arriving at an international consensus to protect the ozone layer," according to the chief US representative involved.[2] Over the past two decades, the varied subjects and sources of international environmental concern have produced a host of regime initiatives and proposals, only a few of which have reached the stage of formal institutionalization. This chapter presents an overview of these initiatives, with special emphasis on those having particular impacts on the major concerns of international business—production and consumption, and trade and investment.

9.1. The Nature of Environmental Regimes

Environmental regime initiatives arise from concerns about fundamental relationships between population and human activity, on the one hand, and the natural condition and resources of the planet, on the other. Some authorities view the fundamental planetary population/resource balance with great alarm (cf. *Global 2000 Report*, 1980; Brown et al., 1990), while others emphasize that human history to date reveals diverse and largely successful responses to resource availabilities and shortages (Simon and Kahn, 1984). Without taking sides in this extensive and often acrimonious debate, it is easy to agree with Pirages that "more and better anticipatory thinking" may be of value (1989, p. 5). This perspective suggests an emphasis on information gathering and on the development of cooperative modes of problem exploration, activities that have both, in fact, been major purposes of international environmental regime development over the past quarter century. If the international trade and exchange regimes discussed in chapter 7 above present the clearest examples of formal and integrated regime development over the postwar decades, the environmental initiatives discussed here present sharply contrasting examples of tentative and fragmented responses to problems that are comparably complex, diverse, and interconnected.

Topics differing widely in both substance and scope appear on the various lists of "international environmental issues" found in the literature (cf. Coate, 1982; Pirages, 1989). Most analysts begin with a broad perspective on population, poverty, and the uneven distribution of resources, climate, and productive capacity throughout the globe. The impact of national security concerns and activities, particularly the production and use of nuclear weapons, is also frequently emphasized. The *Final Report* of the recent American Assembly session on "Preserving the Global Environment" identified three main concerns: human population growth; deforestation and loss of biological diversity; and global atmospheric change (American Assembly, 1990).

A broader framework for considering the status and development of environmental regimes, particularly those relevant to the activities of international business, might integrate the diverse themes from the literature into the following four categories:

1. Renewable resources and their products—agriculture, forests, fisheries.
2. Minerals and other nonrenewable resources, and their products.
3. Secondary impacts of resource use on the unappropriable resources and ambient environment—air, water, climate.
4. Access to and use of hitherto unappropriated environmental domains—the seabed, polar regions, and outer space.

The list of major international environmental regimes shown in figure 9-1 and the tabulation of multilateral environmental treaties signed by the US in figure 9-2 indicate the scope of international environmental policy development at the present time. These data also reveal that major areas of environmental concern discussed in the literature are untouched by contemporary regime initiatives. Global climate change may be the most widely debated issue on which no broad consensus has been achieved, but many other concerns discussed in the literature are entirely unrecognized on the international policy agenda. For example, although many international programs are aimed at improving agricultural production in poor countries, the only important policy regimes involving renewable resources and their products (except as they are involved in world trade such as the international wheat and coffee agreements) are those dealing with fisheries. Similarly, extractive industries (mineral and other) are encompassed by international regimes only insofar as *trade* in their products is influenced by cartels such as the Organization of Petroleum Exporting Countries (OPEC) or narrowly focused intergovernmental agreements such as those for tin and copper. The absence of any institutional forum for addressing broader issues is highlighted by critical occurrences such as the destruction of tropical forests and the wanton waste of petroleum through well burning and sea dumping during the Iraqi occupation of Kuwait (1990–1991). These occurrences, although taking place largely within national boundaries, constitute assaults on the condition and resource base of the planet itself.

Issue-area	Regime
Wildlife (whales, northern fur seals, polar bears)	International Convention for Regulation of Whaling, 1946; Interim Convention on the Conservation of North Pacific Fur Seals, 1957 and subsequent protocols[a]; and Agreement on the Conservation of Polar Bears, 1973.
Marine life	Convention on the Conservation of Antarctic Marine Living Resources, 1980.
Wild fauna and flora	Convention on International Trade in Endangered Species of Wild Fauna and Flora, 1973.
Deep seabed minerals	Regime for the Area (the deep seabed) under Part XI of the United Nations Convention on the Law of the Sea, 1982.
Electromagnetic spectrum (broadcast frequencies, orbital slots)	Regime devised by the World Administrative Radio Conference (WARC) under the International Telecommunications Convention, 1982.
Regional pollution	Convention for the Protection of the Mediterranean Sea Against Pollution, 1976 and subsequent protocols.
Radioactive fallout	Convention on Early Notification of a Nuclear Accident, 1986; and Convention on Assistance in the Case of a Nuclear Accident or Radiological Emergency, 1986.
Stratospheric ozone	Convention for the Protection of the Ozone Layer, 1985 and the 1987 protocol.
Polar regions	
Antarctica	Antarctic Treaty, 1959; Convention on the Conservation of Antarctic Marine Living Resources, 1980; and Antarctic Minerals Convention, 1988.
The Arctic	No comprehensive regime for the Arctic in place at this time.
Acid precipitation	
Europe	Convention on Long-Range Transboundary Air Pollution, 1979 and subsequent protocols.
Other areas	No analogous regime in place for North America or the world as a whole.

[a] The fur seal regime was established initially in 1911 under the terms of the Treaty for the Preservation and Protection of Fur Seals.

Source: Young, 1989b, p. 351.

Figure 9-1.   International Regimes for Natural Resources and the Environment.

Treaty description	Signed
Regulation of whaling	1931
Nature/wildlife conservation for the Western Hemisphere	1940
Regulation of whaling (with schedule of regulations)	1946
Prevention of marine pollution by oil (superceded by 1978 protocol)	1954
Protocol to whaling regulations	1956
Fishing and conservation of living resources of high seas	1958
Antarctica treaty	1959
Conservation of Atlantic tunas	1966
Exploration and use of space	1967
Intervention on high seas in case of oil pollution casualties	1969
Wetlands/waterfowl protection	1971
Prevention of marine pollution from dumping wastes and other matter	1972
Conservation of Antarctic seals	1972
Trade in endangered species	1973
Intervention on high seas for pollution sources other than oil	1973
Military use of environmental modification	1977
Pollution from ships	1978
Long-range transboundary air pollution (LRTAP)	1979
Antarctic marine life	1980
Conservation of North Atlantic salmon	1982
Oil pollution in the Caribbean	1983
Protocol to LRTAP for financing of the monitoring/evaluation of air pollutants in Europe	1984
Vienna convention for protection of the ozone layer	1985
Montreal protocol on substances that deplete the ozone layer	1987
NO_x protocol to convention on LRTAP	1988

Source: Hahn and Richards, 1989, pp. 445–446.

Figure 9-2.   Multilateral Environmental and Natural Resource Treaties Signed by the United States.

Environmental concerns differ from many other international policy issues not only in their variety and dispersion; they may also be mitigated, as well as exacerbated, by the independent actions of individuals, enterprises, and industries. The American Assembly notes that in the "environmental challenge . . . success or failure will not hinge on the actions of governments alone. It will rest equally on the beliefs and actions of billions of individuals, and on the roles played by national and multinational business" (1990, p. 6). Young speaks of "international society" as a "stateless social system" in which individuals are the primary actors (1989a, p. vii). He notes, however, that virtually all the negotiations and agreements take place among nation states, which may or may not represent the interests of the various group of intra- and international participants involved. The role of particular enterprises and industries in recognizing and responding to specific environmental problems may be of special importance (cf. Mahon and Kelley, 1988; Pearson, ed., 1987; UNCTC, 1985).

9.2. The Global Environment: Air, Water, and Climate

Climate results from the interaction between natural phenomena—both the planetary surface of land and water and the external forces of temperature and weather—and human activity; the latter may alter climatic conditions directly (either inadvertently or intentionally) or by their indirect impact on climate-creating resources and processes. Human activities—production, consumption, and environmental alteration—with potential climatic impact take place for the most part within individual national jurisdictions, and the effects of local pollution of air and water may be confined to one or a few adjacent countries and appropriately dealt with by their own national policies and regional agreements among limited numbers of participants. Activities of the Joint (US–Canada) Committee on the Great Lakes or the MEDPLAN for the Mediterranean are of this character. Haas notes that the MEDPLAN "serves as a model for arrangements for nine other regional seas in which over 130 states . . . take part" (1990, p. xx). These regional environmental regimes share many characteristics with the regional economic regimes discussed in chapter 6 above.

Increased knowledge of the forces making for climatic change—including the fact that these forces may arise from numerous and diverse sources, no one of which in itself may have great local significance or independent impact—has led to a series of new and "global" international initiatives concerned with air, water, and climate over the past couple of decades. Figure 9-3, adapted from Hahn and Richards (1989), tabulates the principal features of five of the most important of these agreements. As the detailed data show, these agreements involve significant numbers of countries (and from various parts of the world); they deal with a wide range of global and regional environmental concerns; and they commit signatories to varied responses—cooperation and monitoring in some instances, and specific reductions in environmental discharges in others. None of them contain provisions for international enforcement or sanctions. (Unlike withdrawal of privileges at the International Monetary Fund

	Convention on Long-Range Transboundary Air Pollution (1979)	Sulfur Emissions Protocol (1985)	Nitrogen Oxides Emissions Protocol (1988)	Vienna Convention On Protection of the Ozone Layer (1985)	Montreal Protocol (1987)
Problem addressed	Reduction of transboundary air pollution	Reduction of SO_x emissions (acid rain)	Reduction of NO_x from mobile and stationary sources (acid rain and ground level ozone)	Protection of ozone layer from CFCs	Reduction of CFC use
No. of signatories[a]	34	21	25	41	46
Lag time from negotiation to need for action	4 years	8 years	2 years	No significant action required	19 months
Type of action required	Monitoring, R&D, exchange of information	30% reduction in SO_x from 1980 level	Limitation of NO_x to 1987 (or earlier levels)	Research only	Restriction of CFC consumption
How monitored/enforced	No enforcement	Self-monitored	Self-monitored with reports to executive body	No monitoring	Self-monitored with penalties to be determined at a later meeting
Scope of problem	Regional/global	Regional	Regional	Global	Global
Country-specific concerns addressed	Yes	No	Yes	No	Yes
Initiating body	UNECE[b]	UNECE[b]	UNECE[b]	UNEP[c]	UNEP[c]

[a] Number of signatories includes all countries that had signed the treaty, whether or not they had ratified, plus the number of countries that had deposited documents of accession, as reflected in US State Department records as of February 15, 1989.

[b] UNECE = UN Economic Commission for Europe.

[c] UNEP = UN Environmental Program.

Source: Hahn and Richards, 1989, Table 2, p. 342.

or the World Bank, there is no way to deny a nonconforming nation access to use of the global environment.)

Hahn and Richards conclude from their analysis of such regimes that the likelihood of multilateral agreement in any specific case increases in response to 1) scientific consensus as to the causes and seriousness of the problem; 2) increased public concern; 3) perceived "fairness" of the proposed arrangements; 4) increased short-term political benefits; and 5) existence of previous and related agreements (1989, pp. 433–434).[3] Negotiations among 137 countries concerning a broad "world climate treaty," still in progress at time of writing, will reveal the strength of these factors on a global scale.

The importance of the "fairness" issue is well illustrated by controversies about the treatment of countries that have taken substantial steps toward environmental protection prior to the establishment of relevant international policies. The US, in particular, has argued that its preagreement actions with respect to sulfur oxide emissions and chlorofluorocarbons (CFCs) entitle it to "credit" in subsequent policy implementation. Such "credit" would arise, for example, if policy goals are set in terms of *levels* of discharge (which an environmentally advanced country might already have achieved). By contrast, no "credit" will arise —and, indeed, very difficult and costly tasks may be required—if goals are set in terms of *percentage reductions* from current levels. On the other hand, countries that are less environmentally advanced oppose the granting of credit for past actions, since this approach gives them primary responsibility for the next phase of global improvements.

The importance of the final factor listed—existence of other related agreements—can scarcely be overstated, since acceptance of and (favorable) experience with current regimes undoubtedly contributes to the development of new agreements. The US signed only ten multilateral environmental treaties during the four decades ending in 1969, but then signed nine during the 1970s and seven more during 1980s (Hahn and Richards, 1989, p. 425). There is every reason to believe that the number of such agreements, and the necessary interconnections among them, will continue to increase. French concludes a survey of recent developments by emphasizing that, although continued progress will unquestionably be difficult, "the notion that 'pollution is the price of progress' has become antiquated.... [P]eople on every continent are discovering that pollution control is a sound investment" (1990, p. 42). Optimism about the possibility of enlarging the scope of global environmental consensus is also reflected in the American Assembly report (1990).

The role of individual industries and enterprises in the evolution of regimes with respect to air, water, and climate (and, in a related set of developments, with respect to worker and consumer safety as well) has been problematic. There is plenty of evidence of tendencies to "export pollution," both directly in the form of hazardous wastes and indirectly by shifting environmentally troublesome activities out of countries where protective national regimes are in place and into less restrictive settings. On the other hand, many US-based multinationals claim to have adopted US standards throughout their worldwide operations. Evidence as to the accuracy of these claims is spotty, and incidents such as the Bhopal disaster reveal tragic discrepancies (see discussion in chapter 5 above). However, there is certainly some "export of standards," for the sake of operating efficiency if for no other reason, within most large multinationals.[4]

9.3. Exploiting the Oceans[5]

Much of the international concern with water as an environmental issue is focused on regional water resources—river systems, enclosed seas, and littoral areas—where the primary issues are 1) pollution and 2) conflicting modes of use, access, and control. In dealing with these problems, the prior existence of national jurisdictions and the interests of numerous and diverse constituents are taken as given at the outset. By contrast, since the seventeenth century the open oceans of the world—the "high seas"—have been considered beyond the control of individual states and equally open to all users and uses, i.e., part of a "global commons."

Until late in the nineteenth century, it was generally believed that the resources of the oceans, specifically including fisheries, were literally inexhaustible. However, changes in population and technology altered this perspective, and in 1899 the King of Sweden called a conference of nations concerned with the North Sea and Baltic fisheries. In 1901 the International Council for the Exploration of the Seas (ICES), the first international body concerned with marine conservation, was formed. Throughout the present century, there has been widespread and increasing recognition that the resources of the oceanic "global commons"—both living organisms (fish) and undersea minerals—should be subject to some kind of international policy consideration.

One might imagine, particularly in the light of policy developments concerning the ambient environment discussed in the preceding section, that any international regimes evolving in this area would involve increased regulation of oceanic resource use within a "global commons" framework. However, with one important exception (deep sea mining), the opposite is the case. The main international policy theme with respect to oceanic resources in the postwar half century has been the reduction of the "global commons" through the epxansion of the territorial rights of nation states. As a result, according to Miles, "the structure of the regime under which mankind uses the world ocean has been significantly altered. The most important aspect of this change has been the extension of exclusive coastal state authority over living and nonliving resources to 200 miles beyond the coast" (Miles, ed., 1989, p. 1). (In fact, with respect to nonliving resources, extensions of national authority beyond the 200-mile limit are permissible under some circumstances.) As a result of these extensions of national authority, more than half of the asserted boundaries of states in the territorial sea involve conflicting claims, less than 25% of which have been negotiated to conclusion (Cuyvers, 1984, p. 63). Many of the conflicting claims are currently of little consequence, although some (e.g., Greece versus Turkey) involve strong nationalistic and commercial interests, and many others may become more significant as fish populations shift and technologies for marine resource exploitation change (cf. Sanger, 1986, chapters 5–6).

9.3.1. Renewable Resources: Fisheries

The interests of particular national fishing industries in the exploitation of specific fishery resources—US and Canada in the North Atlantic; Chile, Peru, and Ecuador in the Southeastern Pacific; etc.—have been long recognized in treaties and other agreements among the parties directly concerned. Growing competition in world fishing and the possibility that new "industrial fishing" techniques could exhaust entire fish populations led to more general international concern with the exploitation of fishery resources even prior to World War II.

The first indication that potential damage to the resources of the oceanic commons might be avoided through expanded national jurisdiction, rather than increased international control, came in 1945 when President Truman unilaterally announced that US jurisdiction over undersea minerals extended to the limits of the so-called "continental shelf" and asserted the right to establish fishing conservation zones on the high seas adjacent to US coasts. Chile, Peru, and Ecuador followed quickly with expanded claims for whaling rights in the open ocean; and the decision of the International Court of Justice in the *Anglo-Norwegian Fisheries* case (1951) opened the way for the development of new concepts of jurisdiction and territoriality on the high seas. The first UN Conference on the Law of the Sea

(UNCLOS), intended to deal with these and many other marine environment issues, was convened in 1958; successive UNCLOS sessions and follow-up conferences have continued down to the present. (The early experience, with particular attention to the role of important individuals and national-commercial interest groups, is well summarized in Sanger, 1986, chapters 2–3).

The critical principle of the UNCLOS conferences with respect to fisheries involves recognition of "Extended Fisheries Jurisdiction" (EFJ), the right of coastal states to control access and use of important fishery resources beyond the limits of their territorial waters. Countries with EFJ in a specific area have the authority to limit access to their own nationals, levy charges on the fishing fleets of other countries, and prescribe the harvesting methods employed and the amount and type of fish that may be harvested. The EFJ concept recognizes the fact that the oceanic "commons" with respect to fisheries is regional rather than global in character (cf. Young, 1989a, p. 119); the assumption is that users (nations, enterprises) with the strongest interest in the future productivity of oceanic resources will make the wisest decisions with respect to their preservation and use. (A property rights approach is taken as a corrective to the "global commons" problem.) Unfortunately, natural developments (storms, movements of other sea organisms) and inadequate national policies and enforcement programs, along with inefficient harvesting, have frustrated this objective in some instances.

Whatever the effects of the EFJ concept on the long-run productivity of world fisheries, and however difficult it might be to achieve these or better results through other means, the current international policy regime has transferred large and valuable resources from long-recognized open access (i.e., a "commons") to national jurisdiction and control. Some of the world's best fishery resources are involved, and the results—such as allocation of the rich Georges Bank area of the North Atlantic to the US and Canada, for example—do not necessarily favor poor or developing countries. The world fishing catch is generally believed to be at or approaching its biological limits at the present time; hence, the EFJ arrangement, whatever its merits, has serious implications for the future international distribution of income and wealth.

9.3.2. Nonrenewable Resources: Undersea Minerals

The US proclamations of 1945 put forth important claims for coastal state jurisdiction over the resources of the seabed (specifically oil and gas) as well as over living organisms. These claims, along with the varied and conflicting claims of many other countries in all parts of the world, eventually led UNCLOS III (1982) to recognize the concept of "Exclusive Economic Zones" (EEZs) extending up to 200 miles beyond the conventional territorial limits of coastal states. Within these zones, which remain parts of the high seas as far as navigation and overflight are concerned, coastal states have broad discretionary authority, including the granting or withholding of exploration and extraction rights to their own nationals and others. Thus, although the physical dimensions of EFJs and EEZs are unrelated, their functions are analogous; they grant some, but not all, jurisdictional control over portions of the open sea to individual coastal states.[6]

There is, however, a sharp distinction between EEZ and EFJ concepts with respect to their implications for areas *outside* their respective collective boundaries. It is universally agreed that living organisms (fish, sponges, plant life) outside EFJ boundaries are subject to capture by any party with the necessary capability. However, the same principle is *not* universally applied to undersea mineral resources beyond the limits of all EEZs. The status of such resources is, in fact, one of the most controversial issues on the entire international policy agenda. Three distinct legal positions, each of which involves an analogy between the seabed and some other planetary domain, are put forward:

1. The high seas and the underlying seabed constitute a legal unity that is not subject to appropriation by any state or other entity; in this view, the seabed is an intrinsic element of the "global commons" of the oceans.
2. The sea and seabed are distinct; the seabed, like any unclaimed land, is subject to national appropriation.
3. There is no conventional legal recognition of the bed of the open sea; hence, the legal status of the seabed, like that of outer space, may be determined by competent international authorities without concern for precedent.

The third of these positions was apparently accepted by an overwhelming majority of UN member states (including the US) in 1958 when they declared the seabed outside all national jurisdictions to be part of "the common heritage of mankind." (If the seabed were considered a dimension of the sea itself, there would have been no reason for a vote.) The difference between the first and third concepts became critical in 1982 when another UN majority—this time *not* including the US—approved establishment of an International Seabed Authority (ISA) to control the conditions under which seabed mineral resources can be exploited.

The issue of jurisdiction over the deep seabed has become significant because of increased interest in nodules containing manganese and other minerals on the floor of the open ocean, and the belief that technologies for exploiting these nodules and other deep-sea mineral deposits are or will soon become available. Although exploitation of these resources is not economically justified at present, there has been strong international interest in resolving potential jurisdictional issues well in advance. Schachter believes that general international acceptance of the "common heritage" concept implies a further understanding that there should be some sharing of the benefits of seabed exploitation among "all mankind" (in Pontecorvo, ed., 1986, p. 53). And Krasner declares that UNCLOS III, signed by more than 100 countries in 1982, "gave the coup de grace to an older, weakening regime whose central principle was that the oceans belong to no one," and were thus subject to the rule of capture (1985, p. 231).

However, the remark of a Canadian representative very early in the seabed mining negotiations that "everyone accepts the concept of an international regime, but what isn't agreed are its powers" (Sanger, 1986, p. 167) remains true up to the present. Several governments (particularly the US, UK, and Germany) favor exploitation of undersea deposits by private enterprises, with some portion of the revenue going into a trust fund for the use of less developed countries (LDCs). On the other hand, as noted above, an overwhelming majority of UN member states endorsed the creation of the ISA, which would have an operating branch known as the "Enterprise" to carry out actual mining activities. The current scheme requires that companies wishing to undertake undersea mining submit two similar mining sites to the ISA, one of which will be approved for private exploitation and the other reserved for exploitation by the Enterprise for the benefit of developing nations. These arrangements are unacceptable to the governments of the nations most likely to be capable of engaging in undersea mining, and the whole matter is currently at an impasse that may not be resolved until actual mining operations are imminent or in progress (Cuyvers, 1984, pp. 65–66).[7]

9.3.3.   Pollution of the Sea

Pollution of the sea arises from many sources—discharge of industrial and organic waste from land sources, economic activity and transport on the sea itself, marine accidents, and natural disasters. Unlike previous marine conventions, UNCLOS III (1982) included significant attention to the protection and preservation of the marine environment. The principal emphasis is on the development of guidelines for national policies (particularly including responsibilities of flag states for the status and operations of vessels under their registry); there was also some endorsement of pollution-control authority for coastal states and port states. These principles, both in substance and in modes of implementation, are still in the early stages of evolution (cf. Cuyvers, 1984, p. 159). Pollution of the sea is, of course, a principal concern of the MEDPLAN and other regional agreements modeled on it (Haas, 1990).

A particular problem in sea pollution concerns the transport of hazardous materials, technologies, and wastes (which can also move by land and air across national boundaries). There are no international policy regimes regulating such transport (Handl and Lutz, 1989), which has been left largely to private enterprises and nation states to handle. (For a discussion of the ethical issues involved in such transport, see Singh and Lakham, 1989.)

9.4. The Polar Regions[8]

The polar regions, the Arctic and Antarctica, share some common features with the oceanic "global commons." The Arctic is literally an ocean, although covered by an ice shelf; Antarctica is a land mass, also covered by ice, and like the seabed still largely unexplored and inaccessible. The Arctic region is a host for submarines, and is therefore involved in international security issues as well as in environmental-resource concerns. Antarctica is a demilitarized zone, but both its nonmilitary status and its environmental security may be endangered if, as is expected, its mineral resources prove to be large and exploitable. In both of the polar regions, conflicts arise among the claims and activities of competing users, and in Antarctica the "common heritage of mankind" issue arises as well.

9.4.1. The Arctic

The major conflicts to date over the use of the Arctic have been between the US and Canada; however, the interests of the USSR, European countries, and others are also involved. Setting aside the international security aspects, the principal issues involve the use of the Arctic for transit shipping and the likelihood that Arctic seabeds will become important future sources of oil and natural gas. Concerns include not only physical access to shipping lanes (i.e., distinctions between high seas and territorial waters) but also the environmental protections that may be required for both shipping and exploration/extraction activities. There is also some concern on the Canadian side with the impact of any type of modern economic activity on native populations and wildlife.

Canada attempted to obtain an extension of national authority over the ice-covered area of the Arctic in UNCLOS III (1982), and when this effort was unsuccessful (and the US did not sign the agreement anyway) declared unilaterally all waters of the Canadian Arctic Archipelago to be *internal waters* (i.e., not open seas) in 1985. Many Canadian authorities favor even more extensive claims, all of which are rejected by the US. Additional disputes involving both navigation and fisheries involve Norway, the USSR, Denmark/Greenland, and Iceland.

Young (1989a, pp. 182–187) argues that the time is ripe for creation of a North American Arctic shipping regime negotiated in terms of the intended uses and values of all involved parties, rather than on formal "jurisdictional" principles. He notes that Denmark/Greenland should certainly be included along with the US and Canada, and possibly other potential Arctic shippers as well. The knowledge and interests of native peoples should also be taken into account. Since tanker design and other technical aspects of Arctic shipping are still under development, establishment of standards and criteria in these areas should, in his view, come more easily now than after investments and technical arrangements have been put in place.

9.4.2. Antarctica

Various and often overlapping portions of Antarctica are claimed by seven nations—the UK, Chile, Argentina, Norway, France, Australia, and New Zealand. Most of these nations, plus the US, the USSR, and Poland, also maintain scientific stations on the continent. In spite of all this activity, plus the theoretical claims of other states (Brazil, Peru, Germany), large portions of Antarctica remain unexplored, and some parts of the continent are still unclaimed.

The notion that a special international regime should be established for Antarctica was accepted by the seven territorial claimants, plus five cooperating powers (Belgium, Japan, South Africa, the USSR, and the US) in 1959. The Antarctic Treaty among these 12 nations, which came into effect in 1961, rejected all other territorial claims and declared Antarctica to be a demilitarized zone. This treaty (which currently has 26 signatories), along with its subsequent emendations and satellite agreements, contains provisions for environmental protection (for both living organisms and physical conditions), freedom for scientific research, and open access and inspection of all research facilities to all nations similarly engaged. Nuclear explosions and storage of radioactive materials were barred. A 1975 attempt by nontreaty states to declare Antarctica an international nature park (with guaranteed freedom for research) was defeated in the UN, as was a 1983 proposal by LDCs to establish a UN regime, analogous to the ISA, for the continent.

Nevertheless, in response to these pressures, proposals for the creation of an Antarctic mineral regime reflecting a broad range of international interests continue to be made. There is no formal UN presence in Antarctica, but the territorial waters of the unclaimed portion of the continent would logically fall under the control of the ISA under any circumstance. The International Commission on Antarctica and its satellite agencies currently regulate prospecting, exploration, and development in much the same way that is contemplated for the ISA in the seabed. During the 1990–1991 treaty renewal negotiations, New Zealand and five European countries indicated support for a "world park" with a permanent prohibition on commercial mining activity; the UK, Germany, and Japan favored development of a set of rules to govern possible future mining activity. In the ultimate compromise, the treaty signatories agreed to a moratorium on mining which is subject to review and removal after 50 years (*The Economist*, November 24, 1990; May 10, 1991). Kratochwil notes that although "the Antarctic regime has often been celebrated for its innovative solution to otherwise seemingly insoluble problems . . . , this could change very quickly" in response to resource scarcities and availabilities, LDC pressures for inclusion within the regime, and international political developments (1985, pp. 111–112).

9.5. Outer Space[9]

In terms of both human access and legal status, the air and atmosphere surrounding the earth are divisible into three distinct regions. The immediate airspace enclosing the planet (out to an unspecified level) is considered to be an extension of the underlying land/water territory on the earth's surface. Thus, nation states have jurisdiction of the airspace above their respective territories, and airspace above the high seas and unclaimed land

areas is part of the "global commons." The next broad band, approximately 150–500 miles outward from the earth, is the so-called *low earth
orbit (LEO)*, the location of numerous commercial and scientific satellites.
(Navigational and military satellites operate just above or below this band.)
Finally, a narrow band of space some 22,300 miles directly above the
equator defines the *geostationary orbit*; satellites placed in this orbit remain
positioned at a fixed spot above the equator at all times.

The rotation of the earth alters the relationship between terrestrial
locations and specific sectors of the LEO. Hence, extension of national
jurisdiction outward to include this domain is not feasible. The first article
of the 1967 Outer Space Treaty declared outer space to be "the province of
all mankind." The geosynchronous orbit, however, is uniquely linked with
specific equatorial ground locations, and the Bogota Declaration of 1976
argued that the 27 equatorial countries, all of them LDCs, should have
authority to control the sites above their respective locations. This proposition was not accepted by others, and the countries involved were power-
less to take action to assert their claims (Soroos, in Papp and McIntyre,
eds., 1987, pp. 147–149). Issues involving the allocation of geosynchronous
positions, as well as the reservation of orbital "slots" for future assignment,
are being addressed in the ongoing "Space-WARC" being conducted
under ITU auspices (see the telecommunications case study in chapter 4
above).

The space age began with the flight of the Soviet Sputnik in 1957 and
remained a US–USSR duopoly for more than a decade thereafter.
Additional nations—Japan, China, the European Space Agency (ESA),
and others—gradually entered the field, but satellite launching was a state
monopoly within each jurisdiction until the 1980s. This picture has now
changed dramatically. During 1981–1985, ESA launched 12 Ariane
satellites and NASA an additional 30. China and the USSR began to offer
commercial launching services in 1985, and in the following year the US
began to encourage private companies to enter the space-launch business. Four companies—Martin Marietta, General Dynamics, McDonnell
Douglas, and Hughes/Boeing—have responded to this opportunity. As a
result of all of these developments, commercial space operations are, or
will soon become, highly competitive among both nations and enterprises
(cf. Goodrich, 1989).

The legal status of space operations under these rapidly changing
circumstances has been described by one authority as a "transition of
confusion" (Goldman, in Papp and McIntyre, eds., 1987, pp. 157–177). The
Committee on the Peaceful Uses of Outer Space (COPUOS) was created
by the UN immediately after the initial Sputnik flight, and this organization

has been the primary source of "space law" up to the present. The most recent work of this Committee, the Moon Treaty of 1979, did not receive its necessary ratifications until 1985 and is not recognized by any of the nations with large space programs. Other recent issues have fared little better; problems of liability, safety, sovereignty, and privacy (associated with remote sensing activity), etc., generate controversy and tension rather than cooperation and agreement. Potential military uses of space expand the areas of international concern and conflict. Goldman (in Papp and McIntyre, eds., 1987) believes that national space law will expand, particularly in the US, to deal with problems for which there is no established international consensus, with the likelihood of increased conflict and fragmentation on this most "global" of environmental use issues.

9.6. Conclusion

This review of the recent evolution of international policy regimes for environmental and natural resource issues indicates that the issues motivating these developments are far from resolved. Widespread acceptance of the "global commons" concept does not by itself reduce important scientific uncertainties about optimal usage rates and undesirable secondary effects. Moreover, even where there is both scientific and policy agreement about the need to "take thought for the morrow," feasible and appropriate institutional arrangements and procedures are by no means obvious.

It is often argued that the most efficient way to avoid the "tragedy of the commons" (unrestricted use that reduces long-range benefits) is to allocate property rights and responsibilities among users in such a way that they themselves will try to follow socially optimal usage patterns. However, this approach is not feasible for many important "common" domains, e.g., the ambient environment, high seas, and outer space. Regional regimes based on the common interests of closely involved parties are effective mechanisms in some instances, but truly global issues are outside their scope. In any event, even where feasible, the "property rights/responsibilities" approach eliminates the "commons" itself and has serious distributional consequences. Hence, it seems likely that environmental and natural resource issues will be major foci of international regime development activity and controversy for the foreseeable future.

The problem of the "global commons" illustrates two significant points about international regime formulation. The first point is that national and even regional regimes, while likely to be efficient within their jurisdictions, are not necessarily a net contribution to global integration. Such regimes may permit, and even encourage, spillovers beyond their boundaries. The second point is that international consensus is very likely to be hampered by disagreements. The LDCs have been very active in pushing for control of, or at least sharing in, various global natural resources. The advanced industrial countries have generally resisted such efforts in order to preserve their own claims and interests. It is therefore not likely that any international environmental and natural resource regimes will be functioning effectively for a long time to come, absent a clearly perceived global ecological crisis.

Benedick's recent analysis of the evolution of international policy for protection of the ozone layer highlights situations and problems common to many contemporary environmental issues (Benedick, 1991). He traces the evolving scientific consensus that there is a connection between chlorofluorocarbon use and the integrity of the ozone layer from the initial introduction of the hypothesis in 1974 to its general acceptance by the end of the decade. Although there was widespread agreement that any successful solution to this problem must be found within a global context, there was no existing forum for consideration of the matter and no obvious vehicle for implementation of any policy that might be adopted. The issue was discussed at several international conferences, but according to Benedick "it was UNEP that kept the issue alive" during the early stages (1991, p. 42). Formal negotiations under UNEP auspices began in 1982 and eventually led to the Vienna Convention (1985), with an additional commitment to the subsequent development of a *legally binding* agreement. In this period of heightened interest, private sector groups—affected industries in various countries, citizen organizations, and the media—played active and often adversarial roles. Controversy appeared to be more common that consensus, and many observers felt that the novelty of the subject and the difficulty of the issues precluded a favorable outcome. Nevertheless, in 1987 the Montreal Protocol on Substances That Deplete the Ozone Layer was signed, with eventual participation by more than 60 countries. Benedick, the principal US negotiator, reports that the Protocol "was hailed as 'the most significant international environmental agreement in history'" and sees it as "a prototype for an evolving new form of international cooperation" (1991, pp. 1 and 3). Whether or not this description will prove accurate depends upon future developments.

Notes

1. The concept of the "commons" is widely discussed in the environmental literature, cf. Krasner, 1985, chapter 9; Brown et al., 1977, chapter 1. The classic collection of papers on this theme is Hardin and Baden, eds., 1977. For a comprehensive background on the evolution of international environmental policy, see Caldwell, 1984. For a theoretical perspective on this process of international regime formation, see Young, 1989a and 1989b.

2. Benedick, 1991, p. 40. For a brief description and appraisal of UNEP, see Nanda and Moore, 1983; the creation and evolution of UNEP is also covered in Haas, 1990, chapter 1.

3. Benedick (1991, pp. 5–7) offers a similar list of factors at work in the development of international policy to protect the ozone layer. On the role of scientific knowledge and public opinion in international environmental regime development, see also papers by Andresen, Miles, and Ostreng in Andresen and Ostreng, eds., 1989.

4. For a carefully considered discussion of the decision to adopt uniform vs. diverse standards in various environments, see Donaldson, 1990. A number of specific examples, most of them unfavorable, are discussed in Pearson, ed., 1987.

5. This section is based primarily on the collection of papers edited by Pontecorvo, 1986, particularly the contributions of Pontecorvo and Schachter; Brown et al., 1977; Cuyvers, 1984; Krasner, 1985; Miles, ed., 1989; Sanger, 1986; Smith, 1988; Young, 1989a; and papers by Sahrhage and Floistad in Andresen and Ostreng, eds., 1989.

6. For a discussion of the origin of the EEZ concept from the LDC perspective, see Njenga, in Pontecorvo, ed., 1986, pp. 125–157. As noted above, many of these jurisdictional extensions overlap, and hence increase rather than decrease potentials for international conflict.

7. For an extensive discussion of the power and role of the ISA and the Enterprise, including many of the problematic aspects still outstanding, see Young, 1989a, chapter 5, particularly pp. 125–143.

8. This section is based primarily on Young, 1989a, chapter 7; Krasner, 1985, chapter 9, especially pp. 250–264; Kratochwil et al., 1985, pp. 101–114.

9. This section is based on the collection of papers published in Papp and McIntyre, eds., 1987. Policy issues concerned with the use of space for communications purposes are discussed in the final section (telecommunications case study) of chapter 4 above.

References

American Assembly. 1990. *Preserving the Global Environment*. Final Report of the 77th American Assembly. New York: American Assembly.

Andresen, Steinar, and Willy Ostreng, eds. 1989. *International Resource Management: The Role of Science and Politics*. London: Belhaven.

Benedick, Richard E. 1991. *Ozone Diplomacy: New Directions in Safeguarding the Planet*. Cambridge, MA: Harvard University Press.

Brown, Lester R., et al. 1990. *The State of the World*. New York: W.W. Norton for Worldwatch Institute.

Brown, Seyom, Nina W. Cornell, Larry L. Fabian, and Edith Brown Weiss. 1977. *Regimes for the Ocean, Outer Space, and Weather*. Washington, DC: Brookings Institution.

Caldwell, Lynton K. 1984. *International Environmental Policy: Emergence and Dimensions*. Durham, NC: Duke University Press.

Coate, Roger A. 1982. *Global Issue Regimes*. New York: Praeger.

Cuyvers, Luc. 1984. *Ocean Uses and Their Regulation*. New York: Wiley.

Donaldson, Thomas. 1989. *The Ethics of International Business*. New York: Oxford University Press.

French, Hilary F. 1990. *Clearing the Air: A Global Agenda*. Washington, DC: Worldwatch Institute.

Global 2000 Report to the President. 1980. Washington, DC: US Government Printing Office.

Goodrich, Jonathan N. 1989. *The Commercialization of Outer Space: Opportunities and Obstacles for American Business*. Westport, CT: Quorum.

Haas, Peter M. 1990. *Saving the Mediterranean: The Politics of International Environmental Cooperation*. New York: Columbia University Press.

Hahn, Robert W., and Kenneth R. Richards. 1989. "The Internationalization of Environmental Regulation," *Harvard International Law Journal*, vol. 30, no. 2 (Spring), pp. 422–445.

Handl, Gunther, and Robert E. Lutz. 1989. "An International Policy Perspective on the Trade of Hazardous Materials and Technologies," *Harvard International Law Journal*, vol. 30, no. 2 (Spring), pp. 351–374.

Hardin, Garrett. 1968. "The Tragedy of the Commons," *Science*, vol. 162, no. 3859 (13 December), pp. 1243–1248.

Hardin, Garrett, and John Baden, eds. 1977. *Managing the Commons*. San Francisco, CA: W.H. Freeman.

Kennan, George. 1970. "To Prevent a World Wasteland: A Proposal," *Foreign Affairs*, vol. 48, no. 3 (April), pp. 401–414.

Krasner, Stephen D. 1985. *Structural Conflict: The Third World Against Global Liberalism*. Berkeley, CA: University of California Press.

Kratochwil, Friedrich, Paul Rohrlich, and Harpreet Mahajan. 1985. *Peace and Disputed Sovereignty*. Lanham, MD: University Press of America.

Mahon, John F., and Patricia C. Kelley. 1988. "The Politics of Toxic Waste: Multinational Corporations as Facilitators of National Policy," in Lee E. Preston, ed., *Research in Corporate Social Performance and Policy*, vol. 10, pp. 59–86. Greenwich, CT: JAI.

Miles, Edward L., ed. 1989. *Management of World Fisheries: Implications of Extended Coastal State Jurisdiction*. Seattle, WA: University of Washington Press.

Nanda, Ved P., and Peter T. Moore. 1983. "Global Management of the Environment: Regional and Multilateral Initiatives," in Ved P. Nanda, ed., *World Climate Change: The Role of International Law and Institutions*. Boulder, CO: Westview.

Papp, Daniel S., and John R. McIntyre, eds. 1987. *International Space Policy*. New York: Quorum. See particularly "Introduction" and articles by Soroos and Goldman.

Pearson, Calres S., ed. 1987. *Multinational Corporations, Environment, and the Third World*. Durham, NC: Duke University Press for World Resources Institute.

Pirages, Dennis. 1989. *Global Technopolitics: The International Politics of Technology and Resources*. Pacific Grove, CA: Brooks/Cole.

Pontecorvo, Guilio, ed. 1986. *The New Order of the Oceans*. New York: Columbia University Press.

Sanger, Clyde. 1986. *Ordering the Oceans: The Making of the Law of the Sea*. London: Zed Books Ltd.

Simon, Julian, and Herman Kahn, eds. 1984. *The Resourceful Earth*. Oxford, England: Basil Blackwell.

Singh, Jang B., and V.C. Lakham. 1989. "Business Ethics and the International Trade in Hazardous Wastes," *Journal of Business Ethics*, vol. 8, no. 11 (November), pp. 889–899.

Smith, B.D. 1988. *State Responsibility and the Marine Environment*. Oxford, England: Clarendon.

United Nations Centre on Transnational Corporations (UNCTC). 1985. *Environmental Aspects of the Activities of Transnational Corporations: A Survey*. New York: UNCTC.

Young, Oran R. 1989a. *International Cooperation*. Ithaca, NY: Cornell University Press.

Young, Oran R. 1989b. "The Politics of International Regime Formation: Managing Natural Resources and the Environment," *International Organization*, vol. 43, no. 3 (Summer), pp. 349–376.

Epilogue: The Future of International Policy Regimes

The idea that international policy regimes might be needed to facilitate or control business activities that involve multiple national jurisdictions is scarcely more than a century old. First emerging at the International Telegraph Conference of 1865 and the International Maritime Conference of 1889, this idea has now grown to embrace a wide range of international economic, financial, trade, and environmental issues. This epilogue presents a summary overview of the frontier issues in the major regime areas discussed in the previous chapters, and examines some critical aspects of one area of great current interest—international service industries. The chapter concludes with a brief discussion of the implications of policy regime development for international business management.

E.1. Frontier Issues for Regime Evolution

The data and analysis presented in part I of this book clearly document the contemporary growth and increasing integration of the world economy. It is also argued there that economic and managerial activities have led to the creation and evolution of policy regimes concerned with various areas of international business activity; and that these regimes have, in turn, both supported and controlled the growth and integration processes themselves. Although the scope of specific regimes, and the detailed arrangements to be established within each of them, remain subject to continuing controversy and evolutionary change, there seems to be general agreement that such regimes are likely to become more numerous, more complex, and more important in the future.

The most widely held current view, however, is that comprehensive global regimes embracing diverse aspects of international business activity are *not* likely to evolve in the near future, or perhaps ever. On the contrary, the more popular scenario anticipates the growth of regimes with limited membership and/or limited functions that promise specific benefits and problem-solving capabilities for their participants, both governments and enterprises. According to this scenario, policy regimes concerned with international business will become more numerous and more complex, in response to diverse and not necessarily related specific circumstances in various industries and regions. However, this predicted pattern of evolution raises a further question: what will be the impact of these fragmented developments upon each other, and on the evolution of the total system of international policy regimes over time? The possibility of interregime conflicts, analogous to the conflicts among regulatory jurisdictions that have plagued the US economy in recent decades, is readily apparent.

E.1.1. Global and Comprehensive Regimes

The frontier issue with respect to global/comprehensive regimes remains, as it has for a decade, the refinement and adoption in some form of the long-discussed UN Code of Conduct on Transnational Corporations. It could well be argued that the actual complex of regimes in place, both within and outside the UN framework, has long since evolved beyond the scope of any single integrative concept or document. Indeed, the environment of international business in the 1990s is quite different from the environment of the 1970s that gave initial stimulus to the UN proposals, and the proposed content of the Code has changed substantially as a result. The current draft document (see appendix A) is addressed to both enterprises and governments, and might be more appropriately titled "Statement of Principles Relating to International Business." The argument favoring formal adoption of this (or some similar) version of the Code is not that such an action will actually change arrangements and behaviors that have become established over the last couple of decades, nor even that there is a great need for change in current practices. Instead, the argument is that the formal Code is a summary statement of mutually understood principles. Reference to the Code in this form should encourage anticipatory behavior on the part of both enterprises and governments, and may contribute to the avoidance of problems and misunderstandings in the future (UNCTC, 1990a).

E.1.2. Regional and Associative Regimes

The single most dramatic contemporary development is the growth of regional regimes, particularly the European Community (EC 92) and the potential North American Free Trade Area (NAFTA, composed of the US, Canada, and Mexico). Counterdevelopments are the collapse of the Soviet-dominated Council for Mutual Economic Assistance (CMEA or COMECON) and the continuing weakness and instability of regional collaborations in Latin America, Africa, and the Pacific Rim. There is no doubt that formation of the two major regional economic blocs, EC and NAFTA, is already well underway, and that the benefits expected from these regimes are likely to maintain and strengthen their development over time. There are, however, several critical questions about the future evolution and impact of these regional regimes:

1. How, and how rapidly, will the new regional regimes expand to embrace satellite economies—Eastern Europe for the EC and Latin America for NAFTA—and how will these developments affect less developed countries (LDCs) in Asia and Africa that are unlikely to be included in these arrangements?
2. Will the policies of the two major economic blocs bordering the North Atlantic (the EC and the NAFTA), particularly including agreements and understandings between them, lead to increasingly open and unrestricted worldwide trade and investment, or will they become increasinglsy restrictive over time?
3. In the light of developments suggested by the first two questions, will the two currently evolving regimes inevitably lead to the creation of a third, centered on Japan, and if so with what consequences? The Organization for Economic Cooperation and Development (OECD), consisting of the "Triad" countries, is an associative body, and not a functioning regime. Economic warfare among the Triad countries is a possibility. The Group of 7 (G7) or some other less formal arrangement may be a better forum for collaboration and cooperation among the Triad countries than the OECD.

These detailed questions involve the evolution of particular regional and associative regimes; but what are the implications of subglobal regime developments, whatever their specific form, for the operation of global regimes, whether comprehensive or functional? The answer to this question is by no means clear. It is widely feared that the post-1992 EC may adopt stronger protectionist measures against foreign imports and investment, with particular impact on Japan and the US. Similarly, US policy initiatives in the Western Hemisphere, along with concern over the trade deficit with Japan, may channel attention away from the General Agreement on Tariffs and Trade (GATT) and similar "global" institutions. On the other hand, the evolution of large and prosperous regional economic systems may provide a favorable environment for growth of multinational enterprises (MNEs) and for interregional (and ultimately global) cooperation and integration. As the data presented in chapters 2 and 3 clearly show, global growth and integration trends are much stronger among the Triad countries than elsewhere. Expansion of any of the Triad units through accretion, and/or through the development of additional centers of regional growth and prosperity (e.g., Latin America), would seem more likely to stimulate than to retard worldwide economic development, and hence to promote the development of global regimes. In any event, many critical issues—from agricultural production and prices to environmental protection—are too broad for comprehension within even very extensive regional regimes.

E.1.3. Money and Trade

The postwar international economic regimes centered on the International Monetary Fund (IMF) and the General Agreement on Tariffs and Trade (GATT) have undergone substantial changes over the last couple of decades, and continue to experience severe strains. However, there is universal agreement that an international "bank" to deal with currency exchange problems and an international "forum" for discussion of trade-related issues are essential elements of the global economic framework. Moves by the former USSR and post-Communist East European states to join these bodies show the strength of these economic regimes. Whatever specific agreements and rules may govern these institutions at any point in time, their critical feature is the *process* of mutual consultation and collaboration that they embody, and toward which international commitment remains strong. Of necessity, the leading economic powers—the US, major European countries, and Japan—have dominant roles in these regimes. At the same time, the three institutional elements of these regimes—the World Bank, the IMF, and GATT—are committed to recognition of the special concerns of middle-income countries and LDCs, and to collaborative responses to their problems.

E.1.4. Investment

The missing element in this picture is an identifiable regime for foreign investment. It seems unlikely that a new formal investment regime will emerge in the near future. The more likely prospect is that broad investment guidelines will gradually evolve out of the activities of the International Finance Corporation (IFC, a World Bank affiliate), with enterprise governance and policy arrangements guided by the UN Code (whether or not formally adopted), and by regional and bilateral agreements. Historically, the OECD countries have attempted to gain freer admission for their foreign investment activities, and to provide some measure of insurance or other guaranty against foreign expropriation or other form of loss. Some host countries—as illustrated by the Andean Code, Canada's FIRA process, and France's efforts to control US investment activities—have attempted to restrict foreign investment. Other host countries—as illustrated by the efforts of the ASEAN group—have attempted to encourage foreign investment. Generally, both types of efforts have tended to fail; investment tends to be driven by market dynamics. The two notable exceptions are the COMECON members (whose inward-looking posture is now disintegrating) and Japan, where foreign investment is both discouraged and restricted.

US bilateral efforts with Canada, Israel, and Mexico probably signal the future pattern. Those arrangements all address reduction of restrictions of investment (largely from the US into the other country). The Canada–US agreement eliminated most barriers to both goods and investment flow. Mexico has evinced interest in greater US investment, since European capital (which it previously preferred) may be less available in the future. Formal barriers to capital movements within the EC will disappear at the end of 1992. Such regional developments are far more likely than the emergence of a truly international regime for foreign investment in the foreseeable future.

E.1.5. Transport and Communications

International transport cannot take place at all without some kind of mutual understanding between origin and destination jurisdictions, and policy regimes for air and sea transport have been in place for many decades. The major trend within both regimes is toward increasing liberalization, both with respect to formal arrangements (so that the regimes themselves become less and less restrictive) and with respect to enterprise-level evolution. The result is increasing flexibility in rates and fares, intercarrier links, and service performance, which in turn gives increasing importance to the informational and consultative functions of the regimes. Communication is the "transport service" for information, and communication contacts are both generators of and substitutes for physical movements of both people and goods. International communications is becoming the freest of international business functions, partially because some of the technology in use is simply beyond the control of individual states and even of intergovernmental bodies.

E.1.6. Environment

International environmental regimes are not new phenomena, although earlier historic examples were primarily regional in scope. The shift toward a global perspective on the environment has come about in part because of increasing knowledge about the planet and its characteristics, and in part because increased worldwide resource use gives rise to problems that can only be addressed on a global basis. Since the 1960s there has been a virtual explosion of environmental regime initiatives, some rather tentative and noncontroversial (e.g., the Moon Treaty) and some involving sharp differences in scientific judgment and clashes of interests (e.g., undersea mining). In spite of all this activity, many issues regarded as critical by some authorities—biogenetic diversity, for example—remain largely unadddressed. The two most generally recognized concerns still outside the scope of any identifiable international regime are *climate* and *space*. The latter seems most likely to be approached from the national policy level, with leadership by some countries establishing patterns for others (as in the historic cases of air transport and telecommunications, for example). With respect to climate, however, national and regional (e.g., US–Canada) arrangements, although probably desirable, are clearly inadequate; yet more ambitious international agreements (with respect to planetary warming and the ozone layer, for example) depend at least as much upon advancing scientific knowledge as on the balance of interests among involved parties.

E.2.   A Policy Regime for International Services[1]

An important current example of the difficulty of international policy development in a major line of commerce involves services, defined by *The Economist* as "things one can buy or sell, but not drop on one's foot" (UNCTC, 1990b). The need for international agreements concerning service industries has been a major subject of discussion in business and policy circles since the early 1980s, and service industry issues are major subjects of the Uruguay Round of GATT negotiations, which is still in progress at the time of this writing. International operations in finance and insurance, tourism, and other professional and business services have grown rapidly in recent decades. However, these industries have not been included in GATT negotiations and related discussions up to the present time. The complete list of service industries as defined by the UN International Standard Industrial Classification is provided below (UNCTC, 1989, p. 4). The reader should note that this listing includes transport and communications; other UN publications sometimes include construction within the services sector as well.

Wholesale trade

Retail trade

Restaurants and hotels

Transport (railway, urban, other land, pipeline, water, air, etc.)

Storage and warehousing

Communications

Financial institutions (banks and other institutions providing financial services, except for insurance companies)

Insurance

Real estate

Business services (including legal services, accounting, and auditing; data processing; engineering, architectural, and technical services; advertising; other business services, such as credit-rating agencies and employment agencies; news-gathering and reporting agencies, business management, and consulting services; fashion designers; detective agencies and protective services)

International and extraterritorial bodies (including international organizations, foreign embassies, and other extraterritorial units)

Machinery and equipment rental and leasing

Public administration and defense

Sanitary and similar services

Social and related community services (including education services; research and scientific institutes; medical, dental, other health, and veterinary services; business, professional, and labor associations; religious organizations)

Recreational and cultural services (including motion picture production, distribution, and projection; radio and television broadcasting; theatrical producers and entertainment services; all other amusement and recreational services)

Personal and household services (including repair services, laundry and cleaning services, social escort services, and shopping services)

One reason that services have not been included within the framework of international economic negotiations is their invisible, often nebulous, character. Service transactions may take place without any contact with geographic borders—through telecommunications, for example. They may also occur through the movement of *persons* who subsequently receive services (e.g., tourism) or provide services (e.g., professional work) in another jurisdiction. Such activities do not fit easily into conventional concepts of "trade," although they may have substantial effects on the incomes and international accounts of the enterprises, individuals, and countries involved. At the same time, services are the lubricants of international trade and investment and a major vehicle for the transfer of technology and management processes among countries. In fact, a major problem in the measurement of international service activities is that their value is often embedded in the value of merchandise, equipment, or investments to which the services themselves are applied. The most recent UN estimate is that services account for 50% to 60% of the current world stock of foreign direct investment (FDI), and about 60% of the annual FDI flow (UNCTC, 1990b, p. 2).

The sources of national and international policy concern with respect to services are multiple and interrelated:

1. Although precise definitions and magnitudes are subject to debate, it is generally believed that the volume of international service industry activity is large and growing; hence, the availability of basic information about international services and their possible impact on domestic economies has become a major concern in itself.
2. Many service industries (e.g., financial services and insurance) are tightly regulated within individual states. Some are state monopolies, and in others participation is limited in whole or part to nationals. The connection between such national policies and the operations of foreign competitors performing similar functions is highly problematic, particularly when the magnitude and consequences of the activities involved are imprecisely known.
3. Service industry activities are intimately linked with ownership and use of intellectual property, including artistic creations, data collections, operating routines, and communication procedures. Enterprises and governments seek to control service activities both to *obtain* access to intellectual property originating elsewhere and to *prevent* or *control* access to their own intellectual property holdings by other interests.
4. As the title of Riddle's 1986 publication, *Service-Led Growth*, suggests, many states and enterprises see favorable business development prospects in the service sector. As a result, there is a strong desire to integrate service industries into national development policies and to stimulate and protect nationally based service activities, particularly with respect to financial services.
5. Finally, some countries, particularly LDCs, fear that foreign penetration of their service industries may lead to functional dependence and cultural domination, both of which will ultimately damage their prospects for long-run social and economic development.

E.2.1. Characteristics of a Services Regime

The complexity of the above issues strongly suggests that development of a policy framework for international services is not an easy task, and this impression is reinforced by a wide range of scholarly opinion. Feketekuty (1988) argues that national treatment—the principle that domestic and foreign firms would be treated *alike* in the administration of policy—is the "core concept" in any international regime for services. Krommenacker (1984) notes that both FDI and the mobility of skilled labor are of unusual importance in the services sector, and suggests that the key feature of a services regime should be the adaptation and extension of basic GATT principles: most favored nation (MFN) status, national treatment, and special consideration for LDCs. He sees the development of an international agreement on "telematics"—a combination of telecommunications, data processing, and information services—as a critical development that might provide a focus and model for other service industries developments. Walter (1988) emphasizes the need to remove national protections for financial services that, combined with insurance, account for by far the largest aggregate value of internationally traded services. Dominance of international financial activity by the advanced industrial countries is, of course, a major concern of other governments and enterprises.

Jackson suggests the need for a very broad "umbrella" agreement emphasizing two features:

1. *Transparency*—the obligation of open reporting on actual rules and practices governing foreign participation in service industry activities within individual jurisdictions; and
2. *Regulatory due process*—a commitment to "a certain fair standard of procedure in government dealing with foreign service providers" (1988, p. 25).

Under such a broad umbrella, sequential negotiation of various sectoral —i.e., functional level—agreements involving specific service activities would be expected to evolve. These latter agreements would follow basic GATT-type principles, appropriately adapted to service industry activities.

The difficulties and complexities examined by these analysts strongly indicate that a comprehensive policy regime for international service industries is not likely to emerge in the near future. On the other hand, these service industry issues are simply new versions of the concerns that have been at the center of international policy regime evolution over the past half century. Since international service activities and their consequences, both welcome and problematic, are of growing importance in the economy, it seems that the evolution of policy regimes to deal with them —and probably on a piecemeal rather than comprehensive basis—can be predicted with some confidence.

Experience with international service trade in the context of US bilateral agreements with Israel, Canada, and Mexico is likely to have considerable influence on larger developments. Both the US–Israel and US–Canada agreements, while virtually eliminating barriers to merchandise trade and investment, basically stipulated "best efforts" to negotiate future arrangements for services. These agreements also created special administrative bodies for dispute resolution. The importance and diversity of services within this particular set of trading partners, and the strong US advantage in service industry activities, make these negotiations a microcosm of global service trade problems and opportunities.

E.2.2. Implications of Regime Development for International Management

The enterprise manager of the future will operate within a complex web of international policy regimes. The basic functions of international business —trade, currency exchange, investment, transportation and communication —would be impossible without the existence of supportive agreements and understandings among enterprises and governments. Indeed, the network of formal regimes and looser arrangements forms part of the institutional infrastructure for the global economy. This infrastructure does not consist, for the most part, of a set of *regulations* governing international business. It is more appropriately understood as a reflection of mutual agreement among participating parties about norms and patterns of desirable and acceptable (and undesirable and unacceptable) behavior.

The notion of operating within a network of policy regimes is, however, new and strange to most international managers. Perhaps the most difficult, but also most fundamental, point to grasp is that industries and enterprises are active participants in the formation and operation of regimes, not simply impacted parties. Some regimes originate primarily in response to the specific concerns of industries and enterprises; the air transport regime is perhaps the most conspicuous example. Whatever their origins, effective regimes require collaborative and adaptive behavior on the part of enterprises, and often of several different *kinds* of enterprises operating in various political jurisdictions. The two-decade cycle of social controversy and political–business response concerning international marketing of infant formula, reviewed in chapter 5 above, may be a particularly instructive example for international managers to consider.

Another feature of regimes that is particularly problematic for managers is their highly *dynamic* character. Although most important regimes contain significant institutional elements (formal agreements or organizations) that persist over time, the understandings and norms of behavior that are of primary importance tend to change in response to changing circumstances, and often in very subtle ways. These changes are driven ultimately by the dynamism of international business itself, as well as by domestic and international political developments. The international manager's difficult task is to monitor, anticipate, and even participate in these processes in order to protect and advance enterprise objectives.

From the perspective of international managers, the most conspicuous policy restrictions on business activities are probably those relating to foreign direct investment (FDI) and such specific MNE activities as transfer pricing. Some regimes, such as the CMEA, have essentially prohibited FDI; others have limited foreign ownership (in both percentage and sphere of activity) or placed specific requirements on foreign-owned operations. In general, attempts to limit FDI and restrict MNE activities have not been particularly successful in market-oriented economies. Even where the restrictions themselves have been effective (as in the old CMEA and occasionally in Latin America), they have not typically improved economic conditions within the target environments and have often had perverse effects. Managers confronted with these kinds of issues may need to familiarize themselves with the dismal record of past experience, and then use that information in their negotiations with other involved parties.

A final, and particularly troubling, consideration for managers is the fact that the complex network of policy regimes does not constitute a single, integrated whole and, in fact, contains many inconsistent and conflicting elements. Hence, it is often the case that one principle—say, special consideration for a particular group of countries or interests—prevails in one type of activity, while another principle—say, equal treatment of all participants—prevails elsewhere. This state of affairs is not surprising, since there is no overarching concept or idea uniting the diverse elements of the international policy network, nor is it likely that a comprehensive global regime covering all important aspects of international business activity will appear in the near future. The proposed UN Code, even if adopted, does not have such a unifying character; and, in any event, the more important policy regimes now in place and evolving tend to be functional or regional in focus. Hence, the problems of diversity, and perhaps direct conflict, among the multiple regimes that affect the operations of individual managers and enterprises are likely to become greater, rather than less, in the future.

Notes

1. Principal references for this section include Enderwick, 1989; Fatouros, 1990; Feketekuty, 1988; Jackson, 1988; Krommenacker, 1984; Riddle, 1986; UNCTC, 1989 and 1990b; and Walter, 1988.

References

Enderwick, Peter. 1989. *Multinational Service Firms*. London and New York: Routledge.

Fatouros, Arghyrios A. 1990. "The Code and the Uruguay Round Negotiations on Trade in Services," *The CTC Reporter*, no. 29 (Spring), pp. 7–15.

Feketekuty, Geza. 1988. *International Trade in Services: An Overview and Blueprint for Negotiations*. Cambridge, MA: Ballinger.

Jackson, John H. 1988. *International Competition in Services: A Constitutional Framework*. Washington, DC: American Enterprise Institute.

Krommenacker, Raymond J. 1984. *World-Traded Services: The Challenge for the Eighties*. Dedham, MA: Artech House.

Riddle, Dorothy L. 1986. *Service-Led Growth: The Role of the Service Sector in World Development*. New York: Praeger.

UN Centre on Transnational Corporations (UNCTC). 1989. *Foreign Direct Investment and Transnational Corporations in Services*. New York: UNCTC.

UN Centre on Transnational Corporations (UNCTC). 1990a. *The New Code Environment*. No. 16, Series A. New York: UNCTC.

UN Centre on Transnational Corporations (UNCTC). 1990b. *Transnational Corporations, Services and the Uruguay Round*. New York: UNCTC.

Walter, Ingo. 1988. *Global Competition in Financial Services: Market Structure, Protection and Trade Liberalization*. Cambridge, MA: Ballinger.

APPENDICES

Appendix A. Proposed Text of the Draft UN Code of Conduct on Transnational Corporations

CONTENTS

PREAMBLE

The General Assembly,

Recalling Economic and Social Council resolutions 1908 (LVII) of 2 August 1974 and 1913 (LVII) of 5 December 1974, establishing the Commission on Transnational Corporations and the United Nations Centre on Transnational Corporations with the mandate, as their highest priority of work, of concluding a Code of Conduct on Transnational Corporations.

Convinced that a universally accepted, comprehensive and effective Code of Conduct on Transnational Corporations is an essential element in the strengthening of international economic and social co-operation and, in particular, in achieving one of the main goals and objectives in that co-operation, namely, to maximize the contributions of transnational corporations to economic development and growth and to minimize the negative effects of the activities of these corporations.

Decides to adopt the following Code of Conduct on Transnational Corporations:

DEFINITIONS AND SCOPE OF APPLICATION

1. (a) This Code is universally applicable to enterprises, irrespective of their country of origin and their ownership, including private, public or mixed, comprising entities in two or more countries, regardless of the legal

form and fields of activity of these entities, which operate under a system of decision-making, permitting coherent policies and a common strategy through one or more decision-making centres, in which the entities are so linked, by ownership or otherwise, that one or more of them may be able to exercise a significant influence over the activities of others and, in particular, to share knowledge, resources and responsibilities with the others. Such enterprises are referred to in this Code as transnational corporations.

(b)   The term "entities" in the Code refers to both parent entities— that is, entities which are the main source of influence over others—and other entities, unless otherwise specified in the Code.

(c)   The term "transnational corporation" in the Code refers to the enterprise as a whole or its various entities.

(d)   The term "home country" means the country in which the parent entity is located. The term "host country" means a country other than the home country in which an entity other than the parent entity is located.

(e)   The term "country in which a transnational corporation operates" refers to a home or host country in which an entity of a transnational corporation conducts operations.

2.   For the application of this Code, it is irrelevant whether or not enterprises as described in paragraph 1 (a) above are referred to in any country as transnational corporations.

3.   The Code is universally applicable in all States, regardless of their political and economic systems or their level of development.

4.   The provisions of the Code addressed to transnational corporations reflect good practice for all enterprises. Subject to the provisions of paragraph 52, wherever the provisions of the Code are relevant to both, transnational corporations and domestic enterprises shall be subject to the same expectations with regard to their conduct.

5.   Subject to the relevant constitutions, charters or other fundamental laws of the regional groupings of States concerned, any reference in this Code to States, countries or Governments, also includes regional groupings of States, to the extent that the provisions of this Code relate to matters within these groupings' own competence, with respect to such competence.

6.   In their interpretation and application the provisions of this Code are interrelated and each provision should be construed in the context of the other provisions.

ACTIVITIES OF TRANSNATIONAL CORPORATIONS

A. *General*

Respect for national sovereignty and observance of domestic laws, regulations and administrative practices

7.   Transnational corporations shall respect the national sovereignty of the countries in which they operate and the right of each State to exercise its permanent sovereignty over its natural wealth and resources.

8.   An entity of a transnational corporation is subject to the laws, regulations and established administrative practices of the country in which it operates.

9.   Transnational corporations shall respect the right of each State to regulate and monitor accordingly the activities of their entities operating within its territory.

Adherence to economic goals and development objectives, policies and priorities

10.   Transnational corporations should carry out their activities in conformity with the development policies, objectives and priorities set out by the Governments of the countries in which they operate and work seriously towards making a positive contribution to the achievement of such goals at the national and, as appropriate, the regional level, within the framework of regional integration programmes. Transnational corporations should co-operate with the Governments of the countries in which they operate with a view to contributing to the development process and should be responsive to requests for consultation in this respect, thereby establishing mutually beneficial relations with these countries.

11.   Transnational corporations should carry out their operations in conformity with applicable intergovernmental co-operative arrangements concluded by the countries in which they operate.

Review and renegotiation of contracts and agreements

12.   (a)   Contracts or agreements between Governments and transnational corporations should be negotiated and implemented in good faith. In such contracts or agreements, especially long-term ones, review or renegotiation clauses should normally be included.

(b)   In the absence of such clauses and where there has been a fundamental change of the circumstances on which the contract or agreement
was based, transnational corporations, acting in good faith, should
co-operate with Governments for the review or renegotiation of such
contract or agreement.

Adherence to socio-cultural objectives and values

13.   Transnational corporations should respect the social and cultural
objectives, values and traditions of the countries in which they operate.
While economic and technological development is normally accompanied
by social change, transnational corporations should avoid practices,
products or services which cause detrimental effects on cultural patterns
and socio-cultural objectives as determined by Governments. For this
purpose, transnational corporations should respond positively to requests
for consultations from Governments concerned.

Respect for human rights and fundamental freedoms

14.   Transnational corporations shall respect human rights and fundamental freedoms in the countries in which they operate. In their social and
industrial relations, transnational corporations shall not discriminate on
the basis of race, colour, sex, religion, language, social, national and ethnic
origin or political or other opinion. Transnational corporations shall
conform to government policies designed to extend equality of opportunity
and treatment.

*Non-collaboration by transnational corporations with the racist minority
régime in South Africa*

15.   In accordance with the efforts of the international community
towards the elimination of *apartheid* in South Africa,

(a)   Transnational corporations shall refrain from operations and
activities supporting and sustaining the racist minority régime of South
Africa in maintaining the system of *apartheid*;

(b)   Transnational corporations shall engage in appropriate activities
within their competence with a view to eliminating racial discrimination
and all other aspects of the system of *apartheid*;

(c)   Transnational corporations shall comply strictly with obligations
resulting from Security Council decisions and shall fully respect those
resulting from all relevant United Nations resolutions.

Non-interference in internal affairs of host countries

16.   Without prejudice to the participation of transnational corporations in activities that are permissible under the laws, regulations or established administrative practices of host countries, and without prejudice to paragraph 8 of the Code, transnational corporations shall not interfere in the internal affairs of host countries.

Non-interference in intergovernmental relations

17.   Transnational corporations shall not interfere in intergovernmental relations provided that this provision shall not preclude such activities as are sanctioned within the framework of bilateral or multilateral co-operation.

18.   Transnational corporations should not request Governments acting on their behalf to take the measures referred to in the second sentence of paragraph 65.

19.   With respect to the exhaustion of local remedies, transnational corporations should not request Governments to act on their behalf in any manner inconsistent with paragraph 65.

Abstention from corrupt practices

20.   (a)   Transnational corporations shall refrain, in their transactions, from the offering, promising or giving of any payment, gift or other advantage to or for the benefit of a public official as consideration for performing or refraining from the performance of his duties in connection with those transactions.

   (b)   Transnational corporations shall maintain accurate records of any payments made by them to any public official or intermediary. They shall make available these records to the competent authorities of the countries in which they operate, upon request, for investigations and proceedings concerning those payments.

B.   *Economic, financial and social*

Ownership and control

21.   Transnational corporations should make every effort so to allocate their decision-making powers among their entities as to enable them to

contribute to the economic and social development of the countries in which they operate.

22.   To the extent permitted by national laws, policies and established administrative practices of the country in which it operates, each entity of a transnational corporation should co-operate with the other entities, in accordance with the actual distribution of responsibilities among them and consistent with paragraph 22, so as to enable each entity to meet effectively the requirements established by the laws, policies and regulations of the country in which it operates.

23.   Transnational corporations should carry out their personnel policies in accordance with the national policies of each of the countries in which they operate which give priority to the employment and promotion of its nationals at all levels of management and direction of the affairs of each entity so as to enhance the effective participation of its nationals in the decision-making process.

24.   Transnational corporations should contribute to the managerial and technical training of nationals of the countries in which they operate and facilitate their employment at all levels of management of the entities and enterprises as a whole.

Employment conditions and industrial relations

25.   For the purposes of this Code, the principles set out in the Tripartite Declaration of Principles concerning Multinational Enterprises and Social Policy, adopted by the Governing Body of the International Labour Office, should apply in the field of employment, training, conditions of work and life and industrial relations.

Balance of payments and financing

26.   Transnational corporations shall carry out their operations in conformity with laws and regulations and with full regard to the policy objectives set out by the countries in which they operate, particularly developing countries, relating to balance of payments, financial trans- actions and other issues dealt with in the subsequent paragraphs of this section. These obligations are without prejudice to multilaterally agreed trade rules and sound commercial practices.

27.   Transnational corporations should respond positively to requests for consultation on their activities from the Governments of the countries

in which they operate, with a view to contributing to the alleviation of pressing problems of balance of payments and finance of such countries.

28. Transnational corporations should, where appropriate, contribute to the promotion and diversification of exports in the countries in which they operate and to an increased utilization of goods, services and other resources which are available in these countries.

29. Transnational corporations should be responsive to requests by Governments of the countries in which they operate, particularly developing countries, concerning the phasing over a limited period of time of the repatriation of capital in case of disinvestment or remittances of accumulated profits, when the size and timing of such transfers would cause serious balance-of-payments difficulties for such countries.

30. Transnational corporations should not, contrary to generally accepted financial practices prevailing in the countries in which they operate, engage in short-term financial operations or transfers or defer or advance foreign exchange payments, including intra-corporate payments, in a manner which would increase currency instability and thereby cause serious balance-of-payments difficulties for the countries concerned.

31. Transnational corporations should not impose restrictions on their entities, beyond generally accepted commercial practices prevailing in the countries in which they operate, regarding the transfer of goods, services and funds which would cause serious balance-of-payments difficulties for the countries in which they operate.

32. When having recourse to the money and capital markets of the countries in which they operate, transnational corporations should not, beyond generally accepted financial practices prevailing in such countries, engage in activities which would have a significant adverse impact on the working of local markets, particularly by restricting the availability of funds to other enterprises. When issuing shares with the objective of increasing local equity participation in an entity operating in such a country, or engaging in long-term borrowing in the local market, transnational corporations should consult with the Government of the country concerned upon its request on the effects of such transactions on the local money and capital markets.

Transfer pricing

33. In respect of their intra-corporate transactions, transnational corporations should not use pricing policies that are not based on relevant

market prices, or, in the absence of such prices, the arm's length principle, which have the effect of adversely affecting the tax revenues, the foreign exchange resources or other aspects of the economy of the countries in which they operate.

Taxation

34.   Transnational corporations shall not, contrary to the laws and regulations of the countries in which they operate, use their corporate structure and modes of operation, such as the use of intra-corporate pricing which is not based on the arm's length principle, or other means, to modify the tax base on which their entities are assessed.

Competition and restrictive business practices

35.   For the purposes of this Code, the relevant provisions of the Set of Multilaterally Agreed Equitable Principles and Rules for the Control of Restrictive Business Practices adopted by the General Assembly in its resolution 35/63 of 5 December 1980 apply in the field of restrictive business practices.

Transfer of technology

36.   (a)   Transnational corporations shall conform to the transfer of technology laws and regulations of the countries in which they operate. They shall co-operate with the competent authorities of those countries in assessing the impact of international transfers of technology in their economies and consult with them regarding the various technological options which might help those countries, particularly developing countries, to attain their economic and social development.

(b)   Transnational corporations in their transfer of technology transactions should, in accordance with the criteria set forth in the Set of Multilaterally Agreed Equitable Principles and Rules for the Control of Restrictive Business Practices, avoid restrictive practices which adversely affect the international flow of technology, or otherwise hinder the economic and technological development of countries, particularly developing countries.

(c)   Transnational corporations should contribute to the strengthening of the scientific and technological capacities of developing countries, in accordance with the science and technology established policies and priorities of those countries. Transnational corporations should undertake substantial research and development activities in developing countries and should make full use of local resources and personnel in this process.

Consumer protection

37. Transnational corporations shall carry out their operations, in particular production and marketing, in accordance with national laws, regulations, administrative practices and policies concerning consumer protection of the countries in which they operate. Transnational corporations shall also perform their activities with due regard to relevant international standards, so that they do not cause injury to the health or endanger the safety of consumers or bring about variations in the quality of products in each market which would have detrimental effects on consumers.

38. Transnational corporations shall, in respect of the products and services which they produce or market or propose to produce or market in any country, supply to the competent authorities of that country on request or on a regular basis, as specified by these authorities, all relevant information concerning:

> Characteristics of these products or services which may be injurious to the health and safety of consumers including experimental uses and related aspects;

> Prohibitions, restrictions, warnings and other public regulatory measures imposed in other countries on grounds of health and safety protection on these products or services.

39. Transnational corporations should disclose to the public in the countries in which they operate all appropriate information on the contents and, to the extent known, on possible hazardous effects of the products they produce or market in the countries concerned by means of proper labelling, informative and accurate advertising or other appropriate methods. Packaging of their products should be safe and the contents of the product should not be misrepresented.

40. Transnational corporations should be responsive to requests from Governments of the countries in which they operate and be prepared to cooperate with international organizations in their efforts to develop and promote national and international standards for the protection of the health and safety of consumers and to meet the basic needs of consumers.

Environmental protection

41. Transnational corporations shall carry out their activities in accordance with national laws, regulations, established administrative practices

and policies relating to the preservation of the environment of the countries in which they operate and with due regard to relevant international standards. Transnational corporations should, in performing their activities, take steps to protect the environment and where damaged to rehabilitate it and should make efforts to develop and apply adequate technologies for this purpose.

42.   Transnational corporations shall, in respect of the products, processes and services they have introduced or propose to introduce in any country, supply to the competent authorities of that country on request or on a regular basis, as specified by these authorities, all relevant information concerning:

> Characteristics of these products, processes and other activities including experimental uses and related aspects which may harm the environment and the measures and costs necessary to avoid or at least to mitigate their harmful effects;

> Prohibitions, restrictions, warnings and other public regulatory measures imposed in other countries on grounds of protection of the environment on these products, processes and services.

43.   Transnational corporations should be responsive to requests from Governments of the countries in which they operate and be prepared where appropriate to co-operate with international organizations in their efforts to develop and promote national and international standards for the protection of the environment.

C.   *Disclosure of information*

44.   Transnational corporations should disclose to the public in the countries in which they operate, by appropriate means of communication, clear, full and comprehensible information on the structure, policies, activities and operations of the transnational corporation as a whole. The information should include financial as well as non-financial items and should be made available on a regular annual basis, normally within six months and in any case not later than 12 months from the end of the financial year of the corporation. In addition, during the financial year, transnational corporations should wherever appropriate make available a semi-annual summary of financial information.

The financial information to be disclosed annually should be provided where appropriate on a consolidated basis, together with suitable explanatory notes and should include, *inter alia*, the following:

(a)   A balance sheet;

(b)   An income statement, including operating results and sales;

(c)   A statement of allocation of net profits or net income;

(d)   A statement of the sources and uses of funds;

(e)   Significant new long-term capital investment;

(f)   Research and development expenditure.

The non-financial information referred to in the first subparagraph should include, *inter alia*:

(a)   The structure of the transnational corporation, showing the name and location of the parent company, its main entities, its percentage ownership, direct and indirect, in these entities, including shareholdings between them;

(b)   The main activity of its entities;

(c)   Employment information including average number of employees;

(d)   Accounting policies used in compiling and consolidating the information published;

(e)   Policies applied in respect of transfer pricing.

The information provided for the transnational corporation as a whole should as far as practicable be broken down:

By geographical area or country, as appropriate, with regard to the activities of its main entities, sales, operating results, significant new investments and number of employees;

By major line of business as regards sales and significant new investment.

The method of breakdown as well as details of information provided should be determined by the nature, scale and interrelationships of the transnational corporation's operations, with due regard to their significance for the areas or countries concerned.

The extent, detail and frequency of the information provided should take into account the nature and size of the transnational corporation as a whole, the requirements of confidentiality and effects on the transnational corporation's competitive position as well as the cost involved in producing the information.

The information herein required should, as necessary, be in addition to information required by national laws, regulations and established administrative practices of the countries in which transnational corporations operate.

45. (a) Transnational corporations shall supply to the competent authorities in each of the countries in which they operate, upon request or on a regular basis as specified by those authorities, and in accordance with national legislation, all information required for legislative and administrative purposes relevant to the activities and policies of their entities in the country concerned.

(b) Transnational corporations shall, to the extent permitted by the provisions of the relevant national laws, regulations, established administrative practices and policies of the countries concerned, supply to competent authorities in the countries in which they operate information held in other countries needed to enable them to obtain a true and fair view of the operations of the transnational corporation concerned as a whole in so far as the information requested relates to the activities of the entities in the countries seeking such information.

(c) The provisions of paragraph 52 concerning confidentiality shall apply to information supplied under the provisions of this paragraph.

46. (a) With due regard to the relevant provisions of the ILO Tripartite Declaration of Principles concerning Multinational Enterprises and Social Policy and in accordance with national laws, regulations and practices in the field of labour relations, transnational corporations shall provide to trade unions or other representatives of employees in their entities in each of the countries in which they operate, by appropriate means of communication, the necessary information on the activities dealt with in this Code to enable them to obtain a true and fair view of the performance of the local entity and, where appropriate, the corporation as a whole. Such information shall include, where provided for by national law and practices, *inter alia*, prospects or plans for future development having major economic and social effects on the employees concerned.

(b) Procedures for consultation on matters of mutual concern should be worked out by mutual agreement between entities of transnational corporations and trade unions or other representatives of employees in accordance with national law and practice.

(c) Information made available pursuant to the provisions of this paragraph should be subject to appropriate safeguards for confidentiality so that no damage is caused to the parties concerned.

TREATMENT OF TRANSNATIONAL CORPORATIONS

A. *General provisions relating to the treatment of transnational corporations*

47.   In all matter relating to the Code, States, shall fulfil, in good faith, their obligations under international law.

48.   States have the right to regulate the entry and establishment of transnational corporations including determining the role that such corporations may play in economic and social development and prohibiting or limiting the extent of their presence in specific sectors.

49.   Transnational corporations shall receive fair and equitable treatment in the countries in which they operate.

50.   Subject to national requirements for maintaining public order and protecting national security and consistent with national constitutions and basic laws, and without prejudice to measures specified in legislation relating to the declared development objectives of the developing countries, entities of transnational corporations should be entitled to treatment no less favourable than that accorded to domestic enterprises in similar circumstances.

51.   The importance of endeavouring to assure the clarity and stability of national policies, laws, regulations and established administrative practices is acknowledged. Laws and regulations affecting transnational corporations should be publicly and readily available. To the extent appropriate, relevant information regarding decisions of competent administrative bodies relating to transnational corporations should be disseminated.

52.   Information furnished by transnational corporations to the authorities in each of the countries in which they operate containing confidential business information shall be accorded reasonable safeguards normally applicable in the area in which the information is provided, particularly to protect its confidentiality.

53.   In order to achieve the purposes of paragraph 24 relating to managerial and technical training and employment of nationals of the countries in which transnational corporations operate, the transfer of those nationals between the entities of a transnational corporation should, subject to the laws and regulations of the countries concerned, be facilitated.

54.   Transnational corporations are entitled to transfer all payments legally due. Such transfers are subject to the procedures laid down in the relevant legislation of host countries, such as foreign exchange laws, and

to restrictions for a limited period of time emanating from exceptional balance of payment difficulties.

B. *Nationalization and compensation*

55. It is acknowledged that States have the right to nationalize or expropriate the assets of a transnational corporation operating in their territories, and that adequate compensation is to be paid by the State concerned, in accordance with the applicable legal rules and principles.

C. *Jurisdiction*

56. An entity of a transnational corporation is subject to the jurisdiction of the country in which it operates.

D. *Dispute settlement*

57. Disputes between States and entities of transnational corporations, which are not amicably settled between the parties, shall be submitted to competent national courts or authorities. Where the parties so agree, or have agreed, such disputes shall be referred to other mutually acceptable or accepted dispute settlement procedures.

58. Where the exercise of jurisdiction over transnational corporations and their entities by more than one State may lead to conflicts of jurisdiction, States concerned should endeavour to avoid or minimize such conflicts, and the problems to which they give rise by following an approach of moderation and restraint, respecting and accommodating the interests of Other States.

INTERGOVERNMENTAL CO-OPERATION

59. It is acknowledged that intergovernmental co-operation is essential in accomplishing the objectives of the Code.

60. Intergovernmental co-operation should be established or strengthened at the international level and, where appropriate, at the bilateral, regional and interregional levels.

61. States should exchange information on the measures they have taken to give effect to the Code and on their experience with the Code.

62.   States should consult on a bilateral or multilateral basis, as appropriate, on matters relating to the Code and its application and with respect to the development of international agreements and arrangements on issues related to the Code.

63.   States should take into consideration the objectives of the Code as reflected in its provisions when negotiating bilateral or multilateral agreements concerning transnational corporations.

64.   States should not use transnational corporations as instruments to intervene in the internal or external affairs of other States and should take appropriate action within their jurisdiction to prevent transnational corporations from engaging in activities referred to in paragraphs 16 and 17 of this Code.

65.   Government action on behalf of a transnational corporation operating in another country shall be subject to the principle of exhaustion of local remedies provided in such a country and, when agreed among the Governments concerned, to procedures for dealing with international legal claims. Such action should not in any event amount to the use of any type of coercive measures not consistent with the Charter of the United Nations and the Declaration on Principles of International Law concerning Friendly Relations and Co-operation among States in accordance with the Charter of the United Nations.

IMPLEMENTATION OF THE CODE OF CONDUCT

A.   *Action at the national level*

66.   In order to ensure and promote the implementation of the Code at the national level, States should, *inter alia*:

(a)   Publicize and disseminate the Code;

(b)   Follow the implementation of the Code within their territories;

(c)   Report to the United Nations Commission on Transnational Corporations on the action taken at the national level to promote the Code and on the experience gained from its implementation;

(d)   Take action to reflect their support for the Code and take into account the objectives of the Code as reflected in its provisions when

introducing, implementing and reviewing laws, regulations and administrative practices on matters dealt with in the Code.

B. *International institutional machinery*

67.   The United Nations Commission on Transnational Corporations shall
assume the functions of the international institutional machinery for the
implementation of the Code. In this capacity, the Commission shall be
open to the participation of all States. Consistent with United Nations
practices, it may establish the subsidiary bodies and specific procedures it
deems necessary for the effective discharge of its functions. The United
Nations Centre on Transnational Corporations shall act as the secretariat
to the Commission.

68.   The Commission shall act as the international body within the United
Nations system for all matters related to the Code. It shall establish and
maintain close contacts with other United Nations organizations and
specialized agencies dealing with matters related to the Code and its
implementation with a view to co-ordinating work related to the Code.
When matters covered by international agreements or arrangements,
specifically referred to in the Code, which have been worked out in other
United Nations forums, arise, the Commission shall forward such matters
to the competent bodies concerned with such agreements or arrangements.

69.   The Commission shall have the following functions:

(a)   To discuss at its annual sessions matters related to the Code. If
agreed by the Governments engaged in consultations on specific issues
related to the Code, the Commission shall facilitate such intergovernmental consultations to the extent possible. Representatives of trade
unions, business, consumer and other relevant groups may express their
views on matters related to the Code through the non-governmental
organizations represented in the Commission.

(b)   Periodically to assess the implementation of the Code, such
assessments being based on reports submitted by Governments and, as
appropriate, on documentation from United Nations organizations and
specialized agencies performing work relevant to the Code and non-
governmental organizations represented in the Commission. The first assessment shall take place not earlier than two years and not later than three
years after the adoption of the Code. The second assessment shall take
place two years after the first one. The Commission shall determine
whether a periodicity of two years is to be maintained or modified for

subsequent assessments. The format of assessments shall be determined by the Commission.

(c)   To develop in the light of experience procedures for providing clarifications on provisions of the Code.

(d)   To report annually to the General Assembly through the Economic and Social Council on its activities regarding the implementation of the Code.

(e)   To facilitate intergovernmental arrangements or agreements on specific aspects relating to transnational corporations upon request of the Governments concerned.

70.   The United Nations Centre on Transnational Corporations shall provide assistance relating to the implementation of the Code, *inter alia*, by collecting, analysing and disseminating information and conducting research and surveys, as required and specified by the Commission.

C.   *Review procedure*

71.   The commission shall make recommendations to the General Assembly through the Economic and Social Council for the purpose of reviewing the provisions of the Code. The first review shall take place not later than six years after the adoption of the Code. The General Assembly shall establish, as appropriate, the modalities for reviewing the Code.

Appendix B.   Note on Data and Sources

This book relies primarily on official data sources, especially trade, investment, enterprise, and economic information provided by the World Bank, the United Nations Conference on Trade and Development (UNCTAD), the United Nations Centre on Transnational Corporations (UNCTC), and the International Monetary Fund (IMF). Other data sources have also been used where appropriate. All the data sources on international economic activity include significant omissions and defects. Fortunately, these data deficiencies do not materially affect the basic patterns of international economic activity reported here.

Chapter 2 above explains the general scheme for classification of types of economies employed in this book. The purpose of this note is to provide amplification concerning our data and sources. In chapter 2, we group economies into the five types recognized by UNCTAD. However, the

World Bank and UNCTAD include somewhat different sets of countries in these categories; we have followed the World Bank grouping scheme. The country composition of the five categories of economies is as follows:

1. Industrial (or developed) market economies: US, Japan, European Community (EC) 10, European Free Trade Area (EFTA) 7, and Other (Australia, Canada, and New Zealand). The Organization for Economic Cooperation and Development (OECD) is the same as this category, with the addition of Greece, Portugal, and Turkey (which are classified by the World Bank as developing countries, together with Yugoslavia, which has special observer status with the OECD). South Africa, regarded in some sources as an industrial market economy, is classified by the World Bank as a developing country, and is not a member of OECD.

   a. EC 10: Belgium, Denmark, France, Ireland, Italy, Luxembourg, Netherlands, Spain, United Kingdom, West Germany. Luxembourg is sometimes grouped with Belgium in the data sources. The EC 12 includes Greece and Portugal, classified by the World Bank as developing countries. Data generally do not include East Germany, which was unified with West Germany in October 1990. East Germany had a population of 16.6 million in 1990 and a GNP of $196.9 billion in 1987; *Statistical Abstract of the United States, 1990* (Washington, DC: US Government Printing Office, 1990).
   b. EFTA 7: Austria, Finland, Iceland, Liechtenstein (data often combined with Austria), Norway, Sweden, Switzerland.

2. Eastern Europe: Bulgaria, Czechoslovakia, East Germany (GDR, now unified with West Germany), Hungary, Poland, Romania, and the USSR. These economies were the European members of the now defunct Council for Mutual Economic Assistance (CMEA or COMECON); CMEA also included Cuba, Mongolia, and North Korea (but not Albania). Yugoslavia had special observer status with CMEA.

3. Asian Socialist: People's Republic of China (PRC), Kampuchea (for which data are often not reported), Laos, Mongolia, North Korea, Vietnam.

4. Organization of Petroleum Exporting Countries (OPEC): Algeria, Ecuador, Gabon, Indonesia, Iran, Iraq, Kuwait, Libya, Nigeria, Qatar, Saudi Arabia, United Arab Emirates (UAR), Venezuela. Data for Gabon and Qatar are often not reported. The World Bank category of "oil exporters" consists of OPEC plus Angola, Bahrain, Bolivia, Brunei, Cameroon, Egypt, Malaysia, Mexico, Oman, Trinidad/Tobago, and Tunisia.

5. Other: includes all countries, both "newly industrialized countries" (NICs) and "less developed countries" (LDCs), not members of the previous categories. We use in chapter 2 a selected set of seven NICs: Argentina, Brazil, Hong Kong, Mexico, Singapore, South Korea, and Taiwan. Other countries often classified as NICs include Chile, India, Malaysia, People's Republic of China (PRC), South Africa, and Turkey.

World Bank and UNCTC data are not reported in precisely this same level of detail. The World Bank uses essentially an "industrial countries/developing countries" breakdown, with the few "socialist" economies that are presently reporting members of the World Bank—PRC, Hungary, Poland, Romania, and Yugoslavia—included in the latter category. Membership in the International Monetary Fund (IMF) is a prerequisite for World Bank membership. The USSR and other Eastern European states are now seeking entry into the IMF/World Bank. Limited data for "nonreporting" countries are also included in some World Bank tabulations. World Bank data are generally reported on a country-by-country basis, with "developing" countries also grouped into the following categories:

a. "High-income oil exporters"—Kuwait, Libya, Saudi Arabia, and United Arab Emirates;
b. China and India (separately reported because of their size);
c. Other low-income countries;
d. Lower middle-income countries;
e. Upper middle-income countries, including most of the NICs.

In contrast to both UNCTAD and the World Bank, the UNCTC does not generally publish country-by-country data. Its tabulations utilize three principal categories:

1. Developed market economies;
2. Developing economies (including both OPEC countries and Asian socialist states);
3. Eastern European planned economies, including the USSR.

References

Choi, Frederick D.S. 1988. "International Data Sources for Empirical Research in Financial Management," *Financial Management*, vol. 17, no. 2 (Summer), pp. 80–98.

Graham, Edward M., and Paul R. Krugman. 1989. "US Government Data on Foreign Direct Investment," *Foreign Direct Investment in the United States.* Washington, DC: Institute for International Economics, pp. 135–147 (Appendix A).

Rice, Gillian, and Essam Mahmoud. 1985. "Forecasting and the Database: An Analysis of Databases for International Business," *Journal of Forecasting,* vol. 4, no. 1 (January–March), pp. 89–97.

Thomsen, Stephen. 1990. "Appendix: FDI Data Sources and Uses," in DeAnne Julius, *Global Companies and Public Policy: The Growing Challenge of Foreign Direct Investment.* New York: Council on Foreign Relations (for The Royal Institute of International Affairs), pp. 109–122.

Appendix C.   Appendix Tables

Table A-1.   Growth in World Economic Activity (Current $ Billions, Index: 1970 = 100)

Year	Foreign Direct Investment (FDI Outflows by Origin)		Exports (by Origin)		Gross Domestic Product (GDP)	
	$ Billions	Index	$ Billions	Index	$ Billions	Index
1970	12.956	100	311.9	100	3032.4	100
1975	27.846	215	872.1	280	5934.4	196
1980	57.143	441	1994.5	639	11,790.2	389
1985	53.298	411	1929.5	619	13,640.3	450
1989 (or most recent year)	196.054	1513	2893.2	928	15,241.5	503

Sources: International Monetary Fund (IMF) outflows data series for FDI (dated January 10, 1991) supplied by UN Centre for Transnational Corporations (UNCTC).

Table A-3, supplemented for 1989 by UNCTC data series (August 1991) provided to authors, for exports.

UN Conference on Trade and Development (UNCTAD), *Handbook of International Trade and Development Statistics* (New York: UNCTAD), 1985 *Supplement* for 1970, 1975, various dates for other years.

Notes: Most recent year is 1989 for FDI and exports, 1987 for GDP.

FDI outflows rose in current dollar value from 1970 to 1979, then fell 1980 to 1985, and rose again beginning in 1986. Exports fell from 1980 to 1985.

Exact dollar figures vary with year of source consulted due to subsequent restatements and adjustments.

GDP data include Eastern Europe and the USSR in 1970, 1975, and 1980; but this region was excluded in 1985 and 1987. The region's GDP was valued at $429.3 billion in 1970 (14.2% of world total), $719.6 billion in 1975 (12.1%), and $1698.7 billion in 1980 (14.4%).

Table A-2. Distribution of Gross Domestic Product (GDP) by Type of Economy, 1965 and 1985

	GDP 1965	GDP 1985	Average Annual % Increase 1965–1985	GDP Components					
				Agriculture		Industry		Services	
	\$ Billion (Current)			1965	1985	1965	1985	1965	1985
				Percentage Distribution by Type of Production					
Industrial Market Economies	1367	8569	31	5	3	40	36	55	61
Developing Economies	334	2027	30	29	20	29	34	42	47

Source: World Bank, *World Development Indicators 1987*, diskette data set.

Notes: Developing category includes NIC and OPEC countries, with the exception of four high-income oil exporters (Libya, Kuwait, Saudi Arabia, and UAE). Asian Socialist and USSR and Eastern Europe categories not reported. GDP is gross national product (GNP) less domestic factor payments received by residents from foreign countries plus factor payments by citizens to foreign residents. The factor payments are largely interest and dividends. GDP is the value of output produced in a country, divided here into agriculture, industry, and service components of domestic economic structure.

Table A-3.   Origin and Destination of Exports by Type of Economy, 1970–1985

Origin of Exports	Year	World	Industrial Market	Developing Countries		Centrally Planned	
				OPEC	Non-OPEC	Eastern Europe	Asia
World Total	1970	311.91	218.16	9.58	49.56	28.63	3.65
	1975	872.06	567.69	57.25	147.99	82.60	8.91
	1980	1994.29	1342.96	128.20	335.38	143.80	22.79
	1985	1929.54	1274.79	97.76	341.36	151.14	43.40
Industrial Market	1970	222.56	169.99	7.70	35.03	6.40	2.01
	1975	573.11	396.26	47.22	94.87	26.00	5.89
	1980	1260.63	894.03	100.36	193.03	46.61	14.55
	1985	1262.10	932.94	68.59	187.24	33.72	24.97
USSR and Eastern Europe	1970	30.53	6.98	0.67	3.42	18.39	1.02
	1975	77.36	20.20	2.64	7.73	44.37	1.96
	1980	155.12	47.64	4.94	18.11	78.65	4.19
	1985	173.97	43.61	4.28	26.03	92.00	6.53
Asian Socialist	1970	2.31	0.73	0.11	0.97	0.49	—
	1975	7.26	2.89	0.51	2.61	1.24	—
	1980	19.96	8.73	1.32	7.26	2.65	—
	1985	30.06	11.79	0.81	13.15	3.79	—
OPEC	1970	17.99	13.50	0.13	3.38	0.28	0.02
	1975	113.18	83.44	0.80	23.94	2.10	0.08
	1980	306.65	232.73	4.00	63.98	3.68	0.32
	1985	155.96	96.53	4.56	51.01	2.62	0.16
Other	1970	38.53	26.95	0.98	6.76	3.09	0.60
	1975	101.16	64.89	6.09	18.84	8.89	0.98
	1980	251.93	159.84	17.58	52.99	12.22	3.73
	1985	307.45	189.92	19.52	63.93	19.01	11.21

Source: UNCTAD, *Handbook of International Trade and Development Statistics: Supplement* (New York: 1984, 1987), table A.1.

Table A-4. Origin and Destination of Manufactured Exports for Selected Countries, 1965 and 1985

| | Origin of Exports | | Destination of Exports | | | | | | | | $ Increase 1965–85 | % Increase 1965–85 | Average Annual % Increase |
| | | | Industrial Market Economies | | Nonmember Economies | | High Income Oil Exporters | | Developing Economies | | | | |
	1965	1985	1965	1985	1965	1985	1965	1985	1965	1985	1965–85	1965–85	
NICs	$ Millions		*Percentage Distribution by Destination*								$ Millions		
South Korea	104	27,669	68	68	—	—	—	6	32	26	27,565	26,505	1325
Hong Kong	995	27,540	71	56	—	—	1	2	28	41	26,545	2668	133
Singapore	338	13,317	9	52	—	1	3	4	88	42	12,979	3840	192
Brazil	134	8911	40	52	1	1	—	3	59	43	8777	6550	328
Mexico	165	7129	71	90	—	—	—	—	29	9	6964	4221	211
India	828	5890	55	59	11	10	2	7	32	24	5062	611	31
Argentina	84	1423	45	45	1	5	—	—	54	50	1339	1594	80
OECD	$ Millions		*Percentage Distribution by Destination*								$ Millions		
Japan	7704	171,144	47	58	3	2	2	4	49	36	163,440	2121	106
Germany	15,764	161,304	76	77	2	3	1	2	22	18	145,540	923	46
US	17,833	158,517	58	61	—	—	1	3	40	35	140,684	789	39
Benelux*	8409	76,009	84	83	1	2	—	2	15	14	67,600	804	40
France	7139	72,242	64	69	2	2	1	3	33	26	65,103	912	46
UK	11,346	68,392	61	71	2	1	1	5	36	24	57,046	503	25
Italy	5587	67,292	68	70	3	3	2	5	27	21	61,705	1104	55
Canada	2973	51,523	88	94	—	—	—	—	12	5	48,550	1633	82
Scandinavia*	4386	39,674	81	80	3	2	—	2	16	17	35,288	805	40
Switzerland	2646	25,230	75	74	2	2	1	4	22	20	22,584	854	43
Spain	382	17,227	57	64	9	5	—	3	34	28	16,845	4410	220
Austria	1204	14,628	67	72	12	7	—	2	21	18	13,424	1115	56
Australia/ New Zealand*	485	6036	61	49	—	—	—	1	39.4	50.1	5551	1145	57

Source: World Bank, *1987 World Development Indicators*, 1987 diskette data set.

Notes: *Weighted average used for percentage distribution. Norway especially increased exports to developing countries (from 20% to 28%). PRC fully not reported. Countries ordered by 1985 export value.

Table A-5. Measures of the Role of Foreign Direct Investment in the Economies of the Group of Five Countries, 1977 and 1986

Percentage share of foreign-owned firms in	1977	1986
United States		
Sales	5	10
Manufacturing employment	3	7
Japan		
Sales	2	1
Manufacturing employment	2	1
France		
Sales	24	27
Manufacturing employment	18	21
Germany		
Sales	17	18
Manufacturing employment	14	13
United Kingdom		
Sales	22	20
Manufacturing employment	15	14

Source: DeAnne Julius and Stephen Thomsen, "Foreign-owned Firms, Trade, and Economic Integration," *Tokyo Club Papers* 2, London: Royal Institute of International Affairs, 1988. Cited in Edward M. Graham and Paul R. Krugman, *Foreign Direct Investment in the United States* (Washington, DC: Institute for International Economics, 1989), table 1.8, p. 25.

Index

DATE DUE

JUN 15 '94	
DEC 2 8 1994	
DEC 0 8 1998	
MAY 0 1 2000	
BRODART	Cat. No. 23-221